D1563215

Herodotus and the Origins of the Political Community

Herodotus and the Origins of the Political Community
Arion's Leap

Norma Thompson

Yale University Press   New Haven and London

Designed by James J. Johnson and set in Monotype Baskerville types
by Tseng Information Systems, Inc., Durham, North Carolina.
Printed in the United States of America by BookCrafters, Inc., Chelsea, Michigan.

Library of Congress Cataloging-in-Publication Data
Thompson, Norma, 1959–
Herodotus and the origins of the political community : Arion's
leap / Norma Thompson.
p. cm.
Includes bibliographical references and index.
ISBN 0-300-06260-5 (alk. paper)

1. Herodotus—Political and social views.   I. Title.
JC71.H47T48   1996
938'.007202—dc20   95-260

A catalogue record for this book is available from the British Library.

The paper in this book meets the guidelines for permanence
and durability of the Committee on Production Guidelines for Book
Longevity of the Council on Library Resources.

10   9   8   7   6   5   4   3   2   1

To David Grene,
who saw that Herodotus
is Irish.

"No anchor, no cable, no fences avail
to keep a fact a fact."
—EMERSON, *History*

Contents

Preface

History is all we have. To try to make sense of history is to attempt an explanation of the human situation itself. Herodotus, the "father of history," has never been much associated with ambition or achievement on such a grand scale.

I first came to the study of Herodotus out of mere puzzlement over the distinction of the historian's famous sobriquet, his persisting place in "the canon," and his somewhat dubious stature as compared with Thucydides. Indeed, the two seemed always considered in tandem. To me theirs resembled the relationship of Sherlock Holmes and Dr. Watson, in which Watson's role was to serve as a rather dull foil to the brilliance of Holmes. The older partner may have been professionally certified in his branch of science, but he was regularly and amusingly bested nonetheless by the younger, who was precise, organized, logical, and almost modern in his handling of evidence—the true and only model for intellectual endeavor to follow.

After far too much time spent reading through the battles of myriad commentators on Herodotus and Thucydides, I decided to engage the "father of history" on his terms alone, if I could find him. What has emerged in the form of this book is Herodotus not so much as the contrast to Thucydides, but Herodotus as the pushing-off point for Aristotle as well, perhaps, as the predecessor most despised by Aristotle. When viewed in this way, as I do in this book, Herodotus' work offers a new foundation in support of Aristotle's perception that man is the *political* animal. At the same time, it provides an alternative to Aristotelian-type theory about that fundamental reality.

Herodotus structures his *History* within a hierarchy that first takes shape in Book II, but that can be observed throughout *The History*. A "hierarchy of certitude" is established that comprises the divine, physical, animal, and human worlds. These worlds are distinguished by the degree to which their actions are determined, from the divine realm, which is absolutely fixed, to the human world, which is most uncertain and unfixed in behavior.

It is not open to human beings to decipher the ordering of the divine world. To Herodotus, the divine is suggestively portrayed as a creative intelligence unwilling fully to reveal itself to mortals, but whose essence is relentlessly sought by an exceptional few, most notably Heracles. Throughout his hierarchy, Herodotus favors the seekers and transcenders: Heracles the hero seeks to see Zeus, who, Egyptian-style, hides behind an animal mask; and Arion, the poet, who is saved by dolphins, creatures that symbolize the transcending spirit by endlessly breaking through the surface of their assigned world, the sea. The main significance of Heracles to Herodotus seems to be that of the striving human who dares to quest and learn, even if in doing so he gets so close to the divine that he risks disaster. As G. Karl Galinsky remarks, "Herakles became the living example of the indomitable human spirit and of a humanity engaged in the never-ending struggle to rise above its own limitations" (*Herakles Theme*, 6). Arion, too, struggles to rise above his own limitations. As Seth Benardete says, he "could appeal to the sailor's pleasure in his excellent singing, and rely on his own inventiveness to attract a dolphin. Arion was a poet, and it is not too fanciful, I think, to consider Herodotus as another Arion" (*Herodotean Inquiries*, 15). Stewart Flory adds that just as it is appropriate for a soldier to go down fighting, "it is fitting also—and dignified and equally as brave—for the singer to go down singing" ("Arion's Leap," 419).

Next in the hierarchy is the physical realm, which follows set rules and laws. Even the chaos of the weather is, at its core, a fixed system, as when Herodotus describes the conduct of the sun as it moves from north to south in the winter, encountering winds and affecting evaporation and rainfall. It is a despotic collection of attributes: rigid yet capricious, significant in its effect on human life, but largely unalterable. When Herodotus devotes himself to understanding the properties of the Nile, he recognizes that there, too, some system is at work. He is level-headed enough to know that his world may not have penetrated the mysteries of why the Nile behaves oppositely to every other known river, but that there is a rational explanation he never doubts.

Then comes the animal world. Herodotus describes the behavior of cats, crocodiles, and other creatures. Although each species differs greatly from the others, each is predictable as a consequence of its biologically determined fate. Animals need not, indeed cannot, be political;

their instinctual nature provides them with their communities. But not so with humans. Herodotus informs us that the Egyptians are overcome with grief when cats perish, and then comments, "In whoever's house a cat dies naturally, those who dwell in the house all shave their eyebrows, but only these; if the dead animal is a dog, they shave all their body and head." Suddenly we are in the realm of custom and culture. As this minor example illustrates, human customs and human cultures vary as widely as cats and crocodiles. What is different is that human beings are all of the same species. We are all "cats," yet each human tribe has its own form of behavior. It is in this perception that Herodotus shows us to be the political animal; it is the distinctive and unavoidable human vocation to create community through politics. To Herodotus, as this book seeks to demonstrate, the process of self-definition and description by storytelling is the theme of that politics.

My greatest debt in bringing my work to this point is to David Grene of The Committee on Social Thought of The University of Chicago. Joseph Cropsey has been unfailingly gracious and supportive. Ralph Lerner and James Redfield provided constructive and sharp comments at important moments. The unique intellectual atmosphere of The Committee on Social Thought profoundly contributed to my work.

At Yale, my colleagues in the Department of Political Science—and especially Steven Smith, Ian Shapiro, Rogers Smith, and the members of the Political Theory Workshop—never failed to enlighten me on matters of substance and form. The genial persistence of Jaroslav Pelikan and Frank Turner urged me onward. I appreciate greatly the staff assistance of Mary Anastasio and Kelli Sankow and the facilities provided by the Institute for Social and Policy Studies. Rupert Gordon's research assistance was valued highly.

The Hoover Institution at Stanford kindly offered me the status of Visiting Scholar and the support of its remarkable intellectual and physical resources. My thanks go to its director, John Raisian, for this help as my manuscript was nearing completion.

Abbreviations

I use the following abbreviations in citing selected ancient authòrs. Citations are from the designated translation, with occasional necessary emendations marked by brackets.

DK   Diels, Hermann, and Walther Kranz, eds. *Die Fragmente der Vorsokratiker.* 3 vols. Berlin: Weidmannsche Buchhandlung, 1934.

EE   *Eudemian Ethics.* Translated by J. Solomon in *The Complete Works of Aristotle.* 2 vols. Edited by Jonathan Barnes. For the Greek text, I consulted the Loeb edition, translated by H. Rackham. Cambridge: Harvard University Press, 1935.

GA   *Generation of Animals.* Translated by A. L. Peck. Cambridge: Harvard University Press, 1963.

HA   *Historia Animalium.* 3 vols. Translated by A. L. Peck. Cambridge: Harvard University Press, 1965.

Met   *Metaphysics.* Translated by W. D. Ross in *Complete Works,* ed. J. Barnes. For the Greek text, I consulted the Oxford Classical Text (OCT) *Aristotelis Metaphysica.* Edited by Werner Jaeger. Oxford: Clarendon Press, 1957.

NE   *Nicomachean Ethics.* Translated by W. D. Ross, revised by J. O. Urmson in *Complete Works,* ed. J. Barnes. For the Greek text, I consulted the Loeb edition, translated by H. Rackham. Cambridge: Harvard University Press, 1982.

OH   *On the Heavens.* Translated by J. L. Stocks in *Complete Works,* ed. J. Barnes. For the Greek text, I consulted the OCT *De Caelo,* ed. D. J. Allan. Oxford: Clarendon Press, 1936.

PA   *Parts of Animals.* Translated by W. Ogle in *Complete Works,* ed. J. Barnes. For the Greek text, I consulted the Loeb edition, translated by A. L. Peck. Cambridge: Harvard University Press, 1937.

Poet   *Poetics.* Translated by I. Bywater in *Complete Works,* ed. J. Barnes.

For the Greek text, I consulted the OCT *Aristotelis De Arte Poetica Liber*, ed. Rudolfus Kassel. Oxford: Clarendon Press, 1965.

Pol   *Politics*. Translated by Carnes Lord. Chicago: University of Chicago Press, 1984. For the Greek text, I consulted the OCT *Aristotelis Politica*. Edited by W. D. Ross. Oxford: Clarendon Press, 1957.

Rhet   *The "Art" of Rhetoric*. Translated by W. Rhys Roberts in *Complete Works*, ed. J. Barnes. For the Greek text, I consulted the OCT *Aristotelis Ars Rhetorica*. Edited by W. D. Ross. Oxford: Clarendon Press, 1959.

Introduction

The stories that succeed most compellingly in accounting for the "facts" of a people's past become the core of that people's political community. This recognition is provided to us by Herodotus in his *History*. Herodotus shows—without drawing conclusions, providing explanations, or offering theories—that stories demarcate and bind one polity in distinction to another, and he suggests how that entity may evolve over time in reference to the defining story it tells about itself. He brings us to this insight, speaking in a prephilosophical, pre-Socratic language, as he grapples with the stories current in Greece: of Greeks about Greeks, and Greeks about others. It is a less manageable but more vivid and in some ways more articulated approach than would come with the era of theory to follow. It is also, in its essence, dynamic; each political community incessantly reassesses and reshapes itself through political and cultural discourse about and around its own meaning.

By examining Herodotus as a pre-Socratic figure, I am not seeking to align myself with or to comment on any of the "new" schools that have announced the end of theory or the death of philosophy or that have sought to revivify historicism. I am only trying to engage Herodotus on what I believe are his own terms—terms that a post-Socratic world would have been inclined to regard as amusing at best, ludicrous at worst. My aim is to offer an explanation for why Herodotus includes both "serious" and "ridiculous" stories, and, in doing so, to shed some light on sources of political identities and activities in our own time.

This is also a book about fact and interpretation. Writing these pages while in residence at Berkeley College (where the phenomenalist spirit of Bishop George Berkeley [1685–1753] still dwells) has made me continually aware of the problematic character of "fact." (We Irish, said Berkeley, "are apt to think something and nothing are near neighbors.") Although this essay is not intended as a contribution to that great debate of the centuries or to its contemporary variations, to the extent that those today who think about narrative, truth, history, and subjectivity find interest here I would be pleased. My vocabulary is not, however, a postmodernist one.

For my purposes, a "fact" will be taken, more or less, for what Herodotus puts before us as fact on page one of his *History*. That is, on a given day in the past a number of women, including the king's daughter, came down to the shore where Phoenician sea-traders were selling their wares. The women stopped at the ship's stern to bid for articles that struck their fancy — and then the sailors grabbed them, forced them aboard, and sailed off with them to Egypt. Everything Herodotus tells us thereafter is an exploration, with side excursions, of what became of this fact. My book is an attempt to see, with the simplicity of Herodotus' pretheoretical vision, what he was explaining to himself, to his audiences, and to those who came after, intrigued yet puzzled by his *History*.

Inevitably, in pursuing the inquiries of Herodotus I am brought into contact with issues of historical objectivity. Charges and countercharges regarding the truthfulness of Herodotus have been ever recurring, of course, but what is new is the extent to which these debates, seemingly internal to Herodotean studies, are resonating widely in other intellectual circles. Accordingly, several of my colleagues and readers have advised me to offer guidance as to how my position may be located amid the swirling contemporary debates. I have given serious consideration to this advice, but because these debates include, among others, those over objectivity (Hayden White, Peter Novick), new historicism (François Hartog), deconstruction (Derrida, Foucault), hermeneutics (Gadamer), narrative constructions of political identity (Rorty, MacIntyre), and cultural theory (Said), I have found it impossible to follow them. In the pages that follow, some references to these modern and current intellectual and scholarly debates will be found. But theories and antitheories are produced these days at a bewildering rate. To try to mark a spot on an intellectual map would, I feel, be a fruitless exercise, for by the time the reader came to consult such a map, vast projects of construction and deconstruction will have rendered it obsolete.

My purpose throughout has been to provide a more durable framework for thought. Whether one accepts or rejects the proposition that the world comprises bounded cultures, or whether one such culture can ever represent or understand another, or whether such cultural entities any longer exist in a globalized world,[1] an elemental fact of human life

---

1. Buell, *National Culture*, 35.

can be discerned through the watchful eye and poetic ear of Herodotus: groups exist, defined by their group story. Put this way, it strikes us that perhaps the most significant marker on the intellectual map I referred to earlier has yet to be identified: Martin Heidegger. His appeal to the poetic dimension of the pre-Socratics is motivated by the desire to identify a more authentic experience of thinking—an experience that lay behind philosophy and behind Aristotle. Our attempt to argue for a reading of *The History* that takes it seriously as a work worthy of the malignity of Aristotle is similarly motivated: Herodotus could well represent the same kind of liberating possibility for our thinking that Heidegger identified in Parmenides and Heraclitus. And Heidegger's ontology, in George Steiner's words, is "densely immanent" (and hence Herodotean), for it does not arrive "at the inference of the transcendent, at the attempt to locate truth and ethical values in some abstract 'beyond.' Being is being-in-the-world." [2] This is only to suggest that a Heideggerian reading of Herodotus is plausible; it is not our project here. Rather, we are attempting to recover the voice of Herodotus (not the voice of Being) in the hope of expanding our thinking about storytelling as a mode of political definition.

Beyond the insights Herodotus offers regarding the creation and evolution of political community, *The History* also puts forth the beginnings of an understanding of what we now regard as international relations. His study is of peoples in the plural, how these peoples affect each other, and whether some can be judged more effective and laudable than others. Herodotus does not restrict his attention in *The History* to the major contending powers of the Persian War. Early on, he points out how transitory are the labels "small" and "great" in categorizing the cities of mankind: "For of those that were great in earlier times most have now become small, and those that were great in my time were small in the time before. Since, then, I know that man's good fortune never abides in the same place, I will make mention of both alike" (1.5). [3] He seems to hold that cities small and great will affect each other, but that it is impossible to know the impact of these encounters with finality, even with the clarity of hindsight. The Egyptians, for example, had a negligible role in a military sense in their dealings with the Persians, but their cultural identity surely touched their conquerors. Cook explains, "The

2. Steiner, *Martin Heidegger*, 65.
3. Herodotus, *History*, trans. Grene. Hereinafter references to this edition of *The History* will appear parenthetically in the text.

Egyptians explain the Greeks and the Greeks explain the Egyptians; explaining the Egyptians explains why the Persians were moderately unsuccessful at taking them over, as they were later to be unsuccessful at taking over the Greeks."[4] Herodotus employs the whole world as his stage in order to reserve a place for the mutual influences of intersecting cultures.

This responsiveness to actions and influences among cultures warrants changing Herodotus' name-tag to read "father of international history," for although he attends closely to the unique qualities of peoples, he also represents these peoples in constant interplay. *The History* leaves an unmistakable impression of continuous global movement: his excursions into the different countries appear not as separate anthropological studies, but as parts of a complicated and intricately connected whole, in marked contrast to what we now call national history. *The History* embeds parochial matters in an incessant contact between cultures. For this reason, some of the most fruitful studies of Herodotus are those that, in accounting for Scythia, for example, turn to Egypt or Greece for their means of understanding; or, in accounting for Persia, turn to Athens, Sparta, and Ionia.[5] His focus on individual communities invites rather than closes off further reflections on its context. The diversity of political community form is not set in any larger unity[6]—a problem the solution to which still eludes humankind—but Herodotus' examples of international matters merit our serious attention. If his way of interpreting his

4. Cook, *Myth and Language,* 176.

5. For recent examples, see: Benardete and Cook, previous citations; Gould, *Herodotus;* Hartog, *Mirror of Herodotus;* Konstan, "Persians, Greeks and Empire"; Redfield, "Herodotus the Tourist."

6. Saxonhouse identifies a "fear of diversity" in the ancient Greek world ("a fear that differences bring on chaos and thus demands that the world be put into an orderly pattern. Part of that order is to see the unity underlying the apparent variety of the world we experience with our senses"), of which she has (rightly, I think) exempted Aristotle. But Herodotus and Aristotle are akin on this point. Saxonhouse can make the following claim only by excluding Herodotus from her purview: "it is only Aristotle who, accepting the centrality of sight for understanding, is able to overcome the fear and welcome the diverse" (*Fear of Diversity,* x). There is, in fact, an interesting body of critical literature on Herodotus' embracing of "the world we experience with our senses." Schepens opens his work thus: "Autopsy ($\alpha\dot{v}\tau o\psi\acute{\iota}\alpha$), that is, the personal observation of facts by the historian, constitutes a fundamental starting point for the historiographical activity of antiquity." [*L''autopsie' dans la méthode des historiens grecs,* v; he provides a lengthy review of the relevant literature on "sight" ($\ddot{o}\psi\iota\varsigma$), "inquiry" ($\dot{\iota}\sigma\tau o\rho\acute{\iota}\eta$), and "hearing" ($\dot{\alpha}\kappa o\acute{\eta}$) as bases for historical knowledge in *The History,* 36–94]. See, in addition, Schepens, "Ephore sur la valeur de l'autopsie"; Verdin, *De historisch kritische methode;* and Hunter, *Past and Process.*

world cannot serve as a prescription for ours, still, his example remains instructive. Regional personalities seem to emerge effortlessly, in a way that is both revealing and plausible. To attempt to penetrate Herodotus' mapping of his world, then, stands as a captivating challenge.

At this time, when the Western rationalistic tradition is under challenge, it is being reemphasized that a decisive step in the creation of that tradition was the Greek creation of the idea of a theory. The introduction of the idea of a theory enabled the Western tradition to produce something unique, namely systematic intellectual constructions that were designed to describe and to explain large areas of reality in a way that is logically and mathematically accessible.[7] It is, of course, Aristotle who initiates this tradition of theory and, as I reveal in Chapter 1, it is Herodotus whom Aristotle excoriates as the representative of what his theoretical approach rejects and transcends.

In this way Herodotus seems both pre-Socratic and strikingly postmodern. He seems "against theory" or, more suitably, pre-theory. He does not explain, he shows.[8] To many concerned intellectuals today, the movement against theory is an attack on the Western rationalistic tradition because it attacks linear thinking, that is, thinking straight. Herodotus is not a straight thinker, but neither does he represent the cyclical mode of historical perception in contrast with the progressive—as set out in the familiar description of the fundamental difference between the ancient and modern worlds.[9] Herodotus' mode of historical perception allows for, indeed accounts for, historical change and sometimes even progression. It recognizes a dynamic set of factors and includes individual and collective action that can transform a political community for worse or better.

My conclusion is that Herodotus shows how political communities are formed by humans who, having no choice, must perforce be political animals. In doing so, Herodotus provides us with a different and heretofore unrecognized view of politics and community. It is excessively alarmist, in my view, to regard any stand that differs from the stand

7. Searle, "Rationality and Realism," 58.
8. In this "showing," we shall see, Herodotus stands always in contrast to Aristotle, who favors more explicit formulations. Aristotle can delineate the three ways in which human beings become "good and excellent"—through nature ($\phi\acute{v}\sigma\iota\varsigma$), habit ($\mathring{\eta}\theta os$), and reason ($\lambda\acute{o}\gamma os$): "The other animals live by nature above all, but in some slight respects by habit as well, while man lives also by reason (for he alone has reason); so these things should be consonant with the other" (*Pol* 1332a40–b6).
9. See Manuel, *Shapes of Philosophical History.*

of "theory" as a degeneration of the rationalist tradition. No tradition so fragile could have survived for so long. The Western scientific tradition has taken far heavier blows and still stands; the Western humanistic tradition need not be so fearful. In the present work, Herodotus is not the adversary that Aristotle seemed to wish to make him; rather, his is an enriching version of the same civilization's quest for knowledge and understanding.

Herodotus has been called "most Homeric" (Ὁμηρικώτατος) of authors; aside from stylistic resemblances between the two, both Herodotus and Homer memorialize the character larger than life or the event worthy of remembrance.[10] Time, unresisted, obliterates all; each author understood the art of poetic resistance.[11] This is a fundamental principle for this work, but not a complete one, for it is my contention that Herodotus carries this trajectory to a different and manifestly *political* conclusion. Herodotus listens with the ear of a poet to his Greek audience—for the meaning particular Greeks discern in their past, for the sense it has for their present identity (for who they *are* as a community, and who they are *not*), for the direction of their future. He listens for this meaning, captures it (in ways this work will strive to put to words), and attaches it firmly. In his best hope, it is an act for all time. *The History* is a work for far-ranging minds.

10. Dionysius, *Letter to Pompeius*, 3; Longinus, *On Sublimity*, 13.3. Herodotus has for a long time been considered an heir of Homer and the Homeric tradition: "He has drunk at the Homeric cistern until his whole being is impregnated with the influence thence derived" (Rawlinson, *History of Herodotus*, I, 6; further bibliography will be provided in Chapter 3.) Like Homer, Herodotus is one of those ancients who seem never to have lacked attention from the mind of an educated (and not so educated) public, from his time to ours. Unlike Homer, he has been considered more a figure of curiosity than of awe. It is the purpose of this essay to suggest that a deeper stratum of rich meaning within the Herodotean text also accounts for lively survival through the ages.

11. For interesting elaborations, see Grene on the idea of immortal fame (κλέος) in his introduction to Herodotus, *History*, pp. 16–23; Nagy, "Herodotus the *Logios*"; Hartog, "Herodotus and the Historiographical Operation," 85; and Segal, "*Kleos*," 127–149.

CHAPTER 1

The Decline and Repudiation of the Whole: Notes on Aristotle's Enclosure of the Pre-Socratic World

Herodotus' reputation in the ancient world is something exceptional which must be explained. —ARNALDO MOMIGLIANO

Aristotle defined himself against Herodotus. Plato and Aristotle cannot be understood without recognition that they stand on our side of what has become the great divide in intellectual history: the pre-Socratics, and those who came after them. For his part, Plato famously offers an apology of philosophy against poetry. The maxims associated with the Socratic way ("know thyself," "nothing in excess," "an unexamined life is not worth living") are standing rebukes to what, beginning with Plato, is depicted as the creative madness of the poet. Aristotle then contributes his own apology of the philosophic life in a manner suggesting that he considered the urgent task of defining philosophy unfinished by his teacher, or at least in need of further articulation. Athens, Aristotle is alleged to have said, would not be allowed to sin twice. This Aristotelian enterprise was to be fulfilled at the expense of the pretheoretical, presystematic work of Herodotus. Aristotle scorned Herodotus' "ancient" way of thought as chaotically inclusive of virtually all dimensions of human life. In its place, Aristotle constructed the more controlled, dichotomous, demarcated, and abstract structure that ever since has been taken as the essence of Western and world thought.

This book is an invitation to reexamine that Aristotelian moment in which "The Philosopher" orients his thought against pre-Socratic thinking. When Aristotle eschewed Plato's dialogue in favor of his own monologue, he was advocating the "replacement of myth by logos."[1] This intellectual situation will be explicated in due course; for the mo-

---

1. Rosen, *Quarrel*, viii. In most cases (including hereafter λόγος), I will not transliterate Greek words but will use the Greek characters.

7

ment, I will put a name to it, and claim that the myth that Aristotle's λόγος was intended to replace was Herodotean. Arnaldo Momigliano refers to the near-uniform contempt in which Herodotus was held after his time, and wonders why. He notes that Herodotus began to recover from Thucydides' attack only after two thousand years.[2] In one form or another, this attack has echoed down the ages, and yet it is incomplete, for unmentioned is Herodotus' unremitting critic, Aristotle. My reading of Aristotle's pronouncements on history and historical argumentation indicates that he formulated his views against Herodotus.

Aristotle infrequently names Herodotus as his adversary, masking the character of this defining debate. As a result, commentators have assumed that Aristotle was referring to Thucydides. But a close look at Aristotle's argument reveals that his antagonist was Herodotus. Aristotle directs toward him a series of erroneous or misleading criticisms in the service of promoting his own philosophical conviction: to set definitions, to fix evidence, and to aspire to the theory that holds. The minds of both the philosopher and the historian are revealed to be universal; each seeks to explain all. But Aristotle constantly overestimates his distance from Herodotus and seems oblivious to their common ground. What is remembered is only the theory that holds. It is a triumph of rigorous intellectualization over a way of inquiry more willing and able to comprehend uncertainty, contingency, inconsistency, and the varied sources of human constancy and change. It is the beginning of the academic enclosure of the human commons—the full range of intellectual territory before its demarcation into disciplines and fields.

Aristotle's Double Legacy

Much of political thought as we know it today exists in a universe designed by Aristotle, whose conception of *theoria* and *praxis* is tied up with his notion of the best possible lives for human beings. Aristotle found in the theoretical or contemplative life the possibilities for complete human happiness, and for him the practical life of politics offered happiness of a secondary degree (*NE* 1177b25–1178a9). Even so, in his practical writings Aristotle certainly sought to achieve an integrative conception of theory and practice; in his explication of the φρόνιμος, the practically wise person, for example, we confront the individual who can, through

2. Momigliano, "Place of Herodotus," 10.

experience and wisdom, deliberate correctly about what the best actions are and about how to pursue those actions in particular circumstances. Yet Aristotle's work, as interpreted over the ages, generally came to be understood as justifying the dominance of theory over practice: practice could not be entirely understood or rightly conducted without close attention to theory.

Depending on one's emphasis, Aristotle could be read either as an inspiration for our thinking on theory and practice or as a deleterious influence to be overcome. At the root of this dual reception of Aristotle is his basic association of *theoria* with the divine and *praxis* with the human. This is evident first in his threefold distinction between ways of knowing and his consequent ranking of the theoretical sciences as highest; and second in his tripartite division of the most notable lives and his consequent ranking of the theoretical or contemplative life as best. From these formulations, it is an easy move to construct settled theories, even with regard to such changeable matters as human conduct. I want to emphasize the conscious formulation of this position by Aristotle in his dismissive treatment of Herodotus. In the act of contesting Herodotus' pre-Socratic view, Aristotle reveals with the utmost clarity his tendency to seek the comprehensive explanation even as he counsels against such totalizing theory on practical matters.

Aristotle mentions three forms of intellectual activity (the theoretical, practical, and productive sciences); of these, he grants superiority to the theoretical sciences of theology, mathematics, and physics on account of the necessity and unchanging principles of their subject matter (*Met* 1025b25f.). *Theoria* involves things that cannot be otherwise, and even the "scanty conceptions to which we can attain of celestial things" give us, Aristotle says, "more pleasure than all our knowledge of the world in which we live" (*PA* 644b33–34). His ranking of the human lives most worthy of choosing follows from this estimation of *theoria* and, from the point of view of some readers, is accordingly suspect; it seems to validate the life of the researcher unattached to mere human concerns: "For it would be strange to think that the art of politics (πολιτική), or practical wisdom (φρόνησις), is the [most serious] knowledge, since man is not the best thing in the world" (*NE* 1141a21–23).

The theorizing that Aristotle defends seems to be uninvolved with the world around us, and, as A. W. H. Adkins writes, there seems to be no persuading a *theoretikos* "at a time when he is engaged in *theoria* that he should perform some moral or political action instead." That life is

deemed highest which is in contact with the "unalterable and unmodi-
fied, living the best and most self-sufficient of lives" (*OH* 279a21–22).
The life of contemplation is said to be not only superior to any other
human life but also higher than human: "Human beings are able to live
it in virtue of some divine principle within. . . . Accordingly, we should
athanatizein (play the immortal) so far as in us lies and do our best to
live in accordance with the best part of us."[3] In this way, Aristotle encourages us to associate theory with the divine and practice with the
human, thus leading some readers to conclude that his separation of
theory from practice is so stark as to open the way to extremism: There
is no "sustained attempt to bridge the gulf, to show continuity, between
the principles of justice which all men must respect and the contemplative activities without which no man can be truly happy."[4]

Nevertheless, the gulf between the realms of theory and practice for
Aristotle does not require that there be an absolutist role for theorizing
in human life. Stephen G. Salkever correctly notes that for Aristotle "the
relationship of theory to practice is not direct—not a form of natural law
deductivism—but rather an indirect connection that avoids both dogmatism and relativism."[5] Aristotle accepts the diversity of political life as
given and proceeds to advise us on the means of reforming or maintaining the regime, based not on some transcendent or precisely definable
ideal but on subjects and premises that "are only for the most part true"
(*NE* 1094b21–22). His appeal today seems to be in line with the search
for pluralist thinking with a strong core. Although he recognizes that
political communities define their own versions of the common good,
he also subjects them to scrutiny on the question of their "authoritative
element" (τὸ κύριον, *Pol* 1281a11–15).

As Momigliano observed, Herodotus' reputation in the ancient world
is exceptional, and consequently the recognition of Herodotus "as our
best and most complete document for pre-Socratic philosophy" has not
been widespread, to say the least. This recognition, found in Seth Benardete's *Herodotean Inquiries*, has been long neglected.[6] Herodotus opens his

3. Adkins, *"Theoria* Versus *Praxis,"* 312; NE 117b26, summarized 297–298.
4. Hardie, *Aristotle's Ethical Theory,* 357.
5. Salkever, *Finding the Mean,* 7.
6. For another compelling treatment of Herodotus' *History* as an embodiment of
pre-Socratic wisdom, see Rosen, *Quarrel,* 27–55, and "Herodotus Reconsidered," 332–356.
See also (in addition to the authors cited in the introduction, n 6) Barth, "Einwirkungen
der vorsokratischen Philosophie," 173–183; Humphreys, "Law, Custom and Culture," 219–

history with the quintessentially pre-Socratic notion that because the basic human condition is one of change and instability, the observer of this condition must take in the whole of it. For Herodotus, the challenge is to assure "that time may not draw the color from what man has brought into being," that "those great and wonderful deeds . . .[not] fail of their report" (1.1). It is the proposed Herodotean report that seems to distress Aristotle in every way—for its open-ended nature, its implausible embracing of all the stories of mankind, and its resistance to classification. Aristotle opposes this pre-Socratic view with all his formidable powers. In the process, as Stanley Rosen remarks, he overstates his case for "the reasonableness of nature," and this has had some dramatic and un-Aristotelian consequences. Ultimately, perhaps, "the temptation to master nature by technical devices" is among them; it was an easy step for scientists in the modern age to translate Aristotelian *theoria* as the highest form of cognition into *theoria* as the only form.[7]

The Free-Running Style of Herodotus: "Seeing Nothing in Front of You" and "Getting Nowhere"

Aristotle begins his criticism of Herodotus with the historian's first sentence. In the *Rhetoric* Aristotle remarks that the "free-running" prose style exemplified by Herodotus' opening in *The History* ("Herein is set forth the inquiry of Herodotus . . .") is defined by having "no natural stopping-places, and comes to a stop only because there is no more to say on that subject" (*Rhet* 1409a28f.). Aristotle labels this style the "ancient" one—reminder enough that the writer with the alternative "compact" style represents the way of the future. "Only toward the middle of the [fifth] century," Herington writes, "did the Greek words for 'old' come to acquire the scornful significance of 'outmoded.'"[8] Aristotle's selection of Herodotus as his target is more studied than it may seem at first;

220; Lloyd, "Herodotus on Egyptians and Libyans," 215–244; and Müller, "Herodot—Vater des Empirismus?" 299–318.

7. Rosen, *Quarrel*, xiii.

8. Herington, *Poetry into Drama*, 239. In a way that is pertinent to our own theme, Herington differentiates between a song-culture and a book-culture and remarks that the "single semantic detail"—the newly pejorative sense of "old"—"illustrates this difference in attitudes between the song culture on the one hand and the new culture which emerged in the late fifth century (and our own culture too) on the other" (Ibid.). See also Harris, *Ancient Literacy*, 85: "Who in fact was the first truly bookish individual among the Greeks? . . . The best answer is Aristotle."

he seeks the appearance of an easy dismissiveness, as if the stylistic advance of "compact" writing were obvious. But if the stylistic differences between Herodotus and Aristotle are genuine enough, it is by no means obvious that the latter represent an unquestioned advance.

Aristotle's distinction between the free-running and the compact prose style gives us a fair sense of the discipline and neatness he expects in any theorizing; this is in marked contrast to Herodotus' practice of inserting reminders to his audience of how difficult it is to manage his material in a coherent and effective form. Herodotus' presence in his narrative is conspicuous, and conspicuously unsettling: "I do not know if this is exactly true; I write down just what I am told. Still, anything may happen" (4.195).[9] Aristotle's strong inclination is toward an understanding of the world that controls what is said, and in a way that is readily articulable. Thus his condemnation of the free-running style is that it lacks discipline: "This style is unsatisfactory just because it goes on indefinitely—one always likes to sight a stopping place in front of one" (1409a31f.). It seems that Herodotus' style may even strain our well-being: "it is only at the goal that men in a race faint and collapse; while they see the end of the course before them, they can keep going."

Aristotle grants no philosophic dignity to the style of *The History*, and for the most part the Western tradition has followed suit. Behind the alleged lack of control in Herodotus' prose, however, is a subtle and realistic view of the tentative quality of any theorizing. Philosophers and historians alike must begin with the opinions of humankind, and if, as Aristotle himself says, "every man has some contribution to make to the truth," he also knows that opinions conflict, stories change, and storytellers have ulterior motives; the theorist is on uncertain ground (*EE* 1216b31). No one is more successful than Aristotle in smoothing over this shifting, uneven surface, whereas no one is more assiduous than Herodotus in keeping visible its rough edges. Both enterprises, that of the philosopher and the historian, require discipline of the most exacting sort.

It is not surprising that Herodotus' selection of evidence has often puzzled readers, inasmuch as he seems to lack a well-grounded standard of inclusion; factual and mythical matters are related with equal aplomb. He does look at inscriptions, temple dedications, and battle re-

9. As Dewald remarks, "We do not experience the narrative as an unmediated mimetic event in which we participate as readers. . . . We read it rather as the achievement of an author acting as a master raconteur, subduing difficult and diverse narrative material to his will" ("Narrative Surface," 149).

mains; but he depends predominantly on a widely disparate assortment of human recollections and retellings of much earlier events to form his account of the past. The question "Who?" is prior to every historical "Why?" for Herodotus, and in answering "Who?" he gives expression to all sorts of human remembrances; he recognizes that particular manifestations of the human spirit take their form according to the distinctive *nomoi* of the community. According to Gould, "It is an essential part of the function of the 'social memory' on which Herodotus draws that it should serve to maintain the solidarity of the local community and the distinctive nature of its experiences."[10]

A single theoretical model does not suffice in *The History*, and this gives Herodotus' work a (self-consciously) shifting focus. "This history of mine has from the beginning sought out the supplementary to the main argument" (4.30), he tells us, and although this statement is made in the context of a discussion on mule-breeding, it pertains to the human world as well: no single theory holds to explain all. Accordingly, the evidence that he draws on to characterize a people is constituted differently in each case, in line with the promptings of the people itself. He may stress alternately a people's stories of origin and its rhetorical self-presentations, its embellishments of past events, political forms, heroes, religious beliefs, social customs, or geographical features. He allows the emphasis and animating spirit of his evidence to change with his subjects, keeping him at a far remove from theorists who maintain that a single standard is appropriate and applicable in all places. The stories that people tell of themselves—whether they are Persian or Ionian or Greek—are versions or explanations of their own "goodness." Once the story is told and picked up by the community, it is imitated; it is there as an organizing principle to which people repair in moments of crisis. They may break free of it, but they know when they are doing it.

Aristotle, in contrast, closes off and refines common opinions in an effort to attain an enduring theory. This entails cutting off a whole range of expressions of what is said or believed, or even half-believed, among people. With some understatement, he writes: "To examine all the opinions that have been held would no doubt be somewhat fruitless" (*NE* 1095a29–30; cf. *EE* 1214b29f.); he would like to restrict his attention to those opinions "that are most prevalent or that seem to have some reason in their favor." The impression he perpetuates in this refining pro-

---

10. Gould, *Herodotus*, 38.

cess is that he can explain himself, whereas (unnamed) earlier thinkers could not. Aristotle's enterprise comes across as the higher one because it is more self-conscious and clearer about first principles.

In Aristotle's criticism of the style of Herodotus, he accounts neither for the profundity of the historian's enterprise of crafting social memory nor for his palpable success in containing this mass of material. He encourages the impression that Herodotus somehow does not control what is said, but this is to neglect the ring-composition, analogies, oppositions, and other rhetorical and literary devices that have long impressed readers of Herodotus. The single story of the encounter between Solon and Croesus shows how a paradigmatic figure may illustrate philosophical themes and connect events before, during, and after the Persian War.

As the prosperous and apparently secure individual who falls victim to hubris, Croesus stands equally well as a warning for the great city or the burgeoning empire. As such, he represents a clue to how Herodotus could have made an agreeable unity out of a series of elaborate and convoluted stories, even though these stories might lack the closure that Aristotle favored. When the Herodotean character Croesus asks, "Who is the happiest of mankind?" his question will be answered, but never settled. Croesus connects and illuminates other instances reported by Herodotus that pertain to the question of human flourishing (3.39–43; 7.45–52); the image is repeatedly evoked and further disclosed, yet it never becomes the source for metaphysical propositions. Herodotus indicates (σημαίνω) in the manner of Apollo himself, as Nagy maintains: "The Lord whose oracle is in Delphi neither says nor conceals: he indicates."[11]

In the story of Croesus and Solon, Croesus arranges to have Solon tour his vast stores of treasure and then asks him "whether, of all men, there is one you have seen as the most blessed of all" (1.30). When Solon identifies Tellus the Athenian, Croesus is provoked. Solon explains that Tellus came from a good city, had a prosperous family, lived well, and had a splendid ending in battle: "The Athenians gave him a public funeral where he fell and so honored him greatly" (1.30). Croesus then asks for Solon's opinion of the second happiest man, expecting that at least this honor would be his own. Solon answers with a description of Cleobis and Biton, Argive brothers who had the following story told about them. When a team of oxen did not arrive to take their mother to

---

11. Nagy, *Pindar's Homer*, 234. Nagy translates Heraclitus 22 B 93 DK.

the temple for a religious festival, they hitched the wagon to themselves and brought her the distance: "When they had done that and had been seen by all the assembly, there came upon them the best end of a life, and in them the god showed thoroughly how much better it is for a man to be dead than alive" (1.31). After the mother had prayed to the gods that her sons receive whatever it was best for men to win, the two young men "never rose more" and were laid to rest in the temple. Hearing this second account, Croesus objects that Solon has undervalued his own happiness by estimating so highly the lives of private men. Solon responds that the one who consistently possesses the most "good things" and then dies well may earn the title of happiest, but that this determination cannot be made prematurely: "For to many the god has shown a glimpse of blessedness only to extirpate them in the end" (1.32). And so Croesus sends Solon away, "thinking him assuredly a stupid man who would let by present goods and bid him look to the end of every matter" (1.33).[12]

In Herodotus' portrayal, Croesus' happiness is to be short-lived for all sorts of reasons beyond his control, but there remains an area in which his responsibility for his fate is clearly his own. It is this area that proves so vital to the question of εὐδαιμονία as a whole. Croesus' failing is to define "good things" by measuring them; he proceeds as if there were nothing in the world that could not be known through calculation. Even the gods are subjected to his computations, for he asks the oracles throughout Greece and Libya to report what Croesus, King of Lydia, was doing on a specific day, thereby forcing them to communicate with him in a language he can control. After the Delphic oracle passes this test, Croesus sends massive dedications of gold and silver to the temple, assuming that these quantities matter to the gods.[13] All of this was in preparation for Croesus' asking the significant question: Should he make war against Cyrus, King of Persia? And the Delphic oracle answered honestly again: If you make war, you will destroy a mighty empire. It

12. The Solon-Croesus exchange is one of three anecdotes in *The History* on which most readers will feel compelled to comment (the other two are the "Persian debate" and "Custom is king" passages; accordingly, the bibliographies are overwhelming). For basic references and a discussion of the significance of the name "Tellus," see Immerwahr, *Form and Thought*, 156–161, and Regenbogen, "Die Geschichte von Solon und Krösus."

13. The ordinary Greek might assume that these quantities indeed matter to the gods, but Herodotus drolly restricts his commentary to Croesus' immediate gains: "The Delphians in return gave Croesus and the Lydians the right of primacy of consultation of the oracle, remission of all charges, and the best seats at the festival" (1.54). He seems not (Cephalus-like) to be committed to traditional Greek notions of sacrifice.

turns out, of course, that Croesus did not ask the prior question, which would have led him to discover that the mighty empire to be destroyed was his own.

In his drive to accumulate more goods, more land, more subjects, Croesus defines an end for himself that can have no end. His irrational behavior is corrected only in total defeat; he is not able to appreciate the wisdom of Solon until all is lost. Thus comes into existence the ineffective wise advisor; no ruler in the Croesus paradigm can be affected by good advice until it is too late. However commonly taught, this lesson somehow always remains counterintuitive: self-determination cannot be achieved in a lasting way without actually determining (weighing rather than counting) one's good. The path of least resistance for the rich and powerful ruler, city, or empire is the path toward self-destruction. Hence the Croesus story illuminates the Persian experience, which in turn illuminates the future prospects for the Athenians. But it is a lesson that even readers must determine for themselves; Herodotus nowhere states explicitly what we are to learn from his inquiries. Understanding comes only with our engagement with the story.[14]

Aristotle himself does not eschew the use of well-known stories to fill out his intended meaning ("we must try to get conviction by arguments [λόγοι], using the phenomena as evidence and illustration" [*EE* 1216b26]), but he sharply restricts the length of his examples and sets out his conclusions authoritatively. In Book 1 of the *Politics*, Aristotle recounts the story of Thales, who bought up all the olive presses in the area during the off-season; eventually he benefited immensely from his monopoly (1259a5f.). Aristotle concludes that this is a "piece of business expertise" that is universal. His point (in the context of his contrast between acquisition and use) is less the specific one that philosophers could become wealthy if they only cared to, than the general one: mere accumulation is unnatural ("usury is most reasonably hated" [1259a31]), but

14. And having engaged with the initial story, readers of *The History* will then observe that it does not stand still. We shall see, for example, that when Herodotus comes to write of the Egyptians, his story of the thief and Rhampsinitus stands in provocative relation to the story of Solon's happiest men; this contrast brings out elements of the discernibly Greek and Egyptian characters involved. Furthermore, the Solon-Croesus episode raises other interesting speculations, such as the role of Solon in relation to happiness. What is the relation between the individual seeking wisdom and the possibility for happiness? Is happiness ever possible for public figures, or is it restricted to private individuals? And what of the historian's relationship to his wise character? Of course, there will be no authoritative pronouncements on any of these matters.

accumulation in the service of a higher good—say, for the establishment of political rule within a city—is natural, and a useful insight for rulers (1259a31).[15] The difference is in the defining principle; enrichment is in the service of some higher aspiration, or it is absurd: "Yet it would be absurd if wealth were something one could have in abundance and die of starvation—like the Midas of the fable, when everything set before him turned into gold on account of the greediness of his prayer" (1257b14–17).

Aristotle's story is compact; Herodotus' is free-running. On one level this may be a matter of style. To write compactly is to differentiate one's points, to write in a free-running manner is to seek inclusiveness; the one is not implicitly more satisfying than the other. ("There are some enterprises in which a careful disorderliness is the true method."[16]) But Aristotle may well strike us as rash to take on Herodotus from this perspective in the first place. At the other extreme from Aristotle and his unkind remarks about Herodotean style is Dionysius of Halicarnassus, who writes in his Letter to Gnaeus Pompeius: "Indeed, if we take up [*The History*] we remain enthralled up to the last syllable and always look for more. . . . Herodotus has chosen a number of subjects which are in no way alike and has made them into one harmonious whole."[17] As effusive as Dionysius might be judged to be in regard to his kinsman, he seems to speak more closely to our own experience of reading Herodotus than does Aristotle.

The more predictable charge against Herodotus relates, of course, to his reliability. In the course of connecting dramatic themes, does he compromise the substantive work of writing history? Here, too, Aristotle enters the debate.

Consider the Source: Herodotus the Mythmaker

Herodotus may stand at the beginning of the Western tradition on the subject of historical evidence, but he is a marginal figure in forming it; he is blamed, in James Redfield's phrase, for "failing to be Thucydides."[18] Momigliano claims that the only ancient writer "who never said anything unpleasant about Herodotus" was Dionysius.[19] To be blunt, the

15. See Nichols, *Citizens and Statesmen*, 28.
16. So writes Herman Melville in *Moby-Dick*, 371.
17. Dionysius, *Critical Essays*, 379, 381.
18. Redfield, "Commentary," 251.
19. Momigliano, "The Place of Herodotus," 1.

charge is that Herodotus is a liar. Aristotle, for his part, expresses his ex-asperation with Herodotus in the *Generation of Animals* when he describes the fishermen who "join the chorus and repeat the same old stupid tale that we find told by Herodotus the fable-teller (ὁ μυθολόγος), to the effect that fish conceive by swallowing the milt" (756b4–8). Earlier in this same treatise, Aristotle notes that Herodotus "is incorrect" when he states that "the semen of Ethiopians is black, as though everything about a person with black skin were bound to be black" (736a10–14). Aristotle completes this statement with uncharacteristic pique: "and this in spite of their teeth being white, as he could see for himself."

Factual errors are factual errors, whether they are made by the first historian or the first political scientist. But it is not a matter that should detain us in a discussion of Herodotus.[20] Despite his longstanding double reputation as "father of history" and "father of lies," he is today cred-ited with serious and consistent attempts at historical accuracy: "He was often misinformed, usually by people who themselves believed what was in fact incorrect. But in the elementary duty of a historian, that is, the discovery of how the events actually took place, Herodotus has a good record."[21] In truth, Aristotle's quarrel with Herodotus is not about whether the historian put a high value on historical accuracy, which surely he did. The real source of Aristotle's ire (and that of Thucydides and others) concerns Herodotus' acceptance of hearsay—stories, myths, and opinions of all manner of excess—as valuable historical evidence.

According to Thucydides, it is the responsibility of historians to ex-

---

20. To be sure, this matter *has* detained Herodotean scholars of late. Fehling initiated a new round of skepticism toward Herodotus with his *Die Quellenangaben bei Herodot* (*Herodotus and His 'Sources'*). This was followed in quick succession by works by Armayor and West (to be discussed in Chapter 3). It will be evident that I find the response of Pritchett in *The Liar School* to be adequate to these challenges: in the course of this book, I want to demonstrate further that the typical question posed by the skeptical critics ("Did Herodo-tus really go to . . .") is most appropriately answered, "It doesn't matter."

Fehling performs the remarkable feat of at once denigrating the character of Herodo-tus and exaggerating his influence. It is impossible to believe both that Fehling's thesis could be correct (that Herodotus invented his sources on his way to perfecting the genre of "pseudohistory") and that anyone would ever have paid attention to *The History* as a serious work. Fehling's work ignores a vast body of considerations of the issues he dwells on; critics who are routinely referred to in this book debunk the intellectual boldness that Fehling perceives in his own work (*Herodotus*, 23 n 5, 56, 247).

21. Grene, "Historian as Dramatist," 477. Grene notes, for example, that although Herodotus was often misled by his Egyptian sources, modern Egyptologists are impressed by his diligent efforts to recount what happened. Pritchett elaborates in detail in both *Liar School* and "Appendix," 234–285.

tract from their retellings of events any traces of myth; he therefore rejects those prose-writers (λογογράφοι) who compose their works "more delightfully to the ear than conformably to the truth."[22] It is likely that Thucydides had Herodotus in mind when he has Pericles refer slightingly to those whose work might bring delight "for the moment," only for the truth to come out afterward to "confute the opinion conceived" (2.41). If there were no generally recognized evidentiary boundaries established when Herodotus wrote *The History*, those instituted later were drawn, and often explicitly, with Herodotus in mind as the transgressor. The reader for whom Thucydides wrote is instead someone who would "frame a judgment of the things past" after these things past had been "searched out by the most evident signs that can be" (1.21). If the evidence is circumscribed enough, Thucydides argues, then one might dispense with all irrational or simply untrue elements. In this respect, Aristotle would concur and "blame" Herodotus for not being Thucydides.[23] "But into the subtleties of the mythologists," Aristotle concludes, "it is not worth our while to inquire seriously" (*Met* 1000a18).

Herodotus, ὁ μυθολόγος, was not overly interested in circumscribing evidence; he treated what people thought and said about themselves as if they mattered, ἄλογος or not. Indeed, for Herodotus the accretions of conscious and mythical discourse that build up around the actual moment of action in an event in time past constitute that event insofar as it affects and reveals a community of the present. "History" is not the event but the explanations given to the event. These explanations, however, are not found ready-made; the conscious and mythical discourse—the λόγοι—that interests Herodotus first must be mastered by him. Dewald writes: "The *Histories* Herodotus has given us are the record of his heroic encounter: his exploits in capturing the λόγοι and his struggles to pin them down and make them speak to him the truths they contain."[24] Without the subtle shaping hand of the historian, great and wonderful deeds would "fail of their report."

As all-embracing as Herodotus' inquiries are, they do not aim for knowledge of everything that happened during the Persian War. Indeed,

22. Thucydides, *Peloponnesian War*, Hobbes translation, 1.21. Hereinafter, references will be cited parenthetically in text.

23. Consider Aristotle's injunction to tragedians in the *Poetics*: "There should be nothing [irrational, ἄλογος] among the actual incidents. If it be unavoidable, however, it should be outside the tragedy" (1454b6–8). On this passage, see the essays by Roberts and Frede in *Essays on Aristotle's "Poetics,"* ed. Rorty.

24. Dewald, "Narrative Surface," 147.

in some very basic ways, Herodotus' aim was patently a practical one.[25] As author of *The History*, Herodotus shares points of contact with Aristotle, author of the *Ethics*. The historian both shapes and preserves the Greek memory of the Persian War, for the purpose of affecting the identity and resolve of his contemporary audience. As Clark writes, neither the historian nor the φρόνιμος merely apply general principles; both must be people of experience and "must be able to guess where the principles do not apply, should not be applied (*NE* 1137b26f.) . . . 'history' is the ground of and impossible without the sense to see the best."[26] Just as Aristotle is "not investigating the nature of virtue for the sake of *knowing what it is*, but in order that we may become good, without which result our investigation would be *of no use*" (*NE* 1103b30–32, emphasis mine), so Herodotus does not investigate the past for the sake of simply knowing everything: "Herodotus did not intend to write a history of all that he knew about the epoch he described," concludes Charles W. Fornara: "He wrote about what was (or should be) "well known," "splendid," "worthy of relation."[27] This would seem to be his unstated criterion for narrowing down his professed aim to cover alike the small and great cities of mankind.

This insight may help us to identify where the Aristotelian and Herodotean uses of evidence coincide. Aristotle suggests in his own writing that the theoretical rigor of an opinion may be a less important claim to our attention than its persistence in time, but he is less than generous in granting the point to Herodotus. Much would be learned of Socrates' city-in-speech, Aristotle remarks, from its "actually being instituted" (*Pol* 1264a5f.); Hippodamus' drive for theoretical purity, notes Aristotle, makes him oblivious to the already existing practices in Athens and elsewhere (*Pol* 1268a9–10). It has perhaps not been stressed enough in the case of Aristotle that when he introduces stories for their universal lessons, he often does so quite apart from the factual truth of the story. For instance, as he goes through the various beginning points of revolutions in the *Politics*, he lists contempt of the ruler as one such cause, and says: "as when someone saw Sardanapallus carding wool with the women, if what the retailers of stories (οἱ μυθολογοῦντες) say is true (*though if not of him, this might well be true of another*)" (*Pol* 1312a1–3, emphasis mine). Or we

25. See Raaflaub, "Herodotus, Political Thought, and the Meaning of History," 232, and Dewald, "Practical Knowledge and the Historian's Role," 47–63.

26. Clark, *Aristotle's Man*, 134.

27. Fornara, *Nature of History*, 92.

might well consider his broad use of fictional examples in the *Ethics*.[28] He commonly uses stories told by Herodotus, ὁ μυθολόγος, to make his own point—the footbath of Amasis, *Pol* 1259b8; the egg of a crocodile; there is no attribution and thus no issue of historical veracity. On this point, Lloyd notes other occasions where Aristotle himself is not beyond using dubious Herodotean reports as evidence for "what has been seen."[29]

The Croesus-Solon encounter mentioned earlier is relevant here, for in this instance Aristotle fails to make the accusation that might easily have been made: that the encounter never really happened, and certainly never happened in the form of Herodotus' telling. Instead, he adapts the Solon-character of Herodotus for his own purposes. For reasons we will explore, it is as if Aristotle had quoted from the collected philosophical works of Solon rather than from the famous story in *The History*. The effect is not unlike Socrates' appropriation of Odysseus in the Myth of Er: just enough of his familiar characteristics are preserved in his philosophic transformation for readers to countenance the change.

In his musings on the meaning of εὐδαιμονία in the *Nicomachean Ethics*, Aristotle barely acknowledges the ordinary human inclination to wish to be as rich as Croesus, as the saying goes: "The life of money-making is one undertaken under compulsion, and wealth is evidently not the good we are seeking; for it is merely useful and for the sake of something else" (1096a6–8). His approach in considering the highest good or happiness is to begin by formulating his usual question—what is it? (τί ἐστί). He does not shrink from the challenges of defining happiness (if only in outline); to do so, he consults the opinions of mankind, even though the many and the wise disagree about its nature (1095a23). Aristotle considers the reputable opinions that have come down to him, including that of Solon, which is introduced ("must we, as Solon says, see the end?" [1100a12]), qualified ("Or must we add '[that the happy man must be] destined to live thus and die as befits his life'?" [1101a18–20]),

---

28. Davis, *Aristotle's "Poetics,"* xvii–xviii: "The most startling thing about the account of courage in the *Nicomachean Ethics* is that Aristotle uses almost exclusively fictional examples—Achilles, Hektor, Diomedes, and so forth. Without poetry there is virtually no possibility of seeing that element that makes courage what it is. . . . We need the whole story, and only poetry gives it to us."

29. Lloyd, *Magic, Reason and Experience,* 212. Lloyd refers to the following Herodotean accounts that are then taken up in *HA* 516a19f. and 579b5f.: "There was found a skull without suture, but all of one bone" (9.83); and "To the east of the Nestus . . . you will never see a lion, nor west of the Achelous in the rest of the mainland; but they are found in the land between these rivers" (7.126).

and dismissed ("So much for these questions" [1101a21])—with never a
mention of the author behind Solon's opinion.

Aristotle's strategy has the consequence of transforming the Herodotean, storytelling Solon into a sober Aristotelian philosopher. The
details that Aristotle has left out are apparent; for example, he does not
refer by name to Cleobis and Biton, whose timely dispatch by the gods
is not a subject a "real" philosopher was likely to take up. Aristotle's
final comment on Solon in the *Ethics* brings him precisely in line with
the moral teaching of Aristotle himself: "Solon, too, was perhaps sketch-
ing well the happy man when he described him as moderately furnished
with externals but as having done (as Solon thought) the noblest acts,
and lived temperately" (1179a9f.). Weil comments: "What Aristotle re-
joiced to discover in Solon (and was obliged to discover in one of the
Seven Sages) is the political embodiment of 'nothing in excess,' of the
mean (μεσότης)."[30]

To appreciate the significance of this Aristotelian accomplishment,
it is worth recalling that readers of *The History* have long identified the
character Solon with the views and personality of Herodotus himself.
Solon's tactful instruction of Croesus through stories in which the moral
is indicated rather than asserted, his philosophical bemusement at the
ways of humankind, his eye for marvels—and even his love of travel—
all seem to be essentially Herodotean qualities. Somehow, the wisdom of
Solon seems to illuminate that of Herodotus, until, that is, Aristotle tells
the story. "Every writer creates his own predecessors," Clark observes,
"and so does every philosopher."[31]

Contingency and Necessity

Aristotle has revealed himself as disciplined and principled next to the
free-running and unreliable Herodotus. One final step is required to
clinch Aristotle's superior philosophical identity, and this is for him to
impugn the historian's subject matter as comprising only singular and
contingent events. Aristotle does this in his famous statement about history in the *Poetics*. But here again, all is not as it seems. Aristotle both

---

30. Weil, "Aristotle's View of History," 205. Solon appears in a number of guises in
the works of Aristotle. Weil notes that in the *Politics* Aristotle finds it necessary to transform Solon into a member of the middle class: "on this point as on many others, he strives
to reconcile diverse traditions."

31. Clark, *Aristotle's Man*, 7.

overemphasizes the distinction between history and poetry (thus concealing his more fundamental distinction between theoretical knowledge on the one hand, and practical and productive knowledge on the other), and underemphasizes the common ground between practical philosopher, historian, and poet.

Aristotle claims that poetry is "something more philosophic and of graver import than history, since its statements are of the nature rather of universals, whereas those of history are singulars" (*Poet* 1451a36–b11). A universal statement, he explains, is "one as to what such or such a kind of man will probably or necessarily say or do," whereas a singular statement is "one as to what, say, Alcibiades did or had done to him." This is the passage in which Herodotus is named as the clear representative of the genre of history: "You might put the work of Herodotus into verse, and it would still be a species of history." The true distinction between history and poetry, he states, lies in the fact that the historian "describes what has happened," the poet "what might happen, i.e. what is possible as being probable or necessary." It seems that Aristotle prefers the enterprise of poets to that of historians because historians report not a "single action" (with a coherent beginning, middle, and end) but a "single period," which includes "all that happened in that to one or more persons, however disconnected the several events may have been" (1459a23–24).

In this passage, Aristotle apparently places Herodotus among the ranks of those historians of lesser import or seriousness. A number of commentators have argued that Aristotle's disparagement of history is unfair on his own terms, and others have attempted to defend Herodotus against Aristotle's slur, but these exercises remain largely defensive where a more offensive position is in order.[32] But critics have defended Thucydides with vigor against Aristotle's charge; it has been assumed

32. Moles writes, "Admittedly, Aristotle's critique of historiography is unfair: he chooses Alcibiades as the archetypal historiographical subject because Alcibiades was a supreme individualist, about whom it was indeed difficult to make useful generalizations" ("Truth and Untruth," 108). See also Ste. Croix, "Aristotle on History and Poetry," 46; Glover, *Herodotus*, 230; Gomme, *Poetry and History*, 100–101, 178; and Rosenmeyer, "History or Poetry?" 239–259.

Rosenmeyer believes that Aristotle, in his "careful manner," is "signalling to us that these judgements are relative, and that the same text might, with a moderate shift of emphasis or concern, be moved out of the camp of poetry into the camp of history or vice versa" (240). I am in full agreement with Rosenmeyer on this point; my interest is in why Aristotle has recourse to signals.

more than once (largely because of the Alcibiades allusion) that Aristotle had Thucydides explicitly in mind as he wrote this passage, and
that therefore his argument should be answered from a Thucydidean
perspective.[33] This could be, though it is worth recalling that Aristotle
nowhere mentions Thucydides in this particular passage, elsewhere in
the *Poetics,* or anywhere in the entire Aristotelian corpus. But the name
of Herodotus appears quite prominently, even gratuitously ("you might
put the work of Herodotus in verse"). Aristotle also uses (without attribution) as his example of singular statements events reported in *The
History:* the coincidental overlap of the naval battle off Salamis and the
battle with the Carthaginians in Sicily. Herodotus' appearance here is
no accident; for Aristotle to convince his readers of a decisive break between poetry and history requires him to confront the most poetic of
historians. That confrontation is worth reconsidering.

Aristotle's poetry-history distinction lends itself to misreading. That
is, Aristotle appears to be distinguishing between poetry and history,
and so he is; the basic difference, in Thomas G. Rosenmeyer's words,
is that the historian is constrained within a given time unit, whereas
the poet "creates his own": "The poet creates words, signifiers, a self-
authenticating verbal texture which does not have to be matched with
referents in the mass of facts and events we call the past."[34] Yet for Aristotle, the primary distinction is between poetry and history on one hand,
and philosophy on the other hand, between spheres of knowing that
treat of changeable matters, and those that treat of the unchanging and
the necessary. Hence the questionable aspect of Aristotle's presentation
centers on his choice of words in describing poetry as more philosophic
than history, for it is not his argument that poetry has to do with the
realm of *theoria.*

Like historians, poets imitate men and women of action; like historians, poets are tied to the practical world. But as Gerald F. Else observes,
Aristotle's point is commonly taken to mean that "poetry were actually a
branch of philosophy and the representation of universals were the fundamental concept of ποιητική": "On the contrary, these notions of the
"philosophical" content of poetry grow out of the concept that the work

33. See Pippidi, "Aristote et Thucydide," and von Fritz, "Aristotle's Contribution,"
132.
34. Rosenmeyer, "History or Poetry?" 247.

of art must be *beautiful*. . . . The structure of events "built" by the poet, in order to be beautiful, must be a unified and complete whole."[35]

The poet's work (ἔργον) for Aristotle is in "making plots," not in "making verses." Accordingly, putting anyone's work into verse would not make of them a poet: "the poet must be more the poet of his stories or plots than of his verses, inasmuch as he is a poet by virtue of the imitative element in his work, and it is actions that he imitates" (*Poet* 1451b27). The greater seriousness of poetry is due to the poet's ability to construct a coherent whole of events. And this is quite apart from whether the poet "should come to take a subject from actual history," Aristotle explains: "some historic occurrences may very well be in the probable and possible order of things; and it is in that aspect of them that he is their poet" (1451b29–31).

That some historic occurrences may be in the probable and possible order of things might well suggest to us the feasibility of the mixed genre of "poetic history"—on Aristotle's own terms. To be sure, we could predict that there would be a considerable area of overlap between the works of poet (or tragedian) and historian, without denying the essential distinction between the activities of considering "what might happen" and "what has happened." Historians do not conduct their inquiries without a view of what might happen, nor do poets (or philosophers, in all cases) compose their works unattached to what has happened; the probability and necessity involved in each enterprise are easily blurred.

Even as Aristotle makes this sharp distinction between the realms of the poet and historian, he consciously and subtly qualifies it. G. E. M. de Ste. Croix demonstrates along this line that it is not at all customary in the works of Aristotle for him to limit his terms to the dichotomy between "universal" and "singular" as he does here. There is a third term (the "as-a-general-rule principle") that accounts for the phenomenon of seeing the general in particular events.[36] A historian who worked on the level of this third term would seem to be serious, poetic—even, in a sense, philosophical. The more likely objects of Aristotle's attack would seem to be those who presume to be reporting the facts and nothing but the facts (the Atthidographers have been suggested); this is hardly applicable to Herodotus.

35. Else, *Aristotle's Poetics*, 302.
36. Ste. Croix, "Aristotle on History and Poetry," 51.

There is another, more controversial, indicator that Aristotle undermines his own sharp distinction between poetry and history. In *Poetics* 1459a21 Aristotle remarks that the "usual" histories fail to base themselves on a single action; as Clark notes, perhaps the "unusual" histories would not have this failing.[37] The passage is disputed, both because of the Greek itself, which is difficult, and because of the implication, which is that Aristotle recognizes something of the nature of a poetic history but will not acknowledge it openly. If we are to discount this reading, it should not be because we reject the implication that Aristotle would recognize the accomplishment of his predecessor only in an underhanded way. Rhetoric, Aristotle teaches us, is an art.

We are left with the sense that Aristotle is engaged first and foremost with defending philosophy and the theoretical life, and only secondarily with criticizing history against poetry. His disdain for contingent subject matter, "since man is *not* the highest thing in the world" (*NE* 1141a22), is based on the permanent separation between the realms of *theoria* and *praxis* and on the priority of the former. So historians may connect their material with whatever stories they will; they can do so only up to a point. History "does not deal with coherent wholes with a beginning, middle, and end. Such histories are mere aggregates of isolated facts, and fail to reveal the causes, the organic forms involved in the process of time."[38] To some degree or another, this is for Aristotle the unfortunate attribute of any practical or productive science. The result, as Rosen states, is that there is no accounting for the whole as whole; there are "only separate accounts of distinct families of phenomena. Not even the science of first principles provides us with an account . . . of the unity articulated as the tripartition of theory, practice, and production."[39] Aristotle's signals are plain enough: in the end, the disjunction that was posited at the start between *theoria* and *praxis* reappears.

From the *Poetics*, it evidently follows that the best kind of history would have a universal character, but Aristotle himself does not engage in a constructive analysis of the relative merits of histories. The very contingency of historical events gives the historian what Aristotle will not abide: the space to create, using rational and irrational matter alike. When Aristotle defends the philosophic life as the highest, he does so with the apparent intention of leaving behind him the more creative en-

37. Clark, *Aristotle's Man*, 131.
38. Ibid.
39. Rosen, *Quarrel*, viii.

deavors of poetry and history. It has been observed that Aristotle in the *Poetics* stands the creative process on its head, as he goes about defining tragedy and the rules for its construction; that is, Greek dramatists did not begin with an abstract conception and end with their characters, but began with real people and the stories attached to them.[40] Stephen Halliwell notes that Aristotle's prescriptivism is directed at the philosophical student: "If a young Athenian dramatist had taken the improbable decision of going to Aristotle for instruction in his work, he would have come away with material for reflection, but he would have had to develop his craft elsewhere."[41] Aristotle's recasting of the poetic impulse conceals its status as prior to philosophy, and reminds one of Plato's Socrates, who also demands of the poets that they explain themselves nonpoetically—as a philosopher would.[42] George Steiner considers this phenomenon in which analysis apparently displaces creativity in priority, and determines that "in the truth-hour of his consciousness," there is not "a commentator, critic, (or) aesthetic theorist . . . however masterly, who would not have preferred to be a source of *primary utterance and shaping*."[43] This is to view the quarrel between poetry and philosophy from the point of view of the poet, which is instructive just because it is not Aristotle's view. In the truth-hour of his consciousness, Aristotle would probably have preferred to be The Philosopher.

As The Philosopher, Aristotle is successful in persuading his audience of something remarkable: that the poetic history of Herodotus is inconceivable. Along the way, he diverts our attention from the old quarrel between poetry and philosophy. Perhaps to be seen as involved in this dispute at all would not serve well the reputation of the philosopher; everyday sympathies would likely lie with the poets. Or perhaps he recognized that the seeming attenuation of the quarrel represented the fuller victory of the philosopher. In any case, Aristotle amplifies the distance between poetry and history, and focuses our attention on this rather more recent opposition—notwithstanding the manifestly poetic history of Herodotus.

40. Else, *Aristotle's Poetics*, 309.
41. Halliwell, *Aristotle's "Poetics"*, 38.
42. See Heidegger, *Poetry, Language, Thought*. Herodotus recognizes this in his comments on Hesiod and Homer as poets who provided the early forms for later thought (2.53).
43. Steiner, *Real Presences*, 152. See also Kermode, *Genesis of Secrecy*.

CHAPTER 2

The Development of Social Memory

Fighting Stories

One of Herodotus' more disconcerting admissions comes late in his work: "I must tell what is said, but I am not at all bound to believe it, and this comment of mine holds about my whole *History*" (7.152). In effect, he is insisting here that his readers acknowledge his full control of the narrative, although it is far from clear even at this late stage how this control is exerted; he is silent on his rare ability to marshal "particulars, and even a false particular, into a coherent whole that compels us to reflect on a universal question; how an inquiry and a λόγος are made to join."[1] Whether Herodotus' comments convey doubt or support of his λόγοι, the persistence of his voice suggests that he is accountable for his history, and it is to this mystery of his composition that we now turn. What is to be explored, in the words of Walter Robert Connor, is Herodotus' "technique of breaking out of the immediacy of events and in reaching an audience of unknown dimensions and circumstances."[2] We would like to know how Herodotus succeeds in becoming the voice of what the Persian War signifies for his time—and ours.

To understand Herodotus' accomplishment is to take notice of how he grounds his broad spectrum of evidence; it is to notice that he is ever in contact with what I will call, following David Grene, fighting stories. These are the stories and diverse amplifications about an event of time past that begin immediately to fight their way into the discourse, and that persist over time in this discourse. Grene derives this phrase from a saying of Thucydides, who makes known his regret at the tendency of events of time past to fight their way, "past credence, into the country of myth" (ἀπίστως ἐπὶ τὸ μυθῶδες ἐκνενικηκότα [1.21]). As Grene notes, what Thucydides deems an unfortunate phenomenon is regarded by Herodotus as the occasion for rich meditation: Herodotus "thought that the country of myth for acts and words was just around the corner

---

1. Benardete, *Inquiries*, 6.
2. Connor, "Commentary," 258.

28

from them the moment they were done or uttered. But he was very far from thinking that this rendered them valueless for history."[3]

The importance of fighting stories for us is twofold. First, the country of myth [or "the mythy" ($\mu\nu\theta\hat{\omega}\delta\epsilon\varsigma$, distinct from $\mu\hat{\nu}\theta o\varsigma$)[4]] is said to be "just around the corner," suggesting that Herodotus is confronting a phenomenon that pertains to all historians. Thucydides impugns the historian who inattentively succumbs to this element in his data, but he also admits that he has to make the speeches conform to "what was nearest to the sum of the truth" in that the speeches were hard to remember with certainty even when he was present to hear them (1.22). His aim was for more accuracy—Liddell and Scott translate one of Thucydides' most prized words, $\dot{\alpha}\kappa\rho\iota\beta\dot{\eta}\varsigma$, as "painfully exact"—and it is clear that accuracy is easier to come by in contemporary, as opposed to distant, history. *The History* demonstrates this point, for the closer events are to Herodotus' time, the more informational checks come into play.[5] Nonetheless, it may be that Thucydides (and the tradition following him) does not entertain one daunting thought as fully as does Herodotus: that acts and words enter the realm of $\mu\nu\theta\hat{\omega}\delta\epsilon\varsigma$ instantaneously, and that it is not possible to prevent any act or any words from so doing.[6] This thought would tend to temper one's enthusiasm for seeking out the "painfully exact."

Second, it is undeniable that Herodotus found historical value in fighting stories, and this for reasons moderns should understand; to use Nietzschean terminology, fighting stories link knowledge and life. It is not the informational content of stories that makes them grip the imagination of a political community and serve to perpetuate its goals; the

3. Grene, "Introduction," *History*, 1.

4. Cook, *History/Writing*, 32. As Cook explains, $\mu\nu\theta\hat{\omega}\delta\epsilon\varsigma$ may mean both "story-dominated" and "false"—but for Herodotus the latter meaning attaches to the word $\mu\hat{\nu}\theta o\varsigma$ ("Herodotus: The Act of Inquiry," 41): "Herodotus surpasses his contemporaries in being [story-dominated]."

5. Herodotus wrote of a distant past for which he had almost no written sources, and he wrote for a near past for which his sources were severely limited; could he have managed so well, we wonder, with an excess of sources? That is our own particular problem. Hayden White, referring to Lévi-Strauss, comments: "the more information we seek to register about any given field of occurrence, the less comprehension we can provide for that field; and the more comprehension we claim to offer of it, the less the information covered by the generalities intended to explain it" ("Historicism, History, and the Figurative Imagination," 50).

6. Though, as Dewald notes, once historians have got the $\lambda\acute{o}\gamma o\iota$ right, if they have really got it, they have "at least put a stop to the further exercise of their Protean powers of self-transformation" ("Narrative Surface," 169).

source of its vitality is elsewhere. An example from American history may make clear how a factually inaccurate story might somehow be truer to the event than the factually accurate. The story of Paul Revere is one that continually fights to maintain its once-secure status. The tale of the solitary midnight rider whose alarm roused Middlesex villagers and farmers to rebellion against the British was enshrined by Longfellow ("Listen, my children, and you shall hear"). In contrast, the latest historical study depicts how each succeeding generation has produced its distinctive version of the story, the latest being that the muster of the militiamen in 1775 was the product of careful planning and collective effort rather than an act of spontaneous individuality. Despite these successive onslaughts, Longfellow's version seems firmly in the saddle.[7] The curious mixture of fact and fancy that Longfellow's fighting story contains may outrage the scholar, but it seems to succeed in representing the signature of its community. Such is the abiding interest of fighting stories, for Longfellow's Americans or for Herodotus' Greeks: they impart the origins, character, and destiny of the community, without attending unduly to matters of fact.

As resistant to analysis as fighting stories may be, we can provide a fresh look at Herodotus' criteria of evidence by examining his procedure in three settings that seem to present very different levels of historicity. The first example concerns his opening section in which he relates the stories of the Persian chroniclers, the likes of whom are unknown outside of *The History*. On this matter, Herodotus has been accused either of inventing or embellishing these stories, inasmuch as the scenario he puts forth is utterly implausible and no supporting tradition exists to back him up. In what sense, we ask, is he in contact with stories that fight their way into the tradition if he fabricates them? Our second example is the most famous of Greek military victories, the battle of Marathon. Here Herodotus' rendition is plausible, though few traditions exist to support him. In this case, criticism has largely centered on his reticence; Herodotus' rendition of Marathon has never seemed to measure up to the remembrances of his fellow Greeks. How, then, can he be considered to be attentive to fighting stories if he slights these popular accounts,

7. See Fischer, *Paul Revere's Ride*. Longfellow's Revere is "grossly, systematically, and deliberately inaccurate," as Fischer claims; nevertheless, he is remembered: "the scholars never managed to catch up with Longfellow's galloping hero" (331, 332). In generation after generation, the scholars are shown offering their definitive portraits of Revere, portraits that then serve to date the investigators rather than to fix the story for all time.

exaggerated though they may be, and if he furthermore omits important details? Finally, we will consider the experiment of Psammetichus,
where Herodotus recounts Psammetichus' effort to demonstrate that the
Egyptians are the oldest race of humankind. This story, while not beyond the realm of possibility, contains enough curiosities to keep readers
uncertain of its claims to truth. Does Herodotus presume to know that
this story fought its way into the Egyptian mind? If not, where are the
disclaimers that might easily have been made?

The Persian Chroniclers: A Failed Narrative

In his short opening section to *The History,* Herodotus relates the Persian
chroniclers' version of the origin of the Greek-Persian enmity. The odd-
ness of this section is pronounced, especially given its place of prominence in the work. In the Persian account that Herodotus provides, some
traditional Greek myths are vaguely recognizable in a cause-and-effect
scheme that locates the origins of hostility in a series of long-ago abductions. Io appears in this account, but not the Io of the Greeks, who
as priestess of Argos was loved by Zeus and subsequently transformed
by him to the shape of a heifer; ultimately she was driven to Egypt by
the gadfly sent by Hera to torment her. As the Persians have it, Io was
carried off to Egypt by treacherous Phoenicians while she was innocently
"buying from among the wares" aboard their vessel. The Phoenician
story is more malicious still: "She lay, they say, with the ship's captain in
Argos, and, when she found she was pregnant, in shame for her parents
she sailed with the Phoenicians voluntarily" (1.5).

The points of contact in the Persian account and in the Greek
myths are nevertheless unmistakable: the location (Argos), the genealogy (daughter of Inachus), and the destination (Egypt). And so with each
segment of the Persian explanation. The outlines of the Greek myth are
visible, but the import has been drastically revised. Europa was carried
away by "certain Greeks" who "must have been Cretans" (1.2), not trans-
ported to Crete by Zeus (in the form of a gentle, beautiful bull). And in
perhaps the most startling rendition, Helen, daughter of Zeus and the
most beautiful of women, is carried off by Alexander (Paris) because "he
was certain that he would not have to give satisfaction for it" (1.3), as the
previous aggressors had not.

This passage has all the markings of Herodotean authorship—and
Herodotean humor. We therefore are disinclined to search beyond the

text for any testimony to the physical existence of the Persian chroniclers. Nevertheless, it does not follow that Herodotus has opened his poetic history with a purely poetic invention, much less with an entertaining interlude to warm up his audience. Herodotus demonstrates in his delivery of these stories an unsettling self-consciousness ("that is not how the Greeks tell it. . . . This is still the Persian story" [1.2]) that alerts us to their careful and significant construction. He opens with a puzzle, a puzzle solved only when we see the opening as a parody of his own practice as historian.

If we scrutinize the exaggerated logical account of the Persian chroniclers and the convoluted series of Greek myths at its core, we notice that it stands as the failed model of inquiry for Herodotus, but as a model of inquiry just the same. That is, Herodotus aspires for success just where he has the chroniclers (and the poets) fail. The Persian chroniclers blunder when they associate cause and effect in a strained and implausible way; they are untrue to the shared body of mythical stories as the Greeks knew them. As Aristotle might explain, they patch together facts that are both too large and too discordant for their plot, so that the effect is not serious, not philosophical. Perhaps Herodotean historiography is best approached, at least initially, with this insertion of a failed narrative: the Persian story was not to fight its way into memory.[8] And the Greek poets are also subject to implicit criticism, even though they are only conjured up here as a result of the chroniclers infringing on their material. The Persians may be accused of distorting Greek myths, but the Greeks would be hard pressed to argue that the evidence of the Persians is tainted in regard to Io, Europa, Jason and the Argonauts, or the Trojan War. Herodotus, the historian with the ear for fighting stories, distinguishes himself from poet and chronicler alike.

Herodotus sets himself apart from the poets first because they too easily resort to μῦθος. On the question of the unusual properties of the Nile, Herodotus relates an opinion that is "wonderful in the telling" but "without knowledge," and that is that the Nile "flows from Ocean—and [that] Ocean [flows] round the whole world" (2.21). His subsequent remarks are telling:

8. Vandiver argues that the Persian accounts of the causes (αἴτια) of the earliest wars "rob the Greeks of κλέος." I would emend this: the Persian rendition attempts, but fails, to affect the κλέος of the Greek stories, and the failure is precisely the point. I agree with her larger thesis: Herodotus' "whole work is a demonstration of the errors inherent in the Persian viewpoint" (Heroes, 124).

The person who urged the theory about the Ocean has carried his story, which is indeed only a tale (τὸν μῦθον), back to where it vanishes and so cannot be disproved. For myself, I do not know that there is any river Ocean, but I think that Homer or one of the older poets found the name and introduced it into his poetry (2.23).

Although the poet turns out to be closer to the truth about the Nile than the historian ("So it is my settled thought that the sun is the cause of these matters" [2.26]), Herodotus nonetheless makes clear that the historian remains in contact with his sources and thus is more responsible than the poet; he will not pursue the myth "back to where it vanishes" (ἐς ἀφανές). It may happen that the historian is factually wrong and the poet right, but the distinction between the two—even if less marked than alleged by Aristotle—remains in force. As Aristotle declares in the *Poetics,* if a poet happens to treat of historical occurrences, he may still be a poet for all that (1451b29–30).

Herodotus seems to believe, further, that he does not enjoy the poets' prerogative of ignoring awkward information. So unhampered by inconvenient facts are the poets, according to Herodotus, that Homer could ignore the "well-known" tradition that places Helen in Egypt for the duration of the Trojan War (2.116). In Book II, Herodotus explains that the Egyptians have their own perspective of the Trojan War, which is that the Greeks had fought a futile war in Troy because Helen had been held captive in Egypt for the duration. Paris, they said, had been propelled to Egypt by violent winds after leaving Sparta, and there he had been discovered in his impious deed; the Egyptians had then driven him out while guarding Helen for the eventual return of the Greek host. The Egyptian priests who related this story to Herodotus claimed further that the Greeks themselves had to acknowledge the truth of this account, for when they captured Troy, "there was no Helen!" (2.118). At that juncture, Menelaus had to journey to Egypt and the court of King Proteus, and there "took back Helen, quite unhurt, and all his own possessions as well" (2.119). Then, as Herodotus reports, Menelaus proved himself an unjust man to the Egyptians, for he sacrificed two children of the natives in his attempt to appease the contrary winds which held back his homecoming. Herodotus concludes, "Part of these matters, the priests told me, they learned from their researches; but they said that what happened in their own country *they knew for absolute fact*" (2.119).

Herodotus quite unexpectedly concurs in the judgment of the Egyptian priests: "No, the Trojans did not *have* Helen to give back, and, when they spoke the truth, the Greeks did not believe them" (2.120). He puts forward his Anaximander-like opinion that a divine lesson lay behind these events ("for great wrongdoings great also are the punishments from the gods" [2.120]); Nicholas Ayo correctly notes that the poignant irony of the Trojan War then must be read in "this impossible quest for no actually present women."[9] But the lesson is surely also one of the historian appropriating the work of the poet: "And I think Homer knew the tale; but inasmuch as it was not so suitable for epic poetry as the other, he used the latter and consciously abandoned the one here told" (2.116).[10] Herodotus is allowing for poetic license but will not himself yield to it; hence *The History* seems able to contain the *Iliad,* while the reverse is not true. Herodotus gains in status by engaging with the most serious poetic authority—on his own truth-telling terms. In other words, Herodotus employs Homer as Aristotle was later to employ Herodotus.

If the poets of Herodotus' account tend to undervalue inherited stories (Aeschylus "stole the thing I tell; for he created Artemis as the daughter of Demeter" [2.156]), they can also go wrong by straying too far into the historian's realm. Herodotus writes that "when Phrynicus produced his play *The Capture of Miletus,* the whole audience at the theater burst into tears and fined Phrynicus a thousand drachmas for reminding them of a calamity that was their very own" (6.21). Herodotus could tell the same story to Athens and be rewarded handsomely. The difference seems to be that the historian has prepared his audience to anticipate in the particulars of their own experience the emergence of the most consequential questions.

These reflections on the poets admittedly take us beyond the proemium to *The History,* but the point is that even at this early stage Herodotus conveys his interest in the ways that people ascribe meaning to themselves and to past events through the kinds of stories they tell.[11]

9. Ayo, "Prolog and Epilog," 33. Freeman translates Anaximander's famous saying thus: the "source from which existing things derive their existence is also that to which they return at their destruction, according to necessity; for they give justice and make reparation to one another for their injustice, according to the arrangement of Time." *Ancilla,* 19=DK B1 (I.89, 12).

10. "Herodotus is in effect implying that the events narrated by the *Iliad* are part of a larger scheme of events as narrated by himself." Nagy, *Pindar's Homer,* 228.

11. Krischer perceptively notes that the way critics answer the terminological question of what to call the opening section of *The History* has everything to do with the problems of interpretation that are recognized. "Herodots Prooimion," 159.

The poetic way has been shown to have limitations; the poets appear relatively unbound by their subject matter (and this despite Aristotle's prescription in the *Poetics:* "The traditional stories . . . must be kept as they are, e.g. the murder of Clytaemnestra by Orestes" [1453b23–24]). The conclusion to be drawn from *The History* is that the poets are potentially irresponsible, though this emerges only gradually and piecemeal. The way of the chronicler comes under more immediate attack in the opening section.

Herodotus deconstructs the evidence put forward by his alleged Persian chroniclers by describing it in the most banal, quotidian fashion possible.[12] Through our own familiarity with the Greek understanding and especially with Helen, "the face that launched a thousand ships," we are impressed by how flat and self-serving the Persian rendition that Herodotus produces here is. Gone is the poetry and heroism of the Trojan War; what remains is a view of the Greeks overreacting to a petty squabble over women. The Persians are made to appear as the injured ones, inasmuch as they themselves are willing to overlook the insignificant abductions. They have created an exact chronology out of timeless and mythical figures; they have attributed base and largely economic motives to the most striking personalities; and they have connected these diverse and separate entities into one narrative.[13] They demonstrate in the pages of Herodotus' *History* what turns out to be a marked Persian tendency to simplify and distort the course of events for their own enhancement. Their justification for initiating the Persian War is that they were goaded by a Greek invasion into Asia that took place many centuries before Marathon.[14] What comes across most strikingly in the Persian rendition is that they are able to rationalize their own behavior under any circumstances; they resolutely will not attend to the utterances of others.

Herodotean historiography offers the corrective. Herodotus is acutely sensitive to those indicators in a people's storehouse of memories that differentiate it from all others, and he, in turn, subtly (or not) reproduces these differences. Thus the memorable quality of the opening

12. See Knapp and Michaels, "Against Theory," 723–742, and "Against Theory 2: Hermeneutics and Deconstruction," 49–68.

13. See also Flory, *Archaic Smile*, 25–26.

14. In a similar vein is Darius' cause for making war against the Scythians: "Darius wanted to punish the Scythians because in former times they had taken it upon themselves to invade Media" (4.1). The former times referred to are the end of the seventh century.

section of *The History* is not that it vindicates the Persians in any way, but that it identifies them for the present purposes of Herodotus. We shall see this unflinching rationalism in the Persians again. The crucial message is this: Herodotus has captured in this episode the manner in which a people will put its stamp on recollections, such that the same subject matter will be remembered uniquely by diverse peoples. It follows that different peoples will look at the same past happenings and extract stories that depict a different course of events. The past "as it actually happened" could take as many variations as there were perspectives. Such is the import of the Herodotean methodology, attested to from the start by the unlikely scenario put forward by the Persian chroniclers.

If Herodotus must fill in those memories and in effect invent those Persians, as some might object, our response must be to return to the equilibrium Herodotus establishes between poet and chronicler. His powers of creation do not have free reign. He is not at liberty to invent something out of nothing; he must be open to the emendations to his account that outside contacts bring. When Arnold Gomme observes of great poets that they are bound in some degree by historical fact both because of their own inhibitions and because of what the audience would demand, he then overrides the distinction in a significant afterthought: "for both poet and audience belonged to their age and were in sympathy one with the other."[15] For Herodotus in particular we can assume audience sympathy.[16] His history comes to us already subjected to review by his audience; this is not unlike the review the so-called Persian chroniclers underwent.[17] The difference is that Herodotus emerges as truth-teller: his story fought, and it won.

15. Gomme, *Poetry and History*, 13.

16. It is generally assumed that Herodotus wrote the text for the purpose of public recitation, and a number of stories circulated to this effect. Among the more implausible and oft-repeated examples are first, that Thucydides as a mere boy heard Herodotus recite from his history, and thereupon burst into tears; and second, that for his efforts, Herodotus received ten talents from the city of Athens—enough money, claims Momigliano, for him to eat for about 167 years. (Momigliano, "Historians and their Audiences," 65.) What seems certain is that Herodotus was a transitional figure, standing between the bard who recites without written aid, and the historian who writes without (except on occasion) public oration. It is not clear what physical materials Herodotus used; he describes papyrus growing in Egypt but not its use as paper, on which he presumably wrote.

17. Pritchett makes this point in overturning Fehling's arguments: "many of the alleged fabrications of Herodotus pertain to Greek sources (Samos, Athens, Korinth, etc.), whose people would easily have perceived that Herodotus had fabricated his stories about themselves" (*Liar School*, 80). See also Cobet's review of Fehling, 742.

Monitoring Success: Herodotus' Marathon

We move now from the putative evidence of the Persian chroniclers to the evidence provided by Herodotus in his own name for the battle of Marathon. No one has ever raised any doubts about the occurrence of Marathon as an event. It was close enough to Herodotus' time that he surely could have encountered children of the participants, if not the participants themselves. And there have always been witnesses like Pausanias to attest to the Athenian tomb and other markers of the battle:

> On the plain is the grave of the Athenians, and upon it are slabs giving the names of the killed according to their tribes; and there is another grave for the Boeotian Plataeans and for the slaves. . . . A trophy, too, of white marble has been erected.[18]

For once, the criticism of Herodotus centers not on his tendency to embellish or invent, but on his reticence. He neglects to explain significant details of the battle, namely, why the Persian cavalry seems to have played no role; he does not mention the monuments that were set up to celebrate the Greek exploits; and he refrains from telling the stories that were passed on about the participation of the gods Athena, Heracles, and Theseus and the local heroes Marathon and Echetlus. Even the most sober-minded readers of Herodotus were prompted to observe that his account is "meager and lacking in detail."[19] Gomme avers that everyone knows one thing about Herodotus' narrative of Marathon: it "will not do."[20] How are we to explain the fact that Herodotus dispenses with much of the discourse that grew up around the event as put forth by his contemporary Greeks? Why this version of Marathon, and not a fuller one?

Herodotus' account of Marathon is compact, to be sure, but it should be recognized that in this compact design is revealed nothing less than the unfolding of Athenian identity. Marathon seems to represent for Herodotus the moment in which Athenian political identity is first haltingly enunciated, and the most critical details of this account bring home this point.[21] And this political message is not one that will

18. Pausanias, *Description of Greece*, 1.32.
19. How and Wells, *Commentary*, 2:354.
20. Gomme, "Herodotos and Marathon," 29.
21. I cannot agree with Euben, who claims that "Salamis set the terms in which Athenians defined themselves as a people" ("The Battle of Salamis," 360). Setting the terms of Athenian identity is precisely what is accomplished under the leadership of Miltiades

be served by indulging in the tales of gods and heroes. There may be material for the poets in those traditional stories, but the historian must be more restrained; in no sense is the historian's subject matter found ready-made and serviceable in the stories that circulate among a people. The account of Marathon therefore serves to remind us that Herodotus does not receive λόγοι as if they were in themselves trustworthy gauges of the world. He makes his readers understand that they rely wholly on him as a guide through otherwise equivocal material. He seems to delight in stepping in to expose the contradictions and the untrustworthiness of λόγοι, and presumes that his direction is vital in the transmission of these λόγοι. As Carolyn Dewald remarks, "We are certainly not allowed the illusion that ["the route of the λόγοι"] exists independent of his efforts, or that we can traverse it by ourselves unaided."[22]

The "route of the λόγοι" that Herodotus plots for Marathon is one that will not make the battle larger than life, as the provincial stories had it. The evidence is drawn so as to reveal the enduring meaning of Marathon, not to magnify it beyond all use. Herodotus can thus be seen identifying the deepest causes of Greek victory at the same time that he suggests the import of this victory for that moment and thereafter. As historian of the Persian War, he does not define the Greeks in a way that either incorporates tales of the superhuman strength of Greek combatants or dwells on their supernatural allies on the field.[23]

What, then, of the more mundane matters Herodotus omits, such as an account of the monuments to the dead, or of the timely disappearance of the Persian cavalry? Herodotus gives much less of an account

---

at Marathon, which explains why Herodotus' account in Book VI so unmistakably serves to anticipate events at Salamis in Book VIII. Benardete (*Herodotean Inquiries*, 4) is on the mark: "The victories at Salamis and Plataea are Marathon and Thermopylae writ large, and they complete without altering the argument of the *Inquiries*."

22. Dewald, "Narrative Surface," 149. On one occasion, Herodotus states: "I will write my account according to the evidence of those Persians whose desire is not to make solemn miracles of all that concerns Cyrus but to tell the very truth," and adds intriguingly, "But I know three other ways to tell the story of Cyrus" (1.95). He does not attempt to soften the impact of these assertions ["These are the two reasons given for Polycrates' death; you may believe which you prefer" (3.122)]. Generally speaking, in this type of example Herodotus describes the alternatives such as to leave the reader without any definitive evidence for preferring one version over the other (cf. 5.45).

23. Similarly, he censures the Athenians for being duped by Peisistratus into believing that Athena was orchestrating his return (1.60), and corrects the Dodonaean story which had doves speaking with human voices (2.54–57).

of the former, the physical signs, than he does to the latter; with Athenian speech already tending to magnify their battle deeds, Herodotus has grounds for his reserve. Besides, Marathon was not Thermopylae, where the epitaphs and the pillars to the dead were at the crux of the story (7.227–228). But the matter of the Persian cavalry is more troubling, inasmuch as it would hardly seem to be a matter of indifference to Herodotus that characters he himself introduces on the stage are absent during the main action—without their absence being noted or, apparently, noticed. This is of more than strategic interest, for part of the objection is aesthetic: the narrative lacks closure.

This much said, Herodotus' omissions are hardly grounds for a devastating critique of his historiography. On one hand, if he unknowingly neglects to mention the whereabouts of the cavalry, then we might assume that their original mention is to be attributed to the fact that it was common knowledge among the Greeks that the Persian cavalry had been spotted at some time during the invasion; it would not necessarily be known what happened to them. This would leave Herodotus with a piece of information that dangles awkwardly in the narrative, but it would simultaneously suggest strong confirmation of our claims about the irrepressibility of fighting stories: even incomplete accounts may battle their way into speech. Gomme writes persuasively of this syndrome of the unhitched historical fact forcing its way (unaccountably) into the narrative: in Richard II, he writes, Shakespeare leaves intact "a good deal of incongruous historical residue" in the process of transforming the chronicles into the play.[24] On the other hand, if Herodotus knowingly leaves the cavalry out of his account, then we can speculate that he is anticipating the postmodernists by two millennia by signaling the authorial incapacity to contain the "route of the λόγοι." The History stands up to both readings.

What remains indisputable is that, as a whole, Herodotus' account of Marathon is coherent, and it is coherent because Herodotus projects compelling views of Athenian and Persian characters as a way of illuminating Marathon. The politicized Athenians are prone to great swings in behavior, evident in the distance between the noble urgings of Miltiades

24. Gomme, *Poetry and History,* 10. Herodotus disbelieves in more than one geographical account that nevertheless makes it into his history—for which we are grateful: "For my own part, I do not . . . know of the actual existence of the Tin Islands, from which our tin comes" (3.115).

and the persistent suggestions of Alcmaeonidae treachery. Meanwhile, the apolitical Persians are ever rational and steadfast; consequently they are baffled by their opponents, who so unexpectedly charge them in battle that they think them to be "possessed by some very desperate madness" (6.112). These characterizations are consonant with the Herodotean picture of the Athenians as a people for whom authority ascends from the people, and where discord and dispute are the rule; and of the Persians as a people for whom authority descends from the Great King, and descends predictably and uniformly.

Herodotus' description of the Athenians before Marathon gives us a fairly typical view of their ability—and the ability of their chosen leaders —to move easily between a noble defense of themselves as a people in times of crisis and their base pursuits of gain directly thereafter. Miltiades demonstrates just this pattern. He delivers a stirring speech and impels the Athenians as Athenians to resist the huge invading army; it is an act of creative intelligence on his part that serves to promote the common good of the Athenians. After the danger passes, however, Miltiades just as surely undermines this sense of common good by pursuing his own treacherous ends. This behavior is to be symptomatic for the Athenians, and this explains in part why Herodotus' account of Marathon has proved unpopular: nobility and baseness are presented side by side. Without a doubt, this characterization is meant to resonate with the Athenians as a people.

The most unsavory side of the Athenians portrayed by Herodotus comes across in his rendition of the "Alcmaeonidae slander." According to his account, a story was passed around after the battle of Marathon that alleged that the Alcmaeonidae (sons and descendants of Alcmaeon) had held up a shield to signal to the Persians at Marathon when it was safe for them to make a run on Athens. The accusation is that the aristocratic Alcmaeonidae were ready to betray the city and *demos* for their own private gain among the Persians, and that the Persians fully expected to overrun Athens through the same means used to take Eretria, which is to say, through the treachery of the city's leading men.

It has been customary for interpreters to dismiss this slander as emanating from a source hostile to the Alcmaeonidae, but one critic holds Herodotus accountable for this story: Plutarch. In his diatribe against Herodotus, Plutarch sometimes verges on the hysterical, but he never underestimates him. Here he excoriates Herodotus for his invidious characterizations:

Elsewhere he makes a pretence of defending the Alcmaeonidae, dropping these charges—which he was the very first man to bring against them. . . . This is what you are doing: you make a charge, and then you speak in their defense; you spread slanders against distinguished men which you subsequently withdraw. It must be because you don't trust yourself—because it is your own voice that you have heard saying that the Alcmaeonidae raised a signal. . . . Yes, when you defend the Alcmaeonidae you reveal yourself as a malicious accuser.[25]

Plutarch has surely not exaggerated the ingenuity of the historian's presentation. The seemingly casual sequence of thoughts that Herodotus leads us through is about as effective an indictment against the Alcmaeonidae as could be imagined. He begins, "It is a wonder to me—indeed, I do not accept the story—that the Alcmaeonidae ever showed that shield" (6.121). He argues feebly that the Alcmaeonidae were no friends of despots. Then: "Someone might say that perhaps they betrayed their country in disgust at the democracy in it" (6.124). But "reason" would not have it so, because of the high repute in which these men were held. He concludes, after more diverting observations: "True, a shield *was* so displayed; that cannot be disputed, for it undoubtedly happened; but who it was that was the agent I cannot say, further than what I have declared already" (6.124). If some hostile source were responsible for this story in the first place, Herodotus has made it his own in the retelling.

Yet Plutarch was wrong to conclude that Herodotus was therefore a malicious accuser.[26] There is not vindictiveness in the accusation, but a kind of detached and indulgent humor, and it could reasonably be argued that the truth or falsehood of the slander is not at all the point. Most likely Herodotus believed the slander to be credible, but at the same time he wanted it to represent more than the isolated instance of duplicity that it otherwise might. He made the incident general, and he made it historic. The great vulnerability of the Athenians would ever rise from the same source as their great strength: their common good depended on the will of free individuals. Private inclinations could have overpowered Athens at this moment, but did not. The threat was ingrained.

The counterbalance to this threat to Athens in the account of He-

---

25. Plutarch, "On the Malice of Herodotus," ch. 27.

26. Legrande reaches a similar conclusion in both "De la 'malignité' d'Hérodote" and *Hérodote: Introduction.*

rodotus is the reaffirmation of the Athenian people as articulated by
Miltiades. Herodotus lavishes as much attention on the words he gives
to Miltiades to rouse the Athenians as he did on his drawn-out charges
against the Alcmaeonidae. If this has been less commented on—slander
is, after all, more engrossing than approbation—the portraits nevertheless belong side by side. Herodotus is neither a lover of barbarians, as
Plutarch alleges, nor an idealistic proponent of Athens, as the more common reading has it. Rather, it is a feature of his art that he deepens caricatures through the repetition of many simple but dissimilar contrasts.
At times the contrast involves the tendencies within one people (or one
individual, say, Miltiades); this is supplemented, in turn, by other contrasts—Athenian with Spartan, Greek with Persian, Persian with Egyptian. The cumulative effect of these contrasts is to create multileveled
portraits, portraits that will not sustain charges of either idealization or
malignity on the part of the historian.

Thus it is that the picture of Miltiades and the Athenians at this
one moment is altogether noble. Before Marathon, the Athenians had
every reason to expect the same fate as that of the Eretrians, for events
were unfolding in a like manner. There was division among the leaders
about whether or not to fight, and, according to Herodotus, "it was the
worse opinion that was gaining" (6.109). At this instant Miltiades takes
the initiative and speaks to Callimachus, the polemarch. Miltiades urges
Callimachus to take command in asserting the freedom of Athens; his
appeal is to the greatness of the Athenian city: "It lies in your hands,
Callimachus, whether to enslave Athens or keep her free and thereby
leave a memorial for all the life of mankind, such as not even Harmodius and Aristogiton left behind them. For now the Athenians are in
their greatest danger ever since they were Athenian at all" (6.109).

Miltiades continues in this way to promote a vision of the Athenian
city, "free and the first in Greece." The words are to shape the deeds;
Miltiades forces the reality to fit his conception of the Athenians. "Ever
since they were Athenians at all," the Athenians had not had such an
opportunity to make a name for themselves, and Miltiades seizes this
chance to guide their self-definition. It is a moment of cultural self-
consciousness, and it shows how the words of a single individual may
leave an imprint on and inform that consciousness. Though the moment
is fleeting, it is out of such moments that greatness emerges.

The Persians, in contrast, have no visible crisis at Marathon in formulating their role. What perplexes them is the aggressive position the

Athenians assume. The remark that the Persians believed the Athenians to be mad is the core of the portrait, for Herodotus is pointing to the vulnerability of the authoritarian regime. The Persians of Herodotus' description are accustomed to quantify their goods, such that they are at a loss to explain departures from this Persian way of measuring the world: "After valor in fighting, the goodness of a man is most signified in this: that he can show a multitude of sons. To him who can show most, the King sends gifts every year. For multitude, they think, is strength" (1.136).

The Athenians act in a way that must defy the reasoning of a literal-minded people, for they do not characterize their strength in numbers.[27] The Persians may outnumber them, and the Persians may have the example of Eretria (and the Athenian traitors) on their side, but the Athenians nevertheless "advanced on the Persians at a run" (6.112). The Persians in *The History* never do get a grasp on the Greek mind, and it is their inability to adapt to such foreign behavior that unnerves them in crisis. The Persians, writes Gomme, "had not that aptitude and inclination to put themselves on record consciously and intellectually, and so with an understanding of what the difference between Persia and Greece was."[28] The capacity of a people to transcend the vicissitudes of history seems to be linked by Herodotus to its ability to accommodate the unfamiliar.

The puzzlement with which the Persians regard the Athenians at Marathon is, in Herodotus' depiction, to continue throughout the course of the war. Indeed, this first manifestation anticipates the role that Demaratus will soon play for the Persians, that is, the role of the unheeded interpreter of Greek, and specifically, Spartan, custom. The Persians have in their service a dispossessed Spartan king who willingly details the ways of the Greeks. However, it is axiomatic that Xerxes is amused and not enlightened by Demaratus. When, for instance, Xerxes speculates that the Greeks would be unable to fight him even if they could somehow all agree to assemble, Demaratus attempts to undeceive him; Xerxes then appeals to plain reason: "Now, I would like to see this in plain reason: how could a thousand or ten thousand or even fifty thousand confront so great an army as mine if they were all alike free and not subject to one command?" (7.103). Xerxes will not alter his course, for rationalism is too deeply embedded in Persian custom.

Two features of Herodotus' reconstruction of Marathon emerge

27. See Konstan, "Persians."
28. Gomme, *Poetry and History,* 106.

markedly. First, there is his reserve in describing the Greek victory. His contemporaries and successors alike preferred a more dramatic telling, one that would grant heroic status to the Greek participants.[29] Herodotus does not sanction this outlook, presumably because such an account would not succeed in encouraging individual Greeks to assume responsibility for shaping their future. To affect what would come, they had to be able to draw the appropriate lessons from their past, and this meant recognizing the precarious nature of the victory. The second feature to note in Herodotus' reconstruction is his way of providing dramatic and dramatically balanced peaks in the action that the audience itself must integrate. Herodotus is confident enough in his descriptive powers (his style, says Aristotle, is free-running) not to have to dictate the combined meaning of the shield held up by the traitors and the speech of Miltiades. He provides sufficient clues to enable us to be able to recreate Marathon imaginatively and meaningfully.

The Herodotean evidentiary method thus appears to deserve a predisposed respect rather than disparagement, for his version of Marathon has outlasted all of its corrections.[30] Both the reserve of Herodotus and his choice of significant details point toward the same historiographical end: to employ Marathon as a cautionary and an inspiriting moment in Greek history. Athenian failings as well as Athenian successes must be recognized, Persian vulnerabilities must be evaluated, and, most of all, past actions must be seen in light of present concerns. The fundamental challenge to the Athenian people would not be addressed either by tales of superhuman courage or by a simple chronicling of military events. The Athenian challenge might be met, though, by expressions of another kind: by creative, self-conscious, and bold affirmations of character. This is what Miltiades is shown accomplishing momentarily, and it is what Herodotus himself engages in throughout his history.

29. See Toynbee, *Greek Historical Thought*, 231. In the section "Is Herodotus Malicious," Toynbee quotes from Plutarch's *Moralia:* "It is unpardonable to have spoilt the greatness of the victory and to have made the world-famous achievement of Marathon end in nothing."

30. Single Herodotean critics may presume to decide once and for all the issue of the authority of Herodotus, but the world goes right on reading *The History* just the same. On this point, Will refers to questions that continue to be posed (Is Herodotus a man of science? an artist?); these questions interest readers "who do not accept limiting history only to erudition, only to the establishment of duly authenticated facts." Will, review of *Die Quellenangaben bei Herodot,* 121.

Psammetichus: From Story to History to Essence of a People

Finally, we turn to an Egyptian example that features not a military hero who constitutes the political community as he speaks before the troops, but the King who wants to validate his (prepolitical) community, a community defined by its stability. The Egyptian King Psammetichus seeks to determine the oldest race of humankind in order to assure the Egyptians of their claims to antiquity. Herodotus explains that according to the priests of Hephaestus, the Egyptians before the reign of King Psammetichus had assumed that they were the oldest of mankind. Psammetichus, however, wanted to know in truth, yet could not be satisfied through his inquiries. He therefore arranged for two newborns to be taken away from their ordinary households, and to be raised by a shepherd among his flocks. No humans were to speak to the children, who were to be kept in a lonely dwelling by themselves. The shepherd alone was to care for them, and to bring the goats to them for their milk. The king's intention in this, Herodotus reports, was "to hear from those children, as soon as they were done with meaningless noises, which language they would speak first" (2.2). After two years passed, the shepherd observed the children reaching to him and calling "*bekos.*" When the king was informed and became a witness to their behavior, he set out to learn who of humankind had something by this name. Discovering that the Phrygians called bread "bekos," Psammetichus and the Egyptians "conceded and, making this their measure, judged that the Phrygians were older than themselves" (2.2). The Egyptians were content then to judge themselves second oldest of humankind.

Focusing for the moment on the subject matter and not the transmission of the Psammetichus story, we note its suggestion of an Egyptian character.[31] Elsewhere the Egyptians are revealed as an inquisitive

---

31. The critic with whom I am in most obvious disagreement on this point is Fehling, who identifies the "stories of national origins" as the best examples of Herodotus failing to provide "*any correct information*" (6,7, emphasis mine). Fehling asserts further that "Herodotus never made any effort to obtain genuine information" even though he "must have known perfectly well that other, non-Greek peoples had traditions of their own and that *these had nothing to do with those of the Greeks*. . . . He simply *had no interest* [in such traditions]" (7, emphasis again mine). That Herodotus had no interest in the traditions of non-Greeks indeed comes as a surprise. Aly's assessment strikes a more sane note: "No people has matured without having the closest connection with the drives of its neighbors." Aly, *Volksmärchen, Sage und Novelle bei Herodot*, 2. Fehling's opponents on this point are countless; see, for instance, *Hérodote et Les Peuples Non Grecs*.

people proud of their age and accumulated wisdom, but noticeably lacking in self-awareness. Herodotus makes numerous comments on their
powers of observation: "The Egyptians claim that they know these matters absolutely because they are continually making their calculations
and continually writing down the number of years" (2.145). Similarly, in
the *Timaeus*, Plato has the Egyptian priest remark to Solon, "And whatever happened either in your country or in ours, or in any other region
of which we are informed . . . they have been written down by us of
old and are preserved in our temples." [32] At the same time, though, the
Egyptians are shown to be incurious about the most dramatic natural
phenomenon in their midst: "I was not able to find out anything at all
about [the singularity of the Nile] from the Egyptians, despite my inquiries of them" (2.19). Their lack of comment here is especially notable,
because Herodotus proceeds to report on various Greek theories on the
unique properties of the Nile, including his own.

The Psammetichus story captures just these dual Egyptian characteristics. They are both broad-minded—their king gracefully accepts
an unwelcome result to his experiment—and unquestioning—he designates his people as the second-oldest of humankind, a conclusion made
possible only by their original unfounded assumption. Psammetichus
illustrates this prescribed inquisitiveness later, when he is said to have
proved that the springs of the Nile were unfathomable: "for the king had
twisted a cable thousands of fathoms long and let it down there to the
depths but could not find bottom" (2.28).

The place of the goats in the Psammetichus story further points up
the Egyptians' short-sightedness. They are blind to the flaw in their experiment: that the children, hearing no human voices, would imitate the
sound closest to hand, animal though it was. Herodotus surely means to
underline this point when he criticizes the Greek rendition of this story,
which had the children raised not by a goatherd but by women whose
tongues had been cut out. This version is foolish (2.2), presumably because then the children's articulation of "bekos" truly would be mysterious. [33] Although Psammetichus and the Egyptians take no interest in the
goats, they do at least take note of them, showing themselves again to
be careful if unreflective observers.

---

32. Plato, *Timaeus* in *Collected Dialogues of Plato*, eds. Hamilton and Cairns: 23a. See
also Ronna Burger's reflections on the symbolic opposition between Greece and Egypt in
Plato's Phaedrus, 90–98.

33. See Benardete, *Herodotean Inquiries*, 32–33.

The place of the goats is important, too, because it leads us to question what it means to be human. They are, simply put, just goats; they are not Egyptian or Greek or Persian goats. Goats everywhere organize themselves similarly, goats everywhere make the same sounds. It is human beings who organize themselves in diverse groups and who hear these same sounds differently. What seems to engage Herodotus in this is the way humans are ever curious about their diversity, and ever anxious to give it some order. He shares this passion, although he expresses it in a more discerning and more deeply inquisitive form than do his subjects. Perhaps the Egyptians were misguided in their attempt to rank themselves against others, both in emulating the attribute of age above all, and in their limited probing of it. But other communities will reveal their own vulnerabilities as they engage in this same act of defining themselves. The question is latent: Is there a best way to differentiate one's culture?

This story strikes another universal chord in the way it presents the Egyptians' attempting to uncover the supposed natural language. Goatherd and anonymous newborns aside, this story portrays an impulse which is recognizable across the world. No historical confirmation of the Psammetichus experiment is required for us to recognize the impulse of humankind to separate the natural from the influences of custom. It turns out that there are precisely comparable instances of this attempt to discover the natural language, as when Emperor Frederick II removed newborns from their mothers and had them secluded to determine whether "they would speak the Hebrew language (which had been the first), or Greek, or Latin, or Arabic, or perchance the tongue of their parents of whom they had been born." [34] But even without other cases of this type of experiment available to us on record, we could point to analogous impulses in the modern world. For if the Egyptian impetus toward isolating the natural language is regarded now as almost inconceivably primitive, the beginnings of modern political philosophy itself were marked by contention over the exact unfolding of events within the natural state of humankind. In such a condition, Hobbes asserts, "there is no place for Industry; because the fruit thereof is uncertain: and consequently no Culture of the Earth." [35] Locke insists, rather, that this is "a

34. The infants died before such a determination could be made. Quoted by Sulek, "Experiment of Psammetichus," 647.

35. Hobbes, *Leviathan*, 89.

State of perfect Freedom to order [our] Actions, and dispose of [our] Possessions, and Persons as [we] think fit."[36] Rousseau urges us to force our
thoughts even further back: "The Philosophers who have examined the
foundations of society have all felt the necessity of going back as far as
the state of Nature, but none of them has reached it."[37] And in our own
time the attempt is made to banish customary sex roles to produce the
gender-free or natural child. It is as if we all possess a drive to make out
what we were before we were human; with Psammetichus, we would like
to see demonstrated this imagined natural state. The story causes us to
marvel at the Egyptians, and at human nature itself.

When we turn to focus on the transmission of the Psammetichus
story, we cannot avoid facing a familiar criticism: Herodotus has naively
repeated the deceptive account of (an Egyptian) source. The view that
Herodotus was a passive recipient of his evidence is long-established
and persistent. Its advocates seek to derive a closer approximation of
the original historical moment than what is given in *The History*. These
critics attempt to look through Herodotus to get to the unadulterated
truth, as they have misgivings about leaving the past in the hands of the
historian. Here, the charge is that the priests of Hephaestus that Herodotus mentions as the source of this story have passed on a corrupted
version of the real experiment. Critics have found much in this version
to correct. They do not occupy themselves with what surely occupied
Herodotus: the Egyptians' self-description.

In a recent interpretation of Psammetichus, Antoni Sulek claims that
the most important question to be asked about this passage is "whether
the experiment which Psammetichus had reasons to undertake . . . could
proceed in the way Herodotus described it."[38] Sulek's answer, based on
modern research into the origins of language, is ultimately negative: "It
follows that the poor infants in Psammetichus' experiment could at the
most utter primitive meaningless sounds such as *ma, ba, pa* and their
combinations."[39] Sulek grants that the imagery of this tale is "picturesque" and "appeals to an unenlightened imagination," but he steadfastly refuses to be deluded by these appeals. The implication is that he
and other earnest critics can bring us closer to "what really happened"
than Herodotus could—by resisting the charms that the historian could

36. Locke, *Two Treatises*, 269.
37. Rousseau, *First and Second Discourses and Essay on the Origin of Languages*, 139.
38. Sulek, "Experiment of Psammetichus," 648.
39. Ibid., 649.

not. But the clearer picture he offers is spurious; if he has contributed an exact piece of information, he has also made a muddle of the story as a whole. He creates the same confusion that How and Wells do when they inform us of the following fact: "The Egyptians could have claimed 'bekos' as evidence for their own antiquity, for it resembles one of their words for 'oil.'"[40] Such pronouncements serve to mystify, for they leave us groping for the story's intended meaning. The Psammetichus experiment will never be resolved by patching up its supposed shortcomings. It calls, rather, for a more serious affirmation of the historian who presented the stories of cultures to deepen the experience of humankind.

Less literal, more literary readings of the Psammetichus experiment are in order, if only to supply the corrective to this type of interpretation. For J. A. S. Evans, the significance of this story is largely in the structural markers it sets down, for it represents the historian's famed ring-composition. He draws our attention to Herodotus' remark at 2.15: "If the Egyptians had no land of their own at all, why should they be troubled about whether they were the first of mankind or not?" Herodotus finds cause to allude to the original experiment in the midst of refuting the Ionian judgment that only the Delta is truly Egypt. This allusion alerts us to the literary expertise evident in *The History:* after Herodotus sets out an idea, he develops it in one direction, only to circle back and revive the original sense. Evans concludes, "Psammetichus's experiment was needless, Herodotus reasoned, closing the ring. The Egyptians had always existed, but they could not move on to the land of Egypt until it had been created by the Nile's silting action."[41] Yet whatever such structural disclosures may accomplish for Herodotus' reputation as a writer, they surely detract from his enterprise as a Greek historian seeking to uncover truths about Egypt. Here, too, the appreciation of the balance Herodotus strikes between historical significance and artistic excellence is lacking.

It is doubtless a feature of the modern world that there are intense misgivings about accepting the historian's rendition of another people's stories. The perceived injustice is in not assuring the "Other" a fair hearing; we do not really know that the Egyptians related this Psammetichus story in just this form.[42] This suspicion is in force whether we are consid-

40. How and Wells, *Commentary*, 1: 156.
41. Evans, *Herodotus*, 37.
42. Beyond his role as the father of history, Herodotus has also been titled the founder of anthropology (Myres, *Herodotus*, 43). Today, this title may be unlikely to add

ering Herodotus' sweeping determination of character, or more specific
"speech-acts"—the common stumbling block of Thucydidean scholarship.[43] But, as Charles Fornara writes, we should be clear about where
the problem lies. It is ours, rather than that of the ancient historian,
"the special dilemma of our own traditional scholarship, of a modern
literary and historical criticism disoriented by our habituation to quotation marks."[44] This being the case, we might well indulge our suspicions
more fully for the moment: what if we did possess exact recordings of
the stories of the priests—what then? Surely we are too sophisticated
ever to suppose that words, anyone's words (including those of Egyptian priests), could be trusted to reveal their meaning transparently. Not
since Rousseau's savage roamed the world has language unambiguously
reproduced "the cry of nature."[45] The communications of every messenger must be decoded in a world where all is text. Perhaps we should be
grateful, after all, to have to deal with only one messenger.

As it is, what we have is Herodotus' version of the Egyptians, which
happens to be consonant with other ancient versions.[46] Certainly we are
well-advised to bring some skepticism to Herodotus' portrait—Book II
is notoriously full of inaccuracies and gaps in chronology. But if we are
to have the courage to say anything about the place of people in Herodotus' world (or in our own), we must let go of some of our cherished
suspicions about subjective motives. Herodotus has earned our trust.[47]

---

to his stature, for, as Stocking has noted, "despite anthropology's century as an academic
discipline, its definition is in some respects more problematic today than at the time of
its early institutionalization." The shock of Malinowski's revelations about his views of
Trobriand Islanders and Clifford's study of Maurice Leenhardt's colonialist work among
the Melanesians fueled a still-raging debate over whether one can ever comprehend the
other or whether such relationships can ever be free of exploitation and the distortions of
power. I discuss this issue in Chapter 5. Herodotus' approach, it seems to me, though far
from clinically pure, escapes these issues. His is a method, at least in the ideal, of letting
those observed speak for themselves. Works of further interest include Geertz, "Anti Anti-
Relativism"; Stocking, *Observers Observed*, 5; Clifford, *Person and Myth*; Malinowski, *A Diary
in the Strict Sense of the Term.*

43. See Pratt, *Speech Act Theory* and Searle, *Speech Acts;* the bibliography on this subject is extensive. For a good review of this Thucydidean critical quandary, see Stadter, ed.,
Speeches in Thucydides; Rokeah, "Speeches in Thucydides"; and Wilson, "What Does Thucydides Claim for his Speeches?"

44. Fornara, *Nature of History*, 155.

45. Rousseau, *First and Second Discourse and Essay on the Origin of Language*, 49.

46. See Lloyd's three-volume work, especially *Introduction*, 89–100, 146, as well as the
extensive bibliography cited by Pritchett in both *Liar School* and "Appendix."

47. Of course, not all readers of Herodotus will agree; it is the thesis that this reader

When the Egyptian priest says to Solon: "You Hellenes are never any-thing but children, and there is not an old man among you," it might be useful, for once, to judge that this view is rooted in Egyptian self-perception and not Greek fantasy.[48]

What emerges as the controlling motif in the preceding three ac-counts is Herodotus' examination of character. The accretions at the heart of Herodotus' study deserve our analytic attention so that we may perceive their meaning to the community for which the story is signifi-cant and which it influences. The underpinning of this history is the existence of unique peoples with their own variety of memories. More than anything else, the story of the Persian chroniclers, the battle of Marathon, and Psammetichus and his experiment belong to and reveal particular communities. The meaning of stories for Herodotus is in the collective telling; the "Athenians," "Persians," and "Egyptians" are all actors in *The History* of varying degrees of self-consciousness.

is attempting to demonstrate. West, for example, questions whether Herodotus could have arrived at some of his conclusions in good faith ("Herodotus' Epigraphical Interests," 293); more memorably, she locates in *The History* instances of "meretricious dogmatism" (304). At a certain point, these rival versions of Herodotus must be allowed to fight it out.

48. Plato's, as it happens: *Timaeus* 22b.

CHAPTER 3

The Formation of Persian Political Identity

Aristotelian Quandaries in Evaluating Evidence: The Persian Debate

The episode in *The History* that has attracted more controversy than any other is the Persian debate of Book III. The debate is one of the first theoretical discussions of the three forms of government—monarchy, oligarchy, democracy—we know from the ancient past. No antiquarian interest lies behind this critical interest; what has been recognized here is that this depiction of the conspirators debating the future form of the Persian regime calls into question the historian's procedure altogether. Herodotus introduces the topic without conveying the droll humor that comes across, for example, in the episode of the Persian chroniclers; quite the reverse, he makes an unusually serious remonstration in his account. "Here speeches were made that some of the Greeks refuse to credit," he declares, "but the speeches *were* made, for all that" (3.80). He returns to this issue later in his history when he considers a most wonderful thing:

> When Mardonius, coasting along Asia, came to Ionia, I will tell you of the most wonderful thing that happened—most wonderful, that is, for those Greeks who do not believe that among the Seven Persians Otanes *did* give his judgment that Persia should be ruled by democracy. For here in Ionia Mardonius put down all the princes and set up democracies in the cities (6.43).

The temptation to comment on this passage is irresistible, for Herodotus is nowhere else so insistent about an event that his readers so insistently disbelieve.

The claims of Herodotus are controversial because he defends what is not in dispute and remains silent on his procedure as a whole. Generally speaking, critics have not denied that the Persians could have debated the merits and demerits of various forms of government. Similarly, it is entirely conceivable for most readers that the Persians could have set up democracies in their Greek territories, though not in their own Persian land. And because Herodotus nowhere insists that he has reproduced an exact transcript of the debate, critics have no reason to quibble with his choice of words or expressions. But there is real controversy about the political form of the debate. The form as presented by Herodotus appears to come out of a city-state tradition—a tradition of which the Persians were demonstrably not a part. Everything that we know about Persia suggests a highly bureaucratized, hierarchical regime, one that had no experience with the face-to-face exchange of opinion and participation in rule in which Otanes, Megabyzus, and Darius take part.[1] The charge is that Herodotus had no clear conception of the Persian political regime, and that his persistent claims cannot alter this; if a Persian debate actually occurred, he, for one, did not have unmediated access to its record.

Such is the usual point of departure for readers of this Herodotean passage. It is rehearsed here in order to serve as a reference point as we explore the Aristotelian imprint in the critical literature. I believe that for us to understand the presuppositions that readers typically bring to Herodotus, Aristotle's Herodotus must be kept in view. The Persian debate all but selects itself as a test case, for it combines most uneasily what we tend to label literary and historical points of view. Meier makes the odd (but defensible) observation that Herodotus "was the first to write in the literary genre, which, as far as we know, was first called 'history' by Aristotle."[2] This formulation, which seems to neglect Herodotus' own coherent usage of ἱστορία, in fact rightfully draws attention to the transformation of its meaning in Aristotle's work.

Herodotus opens his work with the phrase "this is the ἀπόδεξις (public presentation, performance) of the ἱστορία" (inquiry, investigation). The combination of these terms allows us to differentiate between the inquiring activity of Herodotus and the object of his activity, but the predominant weight should be seen as attaching to the former, the activity. Hence David Grene's translation: "I, Herodotus of Halicarnassus, am here setting forth my history" (1.1).[3] Gerald Press has made a care-

---

1. Yack objects that the phrase "face-to-face" ill suits even the Athenian political situation; if there were some forty thousand Athenian citizens, they would hardly be recognizable to one another face to face in any significant measure (*Problems of a Political Animal*, 55). Granting him this point, I nevertheless retain the phrase, for it points to a prototypically Athenian (as opposed to Persian) political aspiration: for the citizen "to rule and be ruled in turn" (Aristotle: "For some rule and some are ruled in turn, as if becoming other persons" *Pol* 1261b2–3).

2. Meier, "Historical Answers to Historical Questions," 41. For purposes of consistency, I will use the form ἱστορία throughout.

3. See Erbse, "Das erste Satz," 209–222. Herodotus uses the word and its related forms in a range of ways, but none seems to contradict this basic sense. See Powell, *Lexicon*

ful study of the uses and meaning of ἱστορία at the time of Herodotus,
and concludes that "what ἱστορία means at this time is primarily an activity, inquiring, and only secondarily an object or product, the results
of inquiring, knowledge of some sort."[4] For Aristotle, though, ἱστορία
signifies more the acquired (factual) body of knowledge than the act of
inquiry itself. In the *Poetics* and elsewhere, Aristotle seems intent on em-
phasizing the settled body of material that comes out of the process of
inquiry. His use of this word proves decisive.[5]

It is due in no small part to the influence of Aristotle that Herodotean readers fall so easily into distinct categories. In Herodotus' work
"the fact that in his work we confront full-blown the central problem of
the genre: its mysterious capacity, as both *Wissenschaft* and *Kunst,* to explain and order the world for us."[6] Aristotle does much to demystify this
capacity and to separate the realms. Not surprisingly, we have our ex-
perts on *Wissenschaft* (historical critics) and on *Kunst* (literary critics), and
communication between the two is not the rule. Aristotle's prediction in
the *Ethics* has been borne out: "any one is capable of carrying on and
articulating what has once been well outlined" (*NE* 1098a21–23). But we
shall have our small revenge: those critics who do recognize in Herodotus his confrontation of the central problem of the genre shall be dubbed
"philosophical."

A thorough, scholarly analysis of the massive body of Herodotean
critical literature is the work of another day. There may be many ways of
hunting a crocodile (2.70), but the inclination to recite all of them during
the moment of truth could well be regarded as unpropitious. What follows here is an essay justifying my preference for the philosophic critics
as the readers closest in spirit to Herodotus' own undertaking. Historical
and literary critics both follow Aristotelian leads by focusing on *The His-*

---

to *Herodotus,* for the full listing of these terms. See also Jacoby, "Herodotos," in *RE,* 396;
and most recently, Connor, "The *Histor* in History," 3–15.

    4. Press, *Development of the Idea of History,* 31. See also Gulley, "Concept of ἱστορία," 2.

    5. See Press, *Development of the Idea of History,* 33, where he refers to *HA* 491a7–14 and
Aristotle's statement that it is according to nature (κατὰ φύσιν) to pass on to the discussion
of causes after the investigation of the details (ἱστορία) is complete. Similarly, in the *Prior
Analytics,* "[Aristotle] describes a list of all the true attributes of an object as an ἱστορία."
Weil lists Aristotle's uses of ἱστορία (*Aristote et l'Histoire,* 313).

    I do not intend to minimize the role of Thucydides in this development, for I agree
with Hornblower (against Weil, *Aristote et l'Histoire,* 167–168) that it matters very much indeed that Thucydides did not call his work a ἱστορία (Hornblower, *Thucydides,* 8). The
importance of Thucydides on this point will be taken up in Chapter 6.

    6. Dewald and Marincola, "Selective Introduction," 25.

tory as an object of knowledge to be studied, analyzed, and categorized. Whether critics attempt to identify Herodotus' sources for his information, his stylistic context, various patterns in his writing, or the date of the work's publication, the impulse is often toward contributing hard information for specialist interest in *The History*. In contrast (and against the path indicated by Aristotle) are philosophical approaches that have in common the desire to come to terms with the position of the ἵστωρ (the one who knows right) in *The History* as a still-valid way of ordering the world. For such readers "the *person of the researcher*, with his various possibilities and activities, is central to the historiographical process."[7] If these critical positions of my description are caricatures, they are serious caricatures in the manner of Herodotus himself, for they draw force from their undeniable immersion in what is said.

Critics Historical, Literary, Philosophical

Historical critics are frequently preoccupied with identifying Herodotus' source; they assume that he discovered some physical remnant of the debate and then presented it intact. His innocent reception of this historical document leads these critics to speculate about how Herodotus came to possess these (spurious) speeches, but it leaves them little inclined to reflect on the face value of the debate. His interjection— "the speeches *were* made, for all that"—is therefore welcome. Because Herodotus comes forward to assert his good faith, it is an easy step to absolve him while still rejecting the historicity of the debate. This gives critics an unchecked opportunity to fill in the details to explain how the Persian debate evolved into just this form.

Many critics have suggested that the debate betrays a sophistic influence; specifically, it is thought to be inspired by the methods of Protagoras, whose practice it was to expound on any subject from two opposite and equally justified viewpoints.[8] Herodotus may have come on such a Greek rendition of the Persian debate, the theory goes, and taken it at face value. Its rather jarring effect can be explained by his having forced his information into a foreign historical context. The very act of theorizing about political institutions is recognized as a characteristically Greek

7. Schepens, "Some Aspects of Source Theory," 273.
8. For example, Stroheker, "Zu den Anfängen der monarchischen Theorie in der Sophistik," 385. See also Dihle, "Herodot und die Sophistik," 207–220; and Lasserre, "Hérodote et Protagoras," 55–84.

enterprise, not a Persian one. And if the form and style of the debate
are strikingly Greek, the matter, too, can be seen as directly reflective of
Athenian political life. Critics have been willing to delineate the parallels: "The debate . . . dramatizes the constitutional struggle which was
being fought out at Athens in the first decade of the second half of the
fifth century between the supporters of the Cleisthenic democracy, the
oligarchical party under the leadership of Thucydides, son of Melesias,
and the supporters of Pericles."[9]

Conversely, it has been argued that considering the historical circumstances of Persia at this time, the sentiments expressed in this debate
could be traceable to disaffected Persian nobles; a record of this could
have made its way to Greece. Some critics, like Wells, have been bold
enough to identify the source: "Zopyrus, if Herodotus really met him,
is exactly the informant who satisfies the conditions of our inquiry, for
he was one who was certainly able to give Herodotus the information
desired, and one moreover who was likely to give it just in the form in
which Herodotus reproduces it."[10] Wells's thesis may be unusual in its
specificity, but it is not categorically distinct from the rest. The point for
all of these critics is to explain how it was that Herodotus came to write
just in this form. Someone else is assumed to be responsible, whether
the debate is alleged to have originated from the Persian nobility or the
Greek intelligentsia. These critics tend not to ask further why Herodotus chose to use what he found. In contemporary parlance, there is no
awareness of the world as text, no recognition that "the event, even for
the contemporary observer, is itself a kind of multivalent text that cannot be seen without being read and interpreted differently by different
observers."[11]

These historical critics, then, confirm a kind of objectivity for Herodotus. If they allow that the evidence has been reworked—by any
number of candidates—they congratulate Herodotus for recognizing
that he had a notable find here and for being insightful enough to include

9. Morrison, "Place of Protagoras," 12. For analogous interpretations, see Bringmann, "Die Verfassungsdebatte bei Herodot," 266–279; and Ehrenberg, "Origins of Democracy," 525–547.

According to Connor: "the form, the argumentation, the language of the debate are
all Greek" (*New Politicians*, 200). See as a sample among many proponents of this view:
Brannan, "Herodotus and History," 427–438; Larsen, "The Judgment of Antiquity on
Democracy," 1–14; and Sinclair, *History of Greek Political Thought*, 36–41.

10. Wells, "Persian Friends," 38.

11. Hedrick, "Material Culture," 19.

it as he received it. In other words, his objectivity consists in his preserving intact for us an account of the debate from fifth-century Greece, patently untrue as the account must be. The assumption is that we can see through his sources even if he could not. But this is to commend the historian's inclusiveness and to disregard his intended meaning. Herodotus does not produce a document drafted by another, and thus the nature of the document should not even be at issue; his rendition of the debate remains precisely his. Further, he has told us quite specifically that he is not bound to believe everything he hears, and there is no reason to believe that in this one case he has suddenly suspended his judgment. A preoccupation with identifying Herodotus' sources can have the effect of diverting our attention to futile speculations.

Also recognizable as historical critics are those writers who attend to Herodotus' development as a historian. They distinguish between an early, gullible Herodotus who accepted unconvincing evidence like this debate, and a later, more capable historian who could control his data. For them the most important issue is not where the debate originated but what its place is in the various stages of Herodotus' writing. Felix Jacoby was perhaps the most vigorous spokesman for this approach. In his 1913 article in *Paulys Real-Encyclopädie*, he argues that *The History* developed in stages in conjunction with Herodotus' evolving notions about his subject matter. Thus Jacoby explains the seemingly disparate concerns of the Herodotus of Book II, where geographic and ethnographic details predominate, and the Herodotus of the later books, where political and military events take over, by theorizing that the historian visualizes for himself a steadily more momentous theme. (The Persian debate falls within the less developed stage.) With this thesis, Jacoby drew the battle lines for much of the subsequent Herodotean criticism. Enthusiastic supporters like von Fritz ("we may be able to show how Herodotus gradually became conscious of these requirements of true historiography"[12]) had the effect of solidifying the position.

Although Jacoby and his heirs justifiably focus on the changing narrative strategies evident in *The History*, in the end they do not adequately defend the assumption that Books VII–IX in isolation represent Herodotus' history at its best. Charles Hignett reiterates this assumption in more recent times: "His last three books, describing Xerxes' invasion and its failure, are the most successful from the historical point of view."[13]

12. von Fritz, "Herodotus and the Growth of Greek Historiography," 316.
13. Hignett, *Xerxes' Invasion of Greece*, 33.

Charles Fornara joins those who will distinguish a younger Herodotus
who "is completely at the mercy of his subject," from an older one who
is "an imaginative historian as well as the reporter of tradition."[14] But
to posit this development is to speak the language of a traditional Western historian, that is, someone other than Herodotus. It is to condemn
Herodotus at the outset for breaking the rules of a kind of history writing to which he did not subscribe.

A too generous celebration of Herodotean objectivity should also
raise our suspicions. Kenneth Waters, for instance, offers a variation on
the developmental theme that aims to justify Herodotus' procedure, but
that actually detracts from the significance of his evidentiary method. To
answer the challenge of the Persian debate, Waters infers a sharp division
in the way that Herodotus presents his material. That is, he attempts to
vindicate Herodotus by distinguishing between the pure history and the
mere entertainment. Waters appeals to an unwritten code for historians
according to which Herodotus is so regular and unsurprising a fellow
that his "usual scholarly detachment" can be alluded to without further
comment. When the artistry of a characterization simply cannot be denied, Waters relegates the story to the entertainment category (" 'tell a
joke occasionally so that the audience don't go to sleep' "[15]). And so the
Persian debate assumes an interesting and historically irrelevant stature:
"By and large this debate must be thought a digression, or rather the
insertion at an appropriate moment of an argument of topical interest
about 440 B.C."[16]

Such distinctions create problems where there were none. W. Kendrick Pritchett's critical statement would seem to pertain to Waters: "an
author does not change genres from page to page, writing fiction about
one event and alleged history about another."[17] Yet we might pause over
Pritchett on this question of genres. He represents the interesting case
of someone who is essentially committed to the historical perspective
as we have sketched it, but who is so broadly and deeply educated that
he outsizes the single classification. In responding to Herodotus' more
skeptical critics, Pritchett establishes the authenticity of the historian's
various claims with as much thoroughness as can be conceived, from the
Pillar of Heaven, and the gold-digging ants of India, to Lake Moeris,

14. Fornara, *Herodotus,* 35.
15. Waters, *Herodotos the Historian,* 131, 50.
16. Waters, *Herodotos on Tyrants and Despots,* 58, n 34.
17. Pritchett, *Liar School,* 331.

the Egyptian Labyrinth and the salt-houses in Libya. On the one hand, Pritchett's erudite investigations are welcomed by readers who always knew Herodotus to be trustworthy; Pritchett's intimate feel for the historian (and not his penchant for critical investigation) led him even to check Fehling's assertion that no black doves such as the ones Herodotus describes (2.57) have ever been found.[18] Thus provoked, Pritchett has garnered a staggering amount of evidence to validate Herodotean claims, while still acknowledging the importance to Herodotus of the nonrational factors. Yet one could imagine that the effect of Pritchett's research might be to make us too comfortable with the informational status of the *History*, and to neglect the historian's charge to mistrust the recounted λόγοι.

What is needed to complement this approach is an examination of Herodotus actively confronting his subject matter, subject matter that the historian himself recognizes as fundamentally disputable. Attempts to describe Herodotus as objective historian can never be fully satisfactory. To imagine that only a static and specific kind of relation holds between historian and his material is to distort *The History*. Historical critics tend to be preoccupied with whether the historian and his sources are truthful or not, or whether one or the other is not, but these formulations are obstructive and prevent critics from heeding the historian's own proclivity for sabotaging our expectations for settled truth ("When [Croesus] came to the river Halys, he brought his army across — over existing bridges, in my opinion, though the general report of the Greeks is different. They say that Thales of Miletus brought the army across for him" [1.75]). It is more plausible that Herodotus never intended to reproduce events completely apart from the various biased perspectives of them, that he maintained an interested stance himself and actively sought out interested sources for his own purposes.[19] To view *The His-*

---

18. "The more confident [Fehling] is, the more certain there is error." Pritchett, *Liar School*, 73–74. Pritchett's comments on the Pillar of Heaven, gold-digging ants, Lake Moeris, the Labyrinth, and salt-houses are from this work: 50, 93, 245, 257.

19. The great historiographical debate of the past two centuries is of great value, I believe, for the purposes of this essay. See, for example, Braudel (the Annales school): "every historical landscape — political, economic, social, even geographical — is illumined by the intermittent flare of the event . . . without which we should often find it hard to see anything at all." Braudel, *Mediterranean and Mediterranean World* vol. 2, 901, and *Afterthoughts*, chapter 1. Hunter (*Past and Process*) refers to this debate in her comparison between Herodotus and Thucydides.

tory solely as a source of historical knowledge is to miss the richness and complexity of Herodotus' relation to his material.

The literary critics of my scheme share with historical critics the drive to catalog specific and concrete evidence, but in their case the evidence that is marshaled is internal to the text, and traditional assumptions about historical objectivity are much less likely to be entertained. Insofar as this literary perspective is untrue to the spirit of Herodotus himself (and imitative of Aristotle), it is so when it eschews interpretation, as if there could be findings without interpretations. Eric Havelock has written of a certain classical training that "actively discouraged the use of general concepts and working hypotheses lest they lead to imaginative reconstructions based on assumptions which were not amenable to strict proof."[20] This I will posit as the conventional literary perspective, eventually acknowledging, however, that the truly classically educated will not be contained within such a classification.

On the topic of the Persian debate, literary critics tend either to favor a structural approach that links this event with others or to emphasize the relevance of Herodotus' literary antecedents. As an instance of the former, J. A. S. Evans stresses "that many of the ideas expressed in the debate can be identified elsewhere in the *History*": "Periander, whom the Corinthians hold up as a typical tyrant (5.92) is Otanes' monarch-type, the Athenians deceived by Aristagoras demonstrate the irrational element of democracy, and the monarch corrupted by power is implicit in the picture of Xerxes, who takes his leave of the *History* with the story of Masistes' wife."[21] Donald Lateiner refers to the debate as a master-pattern that "creates a benchmark, shapes expectations for the three theoretical forms of government in action."[22] These approaches are fruitful to the extent that they go on to evaluate the claims of truth that Herodotus is putting forward for the debate. Critics have had more

20. Havelock, *Literate Revolution*, 220.
21. Evans, "Notes on the Debate," 84.
22. Lateiner, *Historical Method*, 167, and "Herodotean Historiographical Patterning," 272. On the enduring worth of the historical method of Herodotus, Lateiner's conclusions are more tentative than my own. He fears that he may be read as overestimating the profundity and originality of Herodotus (*Historical Method*, 218); he sees the work as "groping" toward historical explanation (208), and concludes: "Herodotus cannot now furnish a satisfactory model for historians, but his logic deserves a careful attention" (219). I would prefer to pass by any issues of logic and concentrate on eliciting what is to me a vital model for historians and political thinkers alike.

or less success in confronting this question, but it is a narrow reading of *The History* that avoids it altogether.

If it is true that Herodotus should not be judged on the basis of an abstract and unrealizable standard of objectivity, it is likewise true that we should be able to account for his historical representations. Otherwise our efforts may amount to no more than mere description. Those who accentuate the form of *The History* continually skirt this danger, as is seen in many illustrations that go beyond the Persian debate. Henry Immerwahr best articulated the founding principle: "Since Herodotus is a classic example of the doctrine that thought appears primarily in organization and structure, the interpretation of his work should always proceed from some aspect of organization to the definition of ideas, and not from the opinions of author or critic."[23] Other critics have proceeded from the organization of *The History* exactly in this manner. Ingrid Beck, for instance, explains how Herodotus consolidates his stories through ring-composition, according to which words are repeated at the beginning and end of a section to signify the completion of a theme. Mabel Lang notes variations on this strategy: they "should perhaps better be seen as a kind of spiraling forward, since the wrap-up statement does more than echo the beginning statement; it very frequently builds on the first statement by using material from the digression to make a new directional statement." Critics like Henry Wood employ broader classifications: "How to present the totality of events, not as discrete moments then, but as a continuum? Herodotus' solution is: analogy."[24] Whatever the specific item of categorization happens to be for the literary critic, it is often rendered in a chart or outline of considerable complexity in order to demonstrate beyond a doubt that *The History* is a unified and sophisticated structure.

Because the literary critics predictably preface their investigations with the remark that they will not take on the task of determining precisely what their findings mean, it often appears that the complexity of their findings is somewhat daunting even to them. Immerwahr comments at the outset, "the present investigation is not concerned primarily with the merits of Herodotus as a historian, but attempts to analyze the

23. Immerwahr, *Form and Thought*, 15.
24. Beck, *Die Ringkomposition bei Herodot*, 1 (see also Fränkel, "Eine Stileigenheit der frühgriechischen Literatur," 40–96; and Pohlenz, *Herodot.*); Lang, *Herodotean Narrative*, 5; and Wood, *Histories of Herodotus*, 18.

work as it stands and to define some of its leading ideas." But no matter how successful critics are in conveying the complex unity of *The History* (and Immerwahr's successes have been considerable), their end position may be exceedingly awkward if, after stating that the form of the narrative is decisive for understanding its meaning, they proceed to say almost nothing about what this meaning is. On this point Wood acknowledges: "I have not attempted in these pages to discuss the justification for such use of analogy and its peculiar appropriateness in Herodotus."[25] If the claim is no more than that the form of the work mirrors Herodotus' own conception of the interrelation of events, then the critical efforts seem all out of proportion to the final product.

The "Liar School" of Herodotus (Fehling, Armayor, West) is connected both to the literary and historical critics of my description. They emphasize Herodotus' alleged reliance on earlier literary traditions ("The question is not one of the growth of a scientific and-intellectual achievement . . . but the growth of a literary work"), but instead of considering these literary elements as intrinsically worthy of study, the Liar School uses them to assail the historical authority of Herodotus.[26] However, this notion of historical authority is not explicated. O. Kimball Armayor asks only rhetorically, "What kind of authority is Herodotus?" And again, "Herodotus' historical authority is at stake." Stephanie West writes that the "confident assurance of his historical reconstructions is bluff," and, specifically on the Persian debate: "his whole account of the conspiracy which brought Darius to power bristles with so many blatant improbabilities. . . . It looks as if the story of Darius' ruse (together, no doubt, with much of the immediately preceding narrative) represents a Greek fantasy woven around a conspicuous monument without regard to its real purport."[27] Detlev Fehling claims that Herodotus' "source-fictions do not simply reflect reality . . . what his work reflects instead is a carefully thought-out picture of what any enquiries would have had to

25. Wood, *Histories of Herodotus*, 19; and Immerwahr, *Form and Thought*, 7.

26. Fehling, *Herodotus and his "Sources"*, 249. Pritchett includes Hartog in the "Liar School"—inappropriately, in my view. As I have discussed, Pritchett remains attached to a fairly traditional historical perspective, allowing him to speak of "History proper" or "pure History" without embarrassment (*Liar School*, 205, 264), and to see unfounded cynicism in all literary readings. Thus he overlooks the very significant differences between Fehling/Armayor/West on one hand and Hartog on the other. I will discuss Hartog at length in Chapter 5.

27. Armayor, "Herodotus' Catalogues of the Persian Empire," 1; "Did Herodotus Ever Go to the Black Sea?" 45; West, "Epigraphical Interests," 303, 297.

yield."[28] In all three cases, assumptions are being made and not defended about what constitutes an acceptable historical authority or reconstruction or reality. The silent appeal is to an objective world, perceived by these critics in its absence from *The History*. But Press's rejoinder is relevant to these arguments: "the past was not somehow obscurely 'trying' to be the future, and earlier writers were not trying to say or saying badly what later writers finally did say."[29] It is unlikely that the unexamined assumptions of our own historiographical tradition will prove illuminating of Herodotus; I submit that the reverse could be the case.

As we approach the question of Herodotus' literary antecedents and his transmission of oral material, we are brought into at least partial contact with the preferred philosophical critics. It is not that there is any automatic association between the subject of the transmission of oral material and a philosophic approach. Indeed, there is a real tendency for the word "orality" to stand in as a ready-made and all-purpose explanatory term "for all previously noted developments in ancient literature," as Rosalind Thomas notes.[30] But there are fundamental questions to be answered concerning Herodotus' peculiar literary context, and it is not surprising that some of the best writing on Herodotus poses this question of his relation to and transmission of oral material.

Homer stands as the most renowned predecessor, of course, and studies detailing the Homeric influences on Herodotus abound.[31] But notwithstanding Herodotus' mimetic techniques, dramatic speeches, concern for preserving the κλέος of humankind, and, in general, his title as most-Homeric, Ὁμηρικώτατος, he remains distinctly un-Homeric as well. The pivotal difference between Homer and Herodotus is in their sources of inspiration and in the consequent distance and force of the claims that their creations make on their readers. Homer is the mouthpiece of the Muse, and as such composes his inspired vision of a remote age of Greek heroes and gods in action. Herodotus quite seriously renders his account on the principle that "it is what people severally have

28. Fehling, *Herodotus and his "Sources"*, 152.

29. Press, *Development of the Idea of History*, 143.

30. Thomas, *Literacy and Orality*, 103. Thomas has in mind the work of Havelock, Goody, and (more particularly) their followers; the significance of literacy for the intellectual development of the Greeks will necessarily remain highly disputed. See Havelock, *Preface to Plato*; Goody and Watt, "The Consequences of Literacy"; and the bibliographies in Thomas, *Literacy and Orality*, and Harris, *Ancient Literacy*.

31. Among others, see Strasburger, *Homer und die Geschichtsschreibung* and Huber, "Herodots Homerverständnis."

said to me, and what I have heard, that I must write down" (2.123). To declare what is said—λέγειν τὰ λεγόμενα—might well "constitute the most important of the moments in the evolution of a true historiography."[32] Herodotus recognizes his own and his audience's involvement with the characters in his history, establishes points of contact with them, and trusts this contact to guide him in his depictions. His audience is challenged to judge him in this endeavor in a way that cannot hold for Homer or Hesiod; thus the influences of Homer and Hesiod illuminate, but only partially.

Other obvious influences are similarly limited as means for explaining the work Herodotus produced. Most striking is the sheer number of possibilities that are put forward to locate Herodotus in his proper intellectual setting. We have seen that he may be situated productively in the context both of the pre-Socratics and of the Sophists.[33] It has been observed further that Herodotus self-consciously follows Hecataeus, if always with a hint of disdain toward his predecessor.[34] "Once upon a time Hecataeus, the historian [λογοποιός, maker of λόγοι], was in Thebes," Herodotus begins, and he proceeds to mock Hecataeus' attempts to show descent from a god in the sixteenth generation (2.143). Herodotus does appeal once to the authority of Hecataeus, though more with his usual bow to what is said than with any deference to him as a historian or ethnographer: "The Pelasgians had been driven out of Attica by the Athenians—whether justly or otherwise I cannot say, only that Hecataeus, son of Hegisander, mentions it in his account and says that it was unjustly" (6.137). But after all, even Homer could be appealed to for factual verification (4.29). The two other occasions in which Hecataeus appears confirm his subsidiary function: he serves as the unheeded wise advisor (5.36, 125), that is, as a character integrated in the Herodo-

32. Verdin, "Hérodote Historien?" 682.

33. In addition to works previously cited, see von Fritz, "Der gemeinsame Ursprung der Geschichtsschreibung," and *Die griechische Geschichtsschreibung*, vol. 1; Latte, "Die Anfänge der griechischen Geschichtsschreibung"; and Schadewaldt, "Die Anfänge der Geschichtsschreibung."

34. See Diels, "Herodot und Hekataios"; von Leyden, "Spatium Historicum"; and West, "Herodotus' Portrait of Hecataeus." The charge that Herodotus plagiarized from Hecataeus is raised from time to time; as the next section will show, this accusation would be an interesting one for me to follow, if I could be convinced that there were any substantial evidence to support it. But it seems to be one of those critical refrains that is reiterated almost mindlessly. Other readers of Herodotus who seem to find this refrain tiresome include Hunter, *Past and Process*, 310–313; Lasserre, "L'historiographie grecque," 113–118; and Lloyd, *Introduction*, 127–139.

tean narrative. This treatment, combined with the fragmentary remains of Hecataeus' works, gives us little incentive to pursue further leads in this quarter for signs of substantial influence on Herodotus.

From our point of view, critics have been more successful in finding clues for understanding the enterprise of Herodotus by reflecting on the tradition of archaic poetry. Archaic poets competed with each other and with their predecessors for the attention of their audience, and it is with this in mind that John Herington advises us to read *The History* as an archaic or early classical Greek poem: "almost all will become clear: not only the shaping of the story at every level . . . but the very spirit and intent of the whole."[35] Herington does not neglect Herodotus' concern for eliciting truth (indeed, he suggests that Herodotus comes close to being "the community's philosopher"), but he finds the clues to Herodotus' intent in the compositions of Pindar and other archaic poets and in the settings in which they were performed. The historian's double aim, according to Herington, was also the aim of the poets: to preserve the past and to study "the timeless principles that determine human happiness and human failure."[36] Poet and historian might have shared the aim described earlier as discerning the general in the particular; both would have strived to impart to contingent events a significance worthy enough to appeal to a Panhellenic audience. And the audience would be key as the immediate judge of the success or failure of these enterprises.

Gregory Nagy supports this line of inquiry in his intriguing study of Pindar, where he draws special attention to the ways in which Herodotus designates the performative aspect of his work.[37] Whether or not Herodotus actually read parts of his history before an Athenian audience and induced the child Thucydides to weep, it seems indisputable that its oral delivery had a significance for him as ἵστωρ that was not to hold for later historians. Certainly Thucydides announces a different position; looking past his immediate audience to future readers, he speaks of his work as an everlasting possession (κτῆμα ἐς αἰεὶ), "not to be rehearsed for a prize" (1.22). "So great an increase," remarks Rudolf Pfeiffer, "in the spreading abroad of the written word had apparently taken place between the two generations."[38]

Studies that investigate the links between Herodotus and the ar-

35. Herington, "Poem of Herodotus," 5.
36. Ibid., 8, 12.
37. Nagy, *Pindar's Homer*, 28, n 23; 169; 220.
38. Pfeiffer, *History of Classical Scholarship*, 29.

chaic poets accordingly are valuable for explaining his impulse to appropriate ("stitch together" in a rhapsodic way[39]) disparate traditions.
We have seen Herodotus insisting on the significance of capturing the
stories that are told by various peoples and striving to locate the fighting
versions among them. We can imagine easily enough that an analogous
situation prevailed for poets in a largely oral culture. To endure, their
poems would have had to present compelling and credible retellings of
inherited traditions. "A clumsy or dull poem," writes Herington, "could
not . . . expect even a dubious survival in the dry dock of a printed
book; it would founder without trace at first performance."[40] New poems
would directly compete with old, except that there would be no such distinction between new and old in a time when traditions lived in the telling. Nagy phrases the all-important standard of excellence thus: What is
Panhellenic, ἀλήθεια, and what is not?[41] To prevail in this competition
required putting earlier poets in their place.

Herodotus' repeated efforts to assign his greatest predecessors a
place within his own more expansive work could, then, reflect the fact
that Herodotus lived during a transitional moment between oral and literate cultures. And this view is consonant with the claim, as by Evans,
"that archaic Greece had prose memorialists as well as oral poets, and
that these memorialists retained historical data in trained memories."[42]
Surely the realms of the prose memorialists and poets would have some
overlap, and this understanding could help us to appreciate Herodotus'
unique composition. Thus *The History* could contain ubiquitous references to Greek mythology, poems, or folktales; fables reminiscent of
Aesop (7.152); moral injunctions like that of Anaximander (2.120); rhetorical flairs worthy of a Pericles (7.162); and catalogs of Thales' ingenuity (1.75). Herodotus was no tragedian, but could produce a virtuoso
imitation in the story of Adrastus (1.35–45), and could play handily with
Sophoclean themes (3.119). He was no comic poet, but his timing was
flawless ("About this particular thing [Scyllias' traversing some ten miles
underwater] I would like to record my own opinion, which is that he
came to Artemisium in a boat" [8.8]), and his subject matter proved
worthy of Aristophanes (*Acharnians*). He was no Ionian natural scientist or chronicler, yet he treated these perspectives as living, competing

39. Dewald, "Narrative Surface," 148.
40. Herington, *Poetry into Drama*, 63.
41. Nagy, *Pindar's Homer*, 62.
42. Evans, *Herodotus, Explorer of the Past*, 129.

methods of ordering the world. His own inquiries were created with an eye toward the worthiest of his predecessors.[43] Both within and without his tradition, his selection of λόγοι indeed had much more to do with identifying the serious and authoritative accounts and discounting the frivolous than it did with distinguishing between true and false.[44]

This returns us to our philosophical critics, for to them we attribute the conviction that the Persian debate represents a serious and authoritative episode—analogous to the episodes involving Homer in *The History*. Like Herodotus' revelation about Homer (he "knew the tale" of Helen in Egypt), the Persian debate is not the story we expect. But as in the case of Herodotus' treatment of Homer (or Thales, or Sappho, or Arion), Herodotus puts forth a tenacious idea, one that is very difficult to blot out once expressed; we are made to entertain his ideas. And "tenacity" and "truth" are not far neighbors. Notwithstanding the voluble resistance among readers to Herodotus' depiction of the Persian debate, I would argue that Herodotus succeeds in forcing our compliance in the narrative. His truth-claims remain stronger than our objections—for reasons that may remain mysterious, but which certainly have to do with his successful assumption of the role of ἵστωρ.[45]

However our philosophical critics may disagree on particulars, then, they accept the premise that in the narrated speeches, Herodotus "enforces an intellectual interpretation," advancing instructive intentions that are then up to the reader to discern.[46] Seth Benardete, in his rendition of the Persian debate, stresses that "Otanes relies on the 'middle' characteristic of democracy, Megabyzus on the beautiful, and Darius on the best":

43. For Herodotean references to mythology and folktales, see Aly, *Volksmärchen, Sage und Novelle;* Drews, *Greek Accounts;* Griffin, "Ursprünge der Historien Herodots"; Lachenaud, *Mythologies, religion et philosophie;* Lasserre, "L'historiographie grecque."
 For tragic themes in *The History,* see Chiasson, "Tragic Diction in Herodotus"; Grene, "Herodotus the Dramatist"; Lesky, "Tragödien bei Herodot?"; and Walbank, "History and Tragedy." The Aristophanes reference is *Acharnians,* 46.
 44. Murray, "Herodotus and Oral History," 100.
 45. "The patterns of arbitration associated with the word ἵστωρ provide a powerful metaphor for intellectual activities including the rigorous examination of evidence, choosing between conflicting claims and versions, assessing responsibility, and the consequent building of a consensus within a community." Connor, "*Histor,*" 9. On the Homeric uses of ἵστωρ as adjudicator between conflicting claims (and related connotations), see also Snell, *Ausdrücke für den Begriff des Wissens,* 59–65; Press, 23–25; and Nagy, *Pindar's Homer,* index.
 46. The quotation is based on a similar statement by Kagan in "Introduction" to Parry, *Logos and Ergon in Thucydides,* 6. See also Äpffel, *Verfassungsdebatte bei Herodot,* 91. Needless to say, my listing of philosophical critics is not exhaustive.

These three speeches can be thought of as the most theoretical speeches in Herodotus. They present the possible kinds of
regimes and their corruptions without any regard to local conditions. They consider the nature of each regime as such, in light
of the nature of man as man (his soul), in making their several
claims to superiority. They go most deeply into the nature of man
as a political animal.[47]

Stanley Rosen analyzes the speech for the principles that Herodotus considers to be essential to each regime, considers the natures of the
individual speakers, and then reflects on the Machiavellian teachings
therein.[48] Stewart Flory takes the Persian debate as a point of departure
from which to speculate about Herodotus' ideas on the best and worst
forms of government, maintaining that the historian's point of view can
be deduced by observing how well or poorly the three speeches in the
debate are reflected in the actual regimes as described elsewhere in *The
History*. He concludes that the historian's anecdotes "show that, theoreti-
cally, the best system of government is the tyranny of a quasiphilosopher
king."[49] What these views have in common is, first, the recognition that
Herodotus has issued a broad interpretive challenge, and, second, the
intellectual courage to answer it in kind. Not only does each make a
large claim that depends on a thoughtful mastery of the work, but also
each thereby invites attack (to be supplied on the instant: we must tell
what is said; we are not bound to believe it). To my mind, it is entirely
fitting for readers of Herodotus to match his fighting story with fighting
stories of their own.

Understanding Persia and Persians Through the Persian Debate

In my view of the Persian debate as a serious and authoritative episode, I stress first that Herodotus does not occupy himself with abstract
argumentation. The speeches that he depicts should not be considered
as theories, for there is no sustained reference by Herodotus in his own
name to abstract political regimes. This is a critical point, for it indicates
that the significant component in these combinations for Herodotus is
the particular people. His interest is not in extracting the common fea-

tures of Scythian and Persian and Egyptian kingship; what is compelling to the historian is the completely opposed world views that lie behind those regimes. Second, I emphasize that his ventures into the political workings of the Persian regime may show an unsophisticated apprehension of their politics without this negating his efforts to reveal the Persian character to the Greek mind. I prefer to consider Herodotus in the act of surveying and identifying the Persians as they were set off from and understood by his fellow Greeks, rather than as they were in themselves. If we consider Otanes, Megabyzus, and Darius as prototypically Persian as read by the Greeks—instead of stick-figures mouthing Greek ideas—then a study in character unfolds before us. And this study in Persian character represents just one facet of Herodotus' larger enterprise of exploring human character; in the words of de Romilly, it is historical contrast that interests Herodotus—the "actual acknowledgement, in human events, of the condition of man in its wonderful greatness and its cruel and inevitable limitations." [50] Herodotus' essential accomplishment is to determine character in a historically and philosophically compelling way.

The Persian debate should be read both as an expression of the nature of the Persians that had impinged on the Greek mind and as a vital link in the historian's portrait of the Persian people. In Herodotean historiography, character is determinative of the actions and decisions a people takes during times of crisis; accordingly, Herodotus carefully probes and formalizes the existing Greek understanding of the Persian character to capture the historical occasion. As throughout *The History*, this episode has as its basis inherited thought. At the same time the Persian debate can be seen as integral to the historian's Persian story as a whole. If Herodotus bases his portrait on received stories, still the artistry is his. The Persian types he fills in constitute part of his larger answer to "the reason why [the Greeks and barbarians] fought one another" (1.1). Thus when the Persians are shown questioning and reaffirming their identity in the debate, it prompts both backward and forward glances in *The History*.

The Persian debate is properly viewed as rich in meaning in its own details, and in its vital connection to a larger story of Persia. Each single glimpse of the Persians in this crisis is telling, from the formation of the conspiracy, to the words of the interlocutors, to the final determination

50. de Romilly, *Rise and Fall of States*, 6.

of the Great King. Herodotus is not just describing but construing the course of events, and it is open for us to explore his various levels of meaning. And these discrete moments relate to a broader Persian theme as well: their general failure in truth-telling. Truth-telling is a characteristic that Herodotus traces throughout *The History* as a means of representing the Persian relation to the world. This is the Persian virtue that so appealed to Nietzsche and that led him to designate his own hero Zarathustra: "To speak the truth and to *shoot well with arrows*, this is Persian virtue."[51] Persian truth-telling included a prohibition against speaking of "whatsoever things it [was] not permitted to them to do" (1.138), and has a place in Herodotus' version in the ultimate decline of their empire. The Persian debate is no anomalous episode in this story; it represents one significant marker in the evolution of the Persian character. In the context of Persian truth-telling, the debate appears significant, not inexplicable, not puzzling, not even surprising.

Persian truth-telling is redefined in the course of four Great Kings, yet each of the redefinitions can be seen as implicit in Herodotus' initial formulation of the customs of the primitive Persians. When Herodotus describes the Persians at their most innocent (back when it could be said that "no one, not even the Great King himself, may kill anyone on charge of a single crime" [1.137]), then truth-telling is at the heart of their upbringing. With the steady growth of the Persian empire and the loss of this primitive status, truth-telling is refitted to accord with their new way of life. Both their rising fortunes and their enduring constitution are reflected in this quality. The Persians were never constituted to deliberate on truth, were never in the habit of bringing into line what they thought and what they did, but it is only with their political prosperity that this emerges as a fatal flaw.

Herodotus introduces Persian truthfulness in Book I, when he canvases the Persian customs of which he has personal knowledge. Right from the start, this trait strikes us as singularly contorted, for the Persian love for truth is decisively qualified. Herodotus remarks at 1.136 that the Persians train their boys from ages five to twenty in nothing but horsemanship, archery, and truth-telling. Two chapters later, he adds that for the Persians, "lying is considered among the very basest things" (1.138). But in between these two chapters Herodotus observes, "The Persians declare that never yet has anyone killed his own father or mother. As

51. Nietzsche, *Genealogy of Morals*, 328.

often as this takes place, say they, it must on investigation necessarily appear that the one who did it was either adopted or a bastard" (1.137). There is an engaging simplicity in this disposition that forbids the Persians from speaking about "whatsoever things it is not permitted them to do," but it is a trait that Herodotus renders as ever more menacing.

Herodotus has the crazed King Cambyses mark the incipient changes in this Persian disposition, for Cambyses shows how sinister it can be to equate truth and custom, to measure all of human life with a Persian calculus. Herodotus relates that when Cambyses is in Memphis, the Egyptians suddenly begin celebrating the appearance of Apis. The King summons the leaders to Memphis to explain this festival. They respond that their god has a tendency to appear at very long intervals in the form of a calf. "Cambyses, when he heard that, said that they were lying, and, as liars, he punished them with death" (3.27). This event cannot be accommodated to the Persian way; Cambyses consequently takes care to expunge it.

On a different occasion, Herodotus again has Cambyses reveal the absurdity of the Persian habit of defining as truth whatever can be assimilated to their custom. This occurs when Cambyses seeks legal authorization to commit incest. He assigns to the Persian royal judges the task of finding a Persian law that would justify his inclination to sleep with his sister, a practice that was most assuredly "against usage" for the Persians. The judges well understood their task: "They said they could find no law that ordered brothers to live with their sisters; but they *had* found another law, which said that he who was king of Persia could do anything he wished" (3.31). Herodotus uses Cambyses to illustrate the hypocrisy, for if the Persian king can make incest his own law, this shows that even Persian limits have their limits, at least in the case of the Great King. All others are forbidden from taking that lesson to heart, a situation that would seem to corrupt everyone involved.

Herodotus' tales of the insane king prepare us for the reformulation of the Persian approach to truth-telling that comes with the Persian debate and the accession of Darius. As Darius is urging on his fellow conspirators, he introduces an element of opportunism which seems to have no room for scruples about remaining true to Persian customs:

> Where a lie must be told, let it be told. Those of us who lie
> and those of us who tell the truth are bent upon the same object.
> The liars lie when they would win profit by convincing others

of their lies; the truth-tellers tell truth so that by their truth they
may draw gain to themselves and be the more trusted (3.72).

Darius imagines all the world to be composed of individuals locked
in combat for profit; he is to earn the name "shopkeeper" from his fellow Persians (3.89). His posture may be cynical, but he resembles every
other Great King in *The History*. Among other qualities he exhibits are
initiative and an accompanying impatience with discussion and reflection; from where he stands, it is perfectly clear how the course of events
must unfold.

At the start of the conspiracy, Darius transforms what was an equal
exchange of opinions about the way to proceed into a tyrannical in-
strument against his fellow conspirators: "We must either act today or,
I would have you know, if a single day goes by beyond this, no in-
former will outstrip me myself: I will go and tell the whole matter to the
Magian" (3.71). In the debate scene, too, Darius impedes at every turn
the uncertain and undirected nature of free discourse. Open debate is a
risk he shuns, and he will manage and manipulate it rather than allow
its unpredictable turns. But if this tactic is fitting in the case of an aspiring Great King, we may wonder how it is that debate comes to be
neutralized among the other (momentarily equal) Persians.

The Persian debate itself offers the answer. Darius succeeds because
he masters the peremptory rhetoric of a Great King. It is not that the
Persians could not have acted differently on this occasion; Herodotus'
point doubtless is that this was their pivotal moment to throw off this
controlling mentality. But they did not choose a position of individual
responsibility, and they did not choose it because they could not articulate it. The appeal of Darius is in his ability to describe his best
alternative as the conventional one, whereas the shortcoming of Otanes
and Megabyzus is in their failure to translate their choices ("middle"
or "beautiful") into Persian speech. When Darius sketches his view of
the possibilities for the Persians, they recognize and accept the picture.
Nothing else appeared possible.

Herodotus characterizes the first speaker, Otanes, as someone who
wants the new regime to depart radically from the old, but who does not
put forth a vision of this new regime. He speaks in the terms of one long
used to suffering the whims of a despotic government. This crisis in the
Persian empire was unparalleled; following the murder of the Magian
usurper, the seven conspirators were free to choose the future course of

Persia. At such a time it is unlikely that the Persians would not have considered breaking with their past; the radical times called for radical thinking. But as Otanes demonstrates, they could not escape from their past in an instant. Hence Otanes champions the rule of the multitude because it is as far removed from monarchy as he can imagine. Its best quality is its title: "the fairest of all, namely, equality before the law" (ἰσονομία) (3.80). No description of ἰσονομία follows this pronouncement; Otanes only adds that the rule of the multitude is not guilty of the outrages of monarchy. Ἰσονομία, the fairest title of all, may serve to conceal Otanes' limited political imagination. Spokesman though he is for something as revolutionary as rule by the many, Otanes does not offer a captivating image for his listeners. His chronicle is without the requisite narrative. Primarily, he seems to want an assurance that the ruler will leave him alone. In this he succeeds, for he eventually abdicates from the contest on the stipulation that he will neither rule nor be ruled. His house, Herodotus remarks incisively, "continues as the only free one in Persia" (3.83); it is a voice without an echo.[52]

Otanes closes his speech with words that point up the bleakness of his prospect: "I vote therefore that we abolish the monarchy and increase the power of the people; for in the Many lies All." In the Many lies safety from the One—the One who is a danger to the Many by virtue of his separation from them. We have already heard that individual initiative is mistrusted in the Persian culture: A Persian "may not pray for good things for himself alone, the sacrificer, but only that all shall be well with all the Persians and the king; for among all the Persians is himself also" (1.132). In the debate, Herodotus conveys the idea through Otanes that if a people is educated to be suspicious of individual accomplishment, those people are not likely to have an inspired view of one person's capacities. Otanes, at least, is very clear in his speech that nothing good can come from the ambition of one man. In his diatribe against monarchy, he maintains that the natural quality of the ruler is quite beside the point: "Take the best man on earth and put him into a monarchy and you put him outside of the thoughts that have been wont to guide him." The position of power will corrupt him, for "envy is basic in the nature of man." Monarchy is unacceptable because it allows the ruler to be corrupt with impunity. Conversely, the rule of the multitude

52. See Äppfel, *Verfassungsdebatte bei Herodot*, 87.

is appealing because it must continually bow to the judgment of all; its subjects are thereby protected from one another.

The message that Otanes delivers here is so pessimistic that it may seem curious that he ever initiated the move to overthrow the usurpers. How did he dare to act alone? The answer is that in a decisive sense, he did not. He is memorable as the conspirator who presses always to delay the attack and to gather ever more supporters; eventually, he is compelled to act by Darius. There is room to wonder whether the Persians would have ever regained power if Otanes had continued to lead the conspiracy. And in this sense, his disposition is very much in line with that of other Persians in *The History*. These men invariably recognize the need to correct or respond to some perceived evil, but they are quite hopeless about one man's ability to act on that recognition.

This Persian type who is unable to act in a way that is commensurate with his knowledge is represented in its most extreme form in the Theban banquet anecdote. Here Herodotus reproduces a conversation from a banquet that takes place shortly before the battle of Plataea. The Theban Therander reacts in astonishment when a Persian confides in him that death is imminent for many of the Persians present. "Should you not tell this to Mardonius and to those who are, with him, in great esteem among the Persians?" he asks. But, as the Persian makes clear, recognizing the severity of the situation is not the same as moving to change it: "Sir, what comes from God, no man can turn back. . . . Many of us Persians know all this, but we follow in the bondage of Necessity" (9.16). The Great King faces little chance of a competitor rising from the ranks of such men—men like Otanes. Herodotus portrays these men as disarming themselves before the one who takes it upon himself to master necessity.

The next speaker in the debate, Megabyzus, is a second-rate political opportunist who never stands a chance in this setting. He enters the conspiracy not as an original spirit but as an adjunct, and this remains his defining characteristic. He makes only the slightest motion towards establishing himself as a serious contender for the throne. So lacking in political sophistication is he that he does not even adjust his words according to the predisposition of his listeners, who represent the kind of oligarchy he is proposing. He is the only one to mention knowledge or intelligence, as Rosen notes, but in practical knowledge he is sorely lacking.[53]

53. Rosen, "Herodotus Reconsidered," 348.

Megabyzus begins his speech by embracing the position that Otanes had put forth on monarchy. This is too hasty on his part, for he does not foresee that by accepting the presuppositions of that argument his own position is made less compelling. Megabyzus agrees with Otanes that the monarch is unrestrained and therefore dangerous; he disagrees with him on the rule of the many, which he regards as equally unrestrained but particularly undiscerning. He does not give reason to believe that oligarchy will be different in its unrestrained character than the other two regimes. Consequently, because he concedes that the monarch acts with knowledge, he has not presented a case for choosing oligarchy over monarchy. He seems to have intended to push oligarchy forth by default, but he neglects to show its decisive advantages. He, too, lacks a credible narrative; he is another Persian chronicler.

Megabyzus makes one affirmative statement about oligarchy for his final flourish: "but let us choose a society of the Best Men and entrust the power to them. Among this number we shall be ourselves, and we may reasonably assume that, when the men are the Best, their counsels will be so too" (3.81). Megabyzus does not seize his opportunity to convince his conspirators that an oligarchy would promote the best interests of the majority of the men present. Oligarchy was the most likely path to power for most of them since if a democracy were selected, none of the conspirators would hold a privileged position; if a monarchy, only one would. As an adjunct, Megabyzus had little hope of attaining sole power, and this should have encouraged him to use the numbers to his advantage; Megabyzus merely had to appeal to their desire for power on one hand and their fear of a domineering personality on the other. Or more positively, Megabyzus could have argued for a continuation of the kind of group solidarity that had so far succeeded for them. Herodotus does not have Megabyzus argue in these plausible ways, but instead portrays a type that we can place alongside the timorous Otanes: the ineffectual Persian opportunist. These are the men Darius must silence to assume the throne.

If Otanes and Megabyzus epitomize the Persian nobility, Darius represents the Great King who excels at manipulating their lack of political sophistication. Herodotus gives him his first astute move by having him hold back from speaking until last. As the final speaker, Darius is able to dismiss the first two speeches and put forth his own without subjecting it to anyone's criticism. Because this is a Persian debate with no opportunities for rebuttal, the last speech is intrinsically the accented one. Darius is, furthermore, very assuring in tone when he does speak, because he maintains the predictable Persian position. Otanes is reform-minded but vague, whereas Megabyzus leaves almost everything unsaid. The audience of the debate, the remaining Persian conspirators, had to see this continued uncertainty as the most alarming prospect of all. Before Darius, the fighting story was wanting.

Darius appeals to the quintessential Persian creed that strength in government is generated by eliminating all possibilities of dissent. He makes this appeal in large part in the way he makes room for the Best Man in his speech. With commanding presence, he asserts that of the three forms of government at their best, "monarchy is far superior. Nothing is manifestly better than the one best man" (3.82). Each of the speakers prior to Darius refers to "the Best" in some way: Otanes contends that even the best man will be corrupted by absolute power; Megabyzus accedes to that argument, and adds that in an oligarchy, the Best Men will provide the best counsels. Darius merely reduces that claim to its simpler form: the Best Man must be better than the Best Men. Darius does not fully respond to Otanes; he seems indifferent to the argument that the best man will be corrupted.

Darius is out to persuade his listeners that monarchy is the best regime possible, and he draws on Persian tradition to support this argument. He sets up a strict historical model in which all forms of government eventually lead to monarchy. Persia, by implication, shows her superiority by skipping the intermediary steps. Darius preys on the dual Persian affinity for eminently rational, unambiguous arguments, and for the traditional historical reinforcements. The clarity of the reasoning is cherished above all. His ideal is the single ruler's freedom to pursue one indisputable course of action. There is no place in this scheme for evaluating the monarch's end; Darius just predicts obscurely that the monarch "will have judgment to match his excellence" (3.82). His expectations are not overly high; he foresees only as much advantage as is required to satisfy his Persian listeners. In a monarchy, there will be no discord; everything will be settled.

An immediacy in Darius' argument gives a special twist to the inevitability he claims for monarchy. When he imagines the typical course of an oligarchy, Darius observes that at the start the rule is marked by good intentions on all sides. Then disagreements erupt, for the oligarchs have different ideas about the way to proceed. One can hardly avoid drawing the parallel between this imagined scenario and the debate that is actually taking place among the Persian noblemen. This parallel becomes somewhat more unnerving as Darius follows the course of oligarchy from private quarrels to hatred to faction to murder—and eventually back to despotism. And just as Darius treats this sequence as unquestionable (encouraging his fellow oligarchs to abandon their current status as soon as possible), so, too, does he consider it beyond question that the final stage—despotism—is the culmination: "From murder there is a relapse into despotism—and *there* is an indication again how much despotism is the best" (3.82). Darius looks to the history of Persia for support: "I give my vote that, as we were freed by one man, so we should keep this freedom *through* one man." This combination of the appeal to rational inevitability and to tradition proves irresistible to the Persians.

As Herodotus depicts the Persians' acquiescing in Darius' authoritative, traditional speech, he captures them in their pivotal and lost opportunity to listen to the diverse claims to rule and to appreciate debate as a productive activity. This is the main thrust; the Persian debate is a debate to inhibit all future debates, and it is the predictable end of Persian truth-telling as a possible stimulus to action. Persian truth-telling, self-deceiving even at its inception, ends up signifying the lack of any forum for discussion at all. Thus we observe that when Xerxes invites support for his intentions to attack Greece, the response is preordained: "So spoke Mardonius and stopped, having put a smooth coating on Xerxes' opinion. All the rest of the Persians held their tongues and did not venture to declare a judgment opposite to that which was in discussion" (7.10).

The Persians of Herodotus' description falter by choosing the path of least resistance. The whole premise of their gathering to debate had been that the lot of them could come to a consensus after offering their varied speculations about "the entire condition of affairs" (3.80). If they were convinced of the superiority of Darius' argument, they should have been concomitantly convinced of the value of ἰσηγορία—equal freedom of speech. They should have taken pains to assure some place for ἰσηγορία in the new regime, for they had just witnessed how debate could induce them to select what was to them the best regime possible. The monarch's own limitations might not be decisive if he regularly considered the judicious counsel of others. But the Persians present did not see fit to suggest the obvious emendation of Darius' position, nor to check the situation that they all fully anticipated: the corruption of the monarch. For Herodotus, their resignation at this juncture was to be paradigmatic. The Persians would typically contribute to debate not according to what they know, but according to what they perceived necessity to be. And when some individual like Artabanus or Artemisia contravenes this rule, the rest of the Persians neither regard them as inspirations nor identify them as champions of their own deeply held views. Instead, they cynically await their destruction. The historical and thematic meaning of the Persian debate is that in this moment of crisis, the Persians relinquish what remaining personal stake they may have had in truth-telling.

Thus we conclude that the decline of the Persian empire in this history is inextricably linked to their form of truth-telling, which amounts to a rigidity in holding to custom and to a weakness for neat solutions. That there was little adaptability in their understanding of custom is signified by Herodotus at the start: "Whatsoever things it is not permitted to them to do, of these they must not even speak" (1.138). Without the opportunity to voice alternatives to what is permitted, the Persians gradually lose the ability to conceive of them. Their highly constrained truth-telling easily leads to cynicism and fatalism on the part of the subjects, hardly the inspirational model that Nietzsche would see in the Persians of his Zarathustra. About his Persians, Herodotus knew better.

CHAPTER 4

Political Identities in Conflict:
Herodotus in Contention
with His Characters

That Herodotus presumes to deal in real distinctions among the characters of peoples is noted more often by earlier commentators than those
of late: We "gather from data which he gives here, and from stories
told there, that there was a fundamental difference between Persian and
Greek outlooks, between the silent theories on which the two peoples
severally based life." Glover is so bold as to assert elsewhere that most
readers will readily agree with this unspoken thought of Herodotus:
"Greeks are really in their variety, their restlessness, and their impossi-
bility, the most interesting of all peoples."[1] His candor is of another age.
Writing of ancient historians, Francis Cornford also observed (though
with astonishment) that "*every motive is a first cause, or is determined solely by
character.*" He strove mightily to correct this emphasis to get to the "real,
underlying causes," but it is striking that today his real causes appear as
nothing next to the ones he attempted to negate.[2]

As for the ancient Greeks themselves, we should note that Aristotle
conceived of character as a subject so manifest that one could "ascertain
[it] merely by looking both at those cities among the Greeks that are held
in repute and the entire inhabited [world] as divided by nations" (*Pol*
1327b21–24).[3] The infamous disquisition that follows on the spirited as
opposed to the intelligent and inventive races (which—need we add?—
has its basis in *The History*) is no incidental afterthought to his analysis
of regimes; as P. A. Vander Waerdt remarks, this assertion "considerably
complicates his exposition of political science . . . there are correspondingly different forms of regime and educational programs to promote
the different ways of life of which they are capable."[4]

As late-twentieth-century readers, however, we appreciate with what

1. Glover, *Herodotus,* 64, 195.
2. Cornford, *Thucydides Mythistoricus,* 67, 54.
3. I am designating "character" on the basis of *Pol* 1327b20: "of what quality of persons they should be" (ποίους δέ τινας τὴν φύσιν εἶναι δεῖ).
4. Vander Waerdt, "Political Intention of Aristotle's Moral Philosophy," 82.

circumspection the topic of character must be broached, inasmuch as it is regularly put to such abominable use in modern times. A responsible managing of the subject demands that one maneuver in an undefinable space between fact and fiction, on admittedly precarious ground. But if it is prudent for moderns to beware of irresponsible inquiries on the subject of national character, it is questionable whether the concept should be dismissed out of hand, because it has been used so widely and to such effect among ancient thinkers.[5]

In Herodotus we discern the example of a historian who attempts seriously to identify one people against others; his resulting depictions are neither simplistic nor menacing. In Donald Lateiner's apt phrase, he produces a "transfigured tradition."[6] Contemporary historians, too, Gertrude Himmelfarb argues, might make "the kinds of definitions, discriminations, and qualifications that would serve to distinguish between a sense of national identity and an ideology of nationalism, or between a civilized nationalism and a barbarous one."[7] The goal for the historian might be seen as one of making the people in question transparent to themselves, revealing their past in a way that likewise discloses their most prosperous route for the future. At best, writes Richard Bernstein, such portraits might serve the "vital function of destroying myths about what is deemed necessary or impossible and illuminate . . . what are real possibilities for action."[8]

Without presuming to prescribe in detail how such portraits are accomplished, we note that a prerequisite of Herodotus' success is an awareness of how deeply he is implicated in his characterizations. We have observed throughout that although Herodotus writes his account without ever losing touch with the legacy as he receives it, he never receives it passively. This feature goes beyond his isolated remarks that he is not forced to believe the stories he tells ("These same Chaldeans say— though I myself do not believe their story" [1.182]), or his disinclination to reveal something he hears ("it was one of the Delphians who put that inscription on it because he wanted to win the favor of the Lacedaemonians; I know his name but will not mention it" [1.51]).[9] Herodotus

5. I use the terminology "character" or "national character" anachronistically, cautiously, and without a fitting alternative.
6. Lateiner, "Nonverbal Communication," 103.
7. Himmelfarb, *New History and the Old*, 132.
8. Bernstein, "Hannah Arendt," 155.
9. For the first type, see also: 3.3, 3.9, 3.116, 4.195, 5.86, 7.152; for the second: 1.214, 2.3, 2.65, 2.70, 3.125, 4.43, 7.96, 7.99, 8.85.

actively contends with the particular characters behind these legacies—
the Greeks or Persians who tell the stories they happen to tell—and he
does so in the process of establishing his own credibility as a historian.
He thus has a personal stake in the verdicts he renders against Persians,
Greeks, and others.

Herodotus contends with his characters both by establishing his own
procedure as an implicit contrast to their ways of truth-telling, and by
showing his characters in interaction with each other on this theme. Persian truth-telling is, of course, his broadest subject of attack. Herodotus
mocks Persian pretensions, and by doing so he provides in the *History*
his own definition of truth-telling: how a society characterizes and perpetuates the truest version of itself, in its ability to absorb criticism, to
be open to change, and to show depth in its creative resources. In effect,
truth-telling represents the larger human predicament of demarcating
an estimable spot for oneself in the world. Herodotean historiography is,
then, an exercise in corrective truth-telling; he simultaneously describes
the worldviews as he sees them formulated and establishes the basis for
his own alternative. When he puts Persian and Greek truth-telling in
explicit contrast in the pre-Salamis councils, they are detailed in ways
that prefigure the conflict to come and eventually explain the miracu-
lous Athenian victory. The picture is both heartening and ominous. For
a civilization to sustain the kind of truth-telling that the Athenians momentarily achieve would be the real miracle.

Persian Truth-Telling Exposed

The Persians of Herodotus are peculiarly unquestioning; throughout
The History they are shown accepting what is spoken or written as established fact. Like Gyges, they seem to think that the many fine things
were discovered already by men of old (1.8). This is precisely the way
the Great Kings would have them think; they make every attempt to in-
still reverence for the spoken and written word in order to increase their
own potential powers of manipulation. This is meant in the sense of
Claude Lévi-Strauss's famous pronouncement that "the primary function of writing, as a means of communication, is to facilitate the enslavement of human beings." [10]

---

10. Lévi-Strauss, *Tristes Tropiques*, 393, cited by Thomas, *Literacy and Orality*, 21. It often
has been pointed out that in *The History* it is characteristically tyrants who engage in writ-

Typically, the Great Kings succeed in their attempts to control information; the Persians tend not to suspect a speaker or writer of any ulterior motives, but trust in the inviolability of the words themselves. Thus Cyrus instantly convinces his fellow Persians to revolt against the Medes by dramatically unfolding the papyrus roll and reading (his own) words "to the effect that Astyages had appointed him general of the Persians" (1.125). Darius' order to kill the Persian Oroetes is carried out through the same kind of dispatch-reading: "He saw that their reverence for the dispatches was great and their reverence for the words in them even greater, and so he gave the secretary yet another dispatch" (3.128). Darius himself is assured by Histiaeus' disingenuous speech: "My lord, what a word is this you have spoken! That any plan of mine should be to your hurt, small or great! What would be my object in so doing? What do I lack that I should do it?" (5.106) None of the Persians, Xerxes included, doubt for a moment the truth of Themistocles' note before Salamis (8.76), as though in the midst of a war the words of the enemy were completely reliable. All of this would seem to be incisive commentary for an age enamored of documents; these anecdotes suggest on the part of the receiving persons a relinquishing of the responsibility to interpret.

Herodotus elaborates on this unthinking receptivity among the Persians by underlining how the very act of hearing unduly influences their actions. He indicates that there is a direct link between their hearing and their spiritedness ($\theta\upsilon\mu\acute{o}\varsigma$); the Persians react to words with an immediacy that precludes reflection. Xerxes eventually articulates the connection: "I would have you know that a man's spirit ($\theta\upsilon\mu\acute{o}\varsigma$) dwells in his ears. When he hears what is good, it fills his body with delight; when he hears the opposite, it swells with anger" (7.39). It is the instantaneous impact of upsetting speech on the Persian kings in *The History* that prompts them to their more savage acts of revenge. There is no predilection towards the Heraclitean insight: "The eyes are more exact witnesses than the ears." [11]

In this respect, Cambyses should be conceived of not as a mad King but as a distinctly mad Persian king when he commits atrocities like his arrow experiment with Prexaspes' son. According to Herodotus' ac-

---

ten communication (1.123, 3.40, 5.35); the insight that great power accrues to the one in control of information is long established. Thomas writes: "For Herodotus in the middle of the fifth century, writing tends to be associated with barbarians, especially the Egyptians and Persians, or with tyrants who have a propensity to send messages which are secret and sinister." Ibid., 130.

11. Freeman, *Ancilla*, 31=DK Bı01a (I.173, 15).

count, Cambyses inquired of Prexaspes what the Persians said of him. To this, Prexaspes answers generously, considering what we have already heard of Cambyses: "Master, in all other respects they praise you highly, but they say you are overaddicted to the bottle" (3.34). This answer sets Cambyses off into a rage, and the reason for his fury, as Herodotus tells it, is that previously he had been assured that his reputation was unimpeachable. Cambyses then plays out the role of the insane Great King. He sets up the conditions that will eliminate the contradiction in the accounts; either he will be found to be crazy, or everyone else will: "Your son shall stand there in the doorway; if I shoot and hit him in the middle of the heart, the Persians are manifestly talking nonsense. If I miss him, you may say that the Persians are right and I am not in my senses" (3.35). The outcome is assured; the Great King must be found to be in his senses. For all of its fairy-tale qualities, this story of Cambyses may have uncomfortable resonance in our age: the deranged King manifests his madness in a rage for consistency and control.

In the presence of the Great King, the word out of turn prompts violence and murder. Darius becomes outraged when Oeobazus asks him to leave behind one of his three sons in his campaign against the Scythians; the King responds by leaving all three sons behind—executed (4.84). The thought that Oeobazus implicitly suggested had to be effaced: that familial attachments could be stronger than attachments to the Persia of the Great King. Xerxes is asked by Pythius to spare one son from the Greek campaign; he cuts the son in half and marches his army through him (7.39). And in a Greek story, Demaratus advises Dicaeus: "Hold your peace, and tell this story to no one else; for if these words are carried back to the King, you will lose your head" (8.65). The words themselves carry the danger. In all these examples it is not deep-seated personal resentment that the monarchs are expressing (to Pythius, Xerxes had previously announced "I will make you my friend" [7.29]), but their immediate θυμός when they hear un-Persian speech.

A corollary to this Persian behavior is the often surprising tendency of the monarchs to fail to hold a grudge against those who have assuredly harmed them. Croesus, Psammenitus, and Histiaeus (among others) are each offered a secure and comfortable life in the Persian regime after doing the most in their power to overthrow it. In Herodotus' portrayal, the Persians have closed off the imagination that would fuel resentment; their anger is uncomplicated by any brooding. This characteristic might help to explain why Darius orders one of his servants to repeat three times at every meal, "Master, remember the Athenians" (5.105). The insult must be consciously recalled if Darius is to retain his anger.

Herodotean historiography can be seen as a response in turn to each of these weaknesses in Persian truth-telling. Regarding their general trait of accepting all λόγοι as transparent signifiers of the truth, Herodotus counters by treating λόγοι as highly problematic but still revealing indicators. The difference between the Herodotean and the Persian approach is one of suspicion and uncertainty as opposed to passivity. This is reflected in Herodotus' peculiar terminology, in which he refers to using (χράομαι) λόγοι.[12] It may be that he is himself unsure about how to place certain stories, but he allows for others who might offer another view: "As for the stories told by Egyptians, let whoever finds them credible use them" (2.122). Elsewhere he remarks: "What this was is not credible to me, but perhaps someone else might find it so" (5.86). Herodotus may be arbiter as in the sense of the Homeric ἵστωρ (in the arbitration pictured in *Iliad* 18: The Shield of Achilles), but he is distinct in leaving the grounds for his decision open for debate.[13] Unlike the Persians of his account, Herodotus can imagine a place for the most unlikely of λόγοι.

A second weakness in Persian truth-telling that Herodotus underlines is captured in Xerxes' claim that "a man's spirit dwells in his ears." The point is that the Persian spirit remains on a level that is not self-conscious; it is tied to their nature as Persians only and not as human beings sharing the world with other human beings. Early on, Herodotus separates himself from those who have such purely instinctual bearings by declaring that his hearing is of only partial significance for his understanding. He recognizes that the act of hearing by itself is untrustworthy and that its evidence must be supplemented by every means available and reconsidered in that light. On one hand, it is important for Herodotus simply to hear what a people says of itself, for it will reveal itself in all sorts of unintended ways. On the other hand, he rectifies the distortions inherent in any such speeches by submitting them to his own physical and intellectual vision. The limitations of any one kind of knowledge can be offset by balancing it with other sources:

> So far it is my eyes (ὄψις), my judgment (γνώμη), and my searching (ἱστορίη) that speaks these words to you; from this on, it is the accounts (λόγους) of the Egyptians that I will tell to you

12. See Heidegger's reflections on τὸ χρεών, usage, in *Early Greek Thinking*, 51–57.
13. See Snell, *Ausdrücke für den Begriff des Wissens*, 59–61.

as I heard them (κατὰ τὰ ἤκουσαν), though there will be, as a supplement to them, what I have seen myself (τι αὐτοῖσι καὶ τῆς ἐμῆς ὄψιος) (2.99).

Herodotus exposes and overcomes the distorted view of the Persians, who depend on their Persian hearing alone and therefore cannot suffer challenges to their worldview.[14] He can accommodate other cultures without becoming unglued or without laughing, as Xerxes does at Demaratus' report on the Spartans (7.103).

The best examples of Herodotus' attending seriously to customs that diverge absolutely from his own come when he inspects the religious customs of other cultures. The difficult imaginative leap is not the Persian one, which relates to their physical nature (Median dress or Greek pederasty), but the one that allows Herodotus to appreciate religious sentiment in another people's extraordinary rituals: "The dead man's head [the Issedones] lay bare, and clean out, and gild and afterwards use it as a sacred image, offering great yearly sacrifices in its honor. Each son does so by his father, just as the Greeks celebrate anniversary feasts of the dead" (4.26). We recall that the Persians are less than charitable in regard to the religious practices of others: The Persians "are not wont to establish images or temples or altars at all; indeed, they regard all who do as fools" (1.131). Herodotus shrinks from that kind of conviction ("for I think that all men know equally about the gods" [2.3]).

Similarly, Herodotus is able to accommodate the Egyptian belief that the immortals die as a matter of course. This belief had to be as problematic to Herodotus as it was to any non-Egyptian, and it is therefore interesting to observe how he makes room for it in The History. His main impulse is to avoid speaking of it as much as possible: "Now the part of their account that deals with the divine, and to which I listened, I am not anxious to set forth, save only the matter of the gods' names" (2.3). Herodotus reiterates this sentiment throughout Book II, where he confronts the largest number of religious peculiarities. But it is the same sentiment that he expresses in Book I concerning a "secret and obscure"

14. Hedrick claims that though Herodotus "privileges visual sources in his history, his own history is itself (necessarily) an avowedly verbal production" ("Meaning of Material Culture," 24), and that this constitutes a paradox. But his evidence for the privileging of visual sources centers on Book II, and in Egypt, there may be grounds for the special priority of ὄψις. There everything is "opposite" (2.35), and Herodotus has to start from basics: "The Greeks write and calculate moving their hands from left to right, but the Egyptians from right to left. That is what they *do*, but they *say* they are moving to the right and the Greeks to the left" (2.36).

Persian custom: "So, as far as this custom goes, let it be as it has ever been" (1.140). He is committed to preserving the basic reverence due to "what other men hold sacred and customary" (3.38). Sometimes this requires silence.

Finally, even the Great King's inability to hold grudges comes under scrutiny through Herodotean historiography. The King's forgetting past injuries represents an intellectual failure—the failure to make distinctions among people.[15] The Persians define their enemies in a manner that is perfectly measurable and wholly accidental:

> Most of all they hold in honor themselves, then those who dwell next to themselves, and then those next to them, and so on, so that there is a progression in honor in relation to the distance. They hold least in honor those whose habitation is furthest from their own. This is because they think themselves to be the best of mankind in everything and that others have a hold on virtue in proportion to their nearness; those that live furthest away are the most base (1.134).

The decisive point for the Persians is precisely not in character, just as in their marching orders there is no sense of who is who—the spirited and the intellectual (*Pol* 1327b23f.) are brought together by chance. As Sally Humphreys notes, "Persian kings like to count. . . . By contrast, *nomos* represents an incalculable element in human behavior."[16] Xerxes, who neglected to take the precautions of his father, cannot keep in view the motive of revenge against the Athenians: "So those who are innocent in our sight and those who are guilty will alike bear the yoke of slavery" (7.8).

Herodotus, in contrast, makes no such sweeping pronouncements but deliberates with interest in each case. He does not come to his study of peoples with a predetermined and absolute standard according to which all are judged. Nor does he retire in relativistic despair; cultures make out better and worse in his portrayal. As it happens, the Persians do not come out particularly well, but this is not because Herodotus is incapable of seeing beyond Hellenic greatness; it is, rather, because of specific attributes, primarily those connected with their way of life under

---

15. Derrida would phrase this more positively; the Persians are not logocentric: "The logocentric longing par excellence is to distinguish one from the other" (*Of Grammatology*, 167).

16. Humphreys, "Law, Custom, and Culture," 218.

the Great King. Just as Herodotus names these attributes, so does he contend with them as he articulates his own historical position.

The most prominent attribute of the Persians is their form of rule, not because this is the single most important attribute for all peoples for all time, but because to Herodotus the Great King was the overwhelming factor in the lives of the Persians of his time. And Herodotus responds to this particular, contingent feature as he designates his boundaries as a historian. In other words, he simultaneously undermines the notions of an omniscient historian and omnipotent ruler. He adheres to certain principles as a historian that challenge a man who would live as if unrelated to other human beings, unrelated because of the complete power he wields over them. When assessing human events, Herodotus can hardly conceive of this notion of unrelatedness, "for this history of mine from the beginning has sought out the supplementary to the main argument" (4.30).

Throughout his history Herodotus stresses less what we can know about human events than what we can use in our various remembrances to think meaningfully about the human condition. As the historian who is receptive to a wide range of evidence, Herodotus earns the privilege of judging those who regard humanity from a more restricted perspective. The one with the most restricted viewpoint of all is the (crazed) Persian king. The King alone dictates how his subjects are to understand themselves and their world. This is his great power and great vulnerability, and Herodotus exposes it through his very manner of writing history. This has applications beyond the mad Cambyses. Darius does not understand why the Scythians will not engage him in battle; Xerxes cannot comprehend the placid Spartans combing their hair before battle, or the "mad" Athenians charging at their opponents who hugely outnumber them. In the context of *The History*, their bewilderment is revealing. The King is naturally mystified to discover how limited his way of thinking really is over the course of human events. His ignorance of the imprint of character distorts his judgment to the last, as when Artemisia earns his praise for her bravery after the most ignoble of deeds (8.87–88).

Herodotus knows that there are better ways of ordering one's world than by the whip of a Great King. Artemisia wins Xerxes' praise for sinking an ally ship; in another world in which the story was less resolved than the Persian ["He may not pray for good things for himself alone . . . but only that all shall be well with all the Persians and the king; for among all the Persians is himself also" (1.132)], perhaps her spirit would have been enlisted in more commendable risk-taking. To leave indefinite some parts of the story might be to allow for the Artemisias of the world to a fuller triumph, Arion-like.[17]

Confronting Necessity:
Greeks, Persians, and the Battle of Salamis

The Persian and Greek stories, however, were settled long before Artemisia "charged and rammed a friendly ship." The Persians and Greeks each have had by then their moments of truth in *The History;* these, in turn, ultimately point toward the culminating battle of Salamis, where Persian and Greek characters emerge fully formed. The defining moment for the Persians was the debate in which the Persians failed to transcend their challenge and were induced into a state of resignation by Darius. The Greeks, too, are shown at an early stage debating the future course of their rule. They show themselves adept where the Persians were not—in appreciating the (rare) occasion in which judicious argument and the well-wrought phrase have the potential to shape a constructive action. At this moment the Greeks recognize possibilities that had only been dimly perceived before the clarifying words were spoken.

The defining Greek moment occurs in Book V, when the Spartiates seek to persuade their allies that they are all best advised to restore tyranny in Athens. The Spartiates come to this discussion with sound arguments for overthrowing Athenian democracy; in particular, they point to Athens' recent and alarming increase in power. Furthermore, the Spartiates apologize for their former interference in Athenian politics on behalf of the thankless commonalty and propose to make amends with their new candidate, Hippias. "But," writes Herodotus, "the majority of the allies did not accept their proposals" (5.92). Following the lead of Socles the Corinthian, who seizes the moment to tell a story of Corinth's unjust tyrants, the allies, "when they heard Socles speaking so fearlessly . . . chose the position of the Corinthians and adjured the Lacedaemonians not to do such a revolutionary thing to a Greek city" (5.93). The Greeks are pictured resisting in unison their most powerful ally, and all in the name of their common Greek heritage. If it is to be a

---

17. Herodotus' admiration of Artemisia is genuine enough. She served the Persians out of "pure spirit and manliness" (7.99), there being no compulsion for women to do anything of the kind. Her capacity to transgress conventional wisdom without causing outrage is Herodotean; she is far too large a figure for Xerxes to comprehend.

long time before Greek unity has much substance to it, still, the moment has arrived in which the Greeks give voice to and act upon the concept. It will be well within the bounds of their custom hereafter to talk themselves into resistance.[18]

The respective moments of decision for the Persians and Greeks prepare us for the councils before Salamis, which reveal the true import of national character. The configurations of the Salamis councils for Greece and Persia could not be more antithetical. Herodotus writes that when the Persians assembled, "Xerxes went down to his fleet in person, because he wished to make contact with those who had just sailed in, to learn their opinions" (8.67). The council that follows takes a highly prescribed, ceremonious form. Xerxes assumes his place on a raised throne and assigns the seating of his subjects in accordance with their honor. Our mental image is of the great Persian king about to open his magnificent assembly; yet Herodotus then informs us that it is Mardonius who solicits opinions on the matter: Should Xerxes fight a sea battle? There is to be no public expression, let alone discussion, of views. Xerxes has no more serious objective in learning their opinions than he would in noting their different attire. And this caricature of debate draws to a fitting close as soon as Xerxes has heard his wishes echoed to his satisfaction: "he gave his decision to follow the judgment of the majority" (8.69).

All the Persians except Artemisia seem to recognize their proper place in this ceremony, but it is exactly her presumption that brings out the essential fact here: even apart from the constricting form of the Persian council, it is impossible for Xerxes to hear wise advice with the appropriate impact. The Persians who were present when Artemisia delivered her negative response expected her to be severely punished. Considering the possible responses of the Persian king to unwelcome speeches (4.84, 7.39), their expectations were sound. But clearly there is

---

18. The historian shown here depicting the Greeks talking themselves into resistance is himself in an analogous position. The occasion for mastering the turn of events is unlikely enough, but without a Herodotus to recognize and give his people their voice, the occasion passes unheralded.

In his pathbreaking work on Thucydides, Parry explores the tension between the claims of λόγος and those of ἔργον: "λόγος is only right insofar as it has a clear and immediate relation to reality. . . . But ἔργον without λόγος is disastrous and meaningless. . . . It is the confounding of civilization" (*Logos and Ergon in Thucydides*, 89). He goes on: "The real tragedy of [Thucydides'] *History* is of the human intellect . . . the failure of the intellect, given the conditions of life and the infirmities of human nature, to master the world." (Ibid.) I would replace Parry's "the human intellect" with "constructive storytelling."

no advice that Artemisia can offer in these circumstances that will affect
Xerxes' perspective of the upcoming battle. It does not touch him when
she assesses the Persian naval capabilities, refers to past experiences
fighting against their formidable Greek opponents, or uses her psychological insight to predict their future behavior. Or, more accurately, her
arguments do touch Xerxes because he delights in her unusual forth-
rightness. But he is convinced that he does not have to answer her objections for Persian victory to be assured, for he plans to watch the battle
personally. He believes that his physical presence will have such a dis-
proportionate effect on the outcome of the battle that further strategic
advice is immaterial. But "the eyes and ears are bad witnesses for men if
they have barbarian souls."[19]

Xerxes does not imagine that his men are fighting the battle of Salamis in the name of anything else but their fear of the consequences of
defeat. Because the Persian navy is larger and more powerful than the
Greek, and because Xerxes has the power to oversee the battle, he sees
only the reasonableness of his expectations for conquest. Necessity is
the god; Xerxes does not recognize Persuasion. His subjects correspondingly regard their involvement in this battle as compulsory. The Great
King structures the lives of the Persians and profoundly impresses them
with his capacity to organize, control, and conquer. His power is based
on the conception of his subjects as discrete, countable entities, and they
appear to internalize this image of themselves as figures for the monarch's grand calculations. As David Konstan has suggested, there is undoubtedly a connection for Herodotus "between Persian unity and their
objectified, quantified relation to the world."[20]

Because the Persian king routinely commands acts of sacrifice, he
tends to equate his power with the number of his men rather than their
individual valor. He thus has an exaggerated sense of his control over
events. Typically the King does not anticipate that any supra- or sub-
rational elements will come into play to affect his plans. He is therefore
unable to handle the contingencies which do take him out of the realm
of logic. This is why Darius is thwarted for so long by the Scythians,
who will not encounter him in the man-to-man combat that the Persians
understand, but instead engage in evasive tactics. Darius only acciden-

19. Heraclitus, trans. Freeman, *Ancilla*, 32=DK B107 (I.175, 1).
20. Konstan, "Empire," 73.

tally makes them angry enough to abandon these tactics (4.128), but even then he proves unable to accommodate his style to theirs. Much later in *The History* Xerxes is exasperated by the prospect of having to consider variables in his march across Asia.

The Persian combination of rationalism and slavish obedience makes them the textbook case for a great fall. The King, of course, is the one Persian who is not a slave, and therefore he reflects the most unbalanced rationalism. In Xerxes this disposition is so distorted that he dreams of a Persian empire without borders. Xerxes sets his sight on the super-human, and along the way he loses his ability to read his fellow humans. Herodotus brings this truth home most unforgettably in his descriptions of Xerxes' conversations with Demaratus. As a disaffected Spartan king, Demaratus willingly details the Greek vulnerabilities to the Persians. It is to no avail, though, because when Demaratus speaks of the Spartan character ("they will challenge you to battle, even though all the other Greeks were on your side" [7.102]), Xerxes only laughs. "Joy is almost always ominous in *The History*," Stewart Flory notes, "and foreshadows the unhappy end of the character who feels it."[21] Under the best conditions, the Persians will share their leader's feeling that victory is compulsory. But Xerxes cannot anticipate that his subjects' sense of purpose will prove as assailable as their ships. Fighting with no higher purpose than the order to succeed, the Persians may be especially vulnerable to military setbacks. In Herodotus' portrayal, the Persians fail because they do not define themselves or their aspirations in terms that will withstand an aggressive challenge.

The historian is providing more than a hint of the nature of his own act of defining the Greeks. It is not the case that any definition will do for inspiriting this or any political community, for there are both internal and external checks to this process. The checks are internal because, as Herodotus demonstrates relentlessly, the Greeks are not a recognizable unit until that unity is forced on them by leaders they will recognize as such, and until they accept the imprint. (Their acceptance is always provisional, and "they" is never fully inclusive, as we conclude from the outcome of the messengers sent to Argos, Sicily, Corcyra, and Crete, "all asking for help for Greece" [7.145ff.]) It is an easier matter to insist on difference, not sameness. The checks are external because just as the

---

21. Flory, "Laughter, Tears and Wisdom," 150.

Greeks are not Greeks until they accept themselves as such, so their profoundest recognition comes only with validation by the outside world.[22] They require the Persians for their political identity.

As opposed to the Persian council, which follows a predictable procedure and has a clear beginning and end, the gathering of the Greek council before Salamis is marked by its lack of structure and its irresolution. Eurybiades opens the debate by declaring, "anyone who pleased should declare where, among the territories of which the Greeks were master, would be the most suitable place to fight their sea battle" (8.49). The Greek commander is so receptive to the opinions of others that he cannot bring the debate to a proper close, for even when all seem decided on a course of action, there turns out to be an opening for further debate. This inability of the Greeks to agree on and stick to one decision results directly from their perception of their leadership as both compliant and fallible. Eurybiades himself certainly perceives his role in this way; he, unlike Xerxes, truly listens to opposing ideas and recognizes their merit. Thus he is shown not only acceding to Themistocles' unpopular view, but also making room for him in his command to execute the plan.

It is a typical Herodotean touch to observe further that it was not, indeed, Themistocles who originally grasped that a retreat to the Isthmus would mean the dissolution of the Greek resistance. Themistocles heard it first from Mnesiphilus, and "recounted it as though it were his own idea" (8.58). In the final analysis, the source of the wise advice would not seem to matter, so long as it receives a genuine hearing; this is truth-telling of the most vigorous sort. As always, the notion of truth-telling encourages us to reflect on Herodotus' own procedure. It seems to be fair enough to say of him, too, that the source of wisdom is less im-

22. This point is easily misunderstood. I am not conflating military success with strong self-definition; quite the reverse. There is no lack of examples of leaders of political communities pushing their people forward, through stories and myths, in shameless acts of self-aggrandizement (e.g., "The Nightmare's Roots: The Dream World Called Serbia," *New York Times* May 16, 1993, sec. 1, p. 1). The lesson to be drawn from Herodotus is not that this does not occur or that it will not succeed on many occasions. The point is merely that this self-aggrandizement or nationalism or hatemongering is identifiable and vulnerable to external censure, whether the world community chooses to censure it or not. The stories of mankind do not stand in relativistic isolation for Herodotus; they are never immune from criticism. ["Nothing can serve as a criticism of a person save another person, or of a culture save an alternative culture." Rorty, *Contingency, Irony, and Solidarity*, 80.] This recognition may do little or nothing to console the subjects vilified by the ruling powers. But whether for good or for evil, Herodotus makes us more capable of understanding this phenomenon.

portant than the use to which it is put. Even lying stories can educate; there are noble and ignoble lies.

Herodotus establishes a humorous contrast in the way that the Greeks and Persians treat their sources of wisdom. As we have seen, Xerxes praises Artemisia unreservedly for her insights and then ignores them. Themistocles ignores Mnesiphilus utterly and then propounds his ideas. And Themistocles in turn is maligned for his suggestions. Adimantus the Corinthian, for one, delights in disparaging the words of Themistocles at every turn. And regarding his Greek audience as a whole, Themistocles is so far from being able to dictate his (reasonable) wishes that he has to enlist Aristides, "the best and the justest man in Athens" (8.79), as a spokesman for his ideas. The Greeks, who never stand on ceremony, are a tough audience; they do not accept the words of Aristides at face value either. Meanwhile, in Persia, where they are accustomed to respect every utterance of the King, the Persians trust so implicitly in the message brought by a Greek slave that they make immediate preparations for war (8.76).

Themistocles' whole enterprise may be seen as his attempt to force his fellow Greeks to the conviction that fighting the battle of Salamis would be in their common interest. He will not be satisfied with accomplishing half of this project, which would be to convey the necessity of fighting (in the manner of Xerxes). The Greeks had to be persuaded in addition that to fight this battle would be to attend to their higher nature and to work for the common good. For this purpose Themistocles has to summon those "two great gods" of the Athenians: Persuasion and Necessity (8.111). Moreover, he has to choose precisely the right moment. By invoking necessity too soon, Themistocles would fail as Xerxes did to inspire his listeners with a firm sense of purpose. By not invoking necessity soon enough, Themistocles would see the Greeks disperse without a fight. In Herodotus' portrayal, Themistocles accomplishes his task with masterful equanimity.

Themistocles' skills are evident first when he persuades Eurybiades to disembark and call another meeting, although the generals are set on retreating to the Isthmus. In the debate that follows, Themistocles refrains from criticizing the advocates of retreat for their self-interested motives: "for in the presence of the allies it would not have been suitable to make accusations against anyone" (8.60). Instead, he imagines the most positive role for the Greek commander at Salamis (Eurybiades could be the savior of Greece) and the most appealing outcome of the event (the barbarians would retreat in disorder). His arguments are sound as well as inspirational. Nevertheless, he succeeds only in prompting Adimantus' further taunting. At this point Themistocles directs the scene to its necessary end, first casting Eurybiades in his grand role, and then forcing him to accept it: "Eurybiades, if you stand your ground here, by such standing you will be a good man; if you go away, you will utterly destroy Greece" (8.62). Themistocles adds pointedly that should Eurybiades refuse to stand firm the Athenians would desert to Italy. This is the timely addition of necessity to his argument. The result is that in the same moment that the Greeks (temporarily) accept the necessity of fighting at Salamis, they also accept the meaning that Themistocles attributes to this action.

There is never any doubt about the precarious nature of the balance Themistocles has struck between necessity and persuasion. Herodotus intimates that it is the conjunction of qualities in Themistocles himself that made the balance possible at all. For the Greeks, at first "standing close together, man with man . . . whispering their bewilderment at the stupidity of Eurybiades" (8.74), and then in a larger meeting, manage to redefine the situation such that sailing off to the Peloponnese is their only logical move. Once again, Themistocles takes on the role of the one who corrects their interpretation of events and effectively enforces his vision. But to make the Greeks reinterpret their position requires no less of him than to incite the Persian attack. In this he succeeds, though it is quite some time before the Greeks accept this reality. When they do accept the necessity of fighting, Themistocles is at hand to attach the proper meaning to their actions: "Themistocles spoke well, better than all the others; for all his words were a contrast of the worse and the better side in man's nature and position in the world, and he bade them ever choose the better, and wound up his oration by urging them to board their ships" (8.83). It is a rare moment when the Greeks agree to define themselves as exceptional; thus they prepare themselves to perform extraordinary deeds.

Themistocles' actions have an intriguing relation to Herodotus' own procedure; as Carolyn Dewald remarks, "there are obvious parallels to be drawn between the author's presentation of his own role and that of the most intelligent individuals of his narrative."[23] Themistocles uses inventive means to get the Greeks to perceive their situation in a life-

23. Dewald, "Practical Knowledge and the Historian's Role," 60.

affirming way. The Greeks apprehend at least partially that they will fight at Salamis because they are good men whose way of life should be defended at all cost; incidentally, they also happen to be surrounded. On a grander scale, Herodotus likewise promotes a vision of the Greeks that encourages them to apprehend their exceptional status as a people over their link to the realm of necessity. For they, too, as contemporaries of Herodotus, are surrounded, surrounded by an empire with all too many resemblances to the one of Herodotus' description. If they are not to succumb to the same decline, they must be true to their politicized custom—which allows and rewards great exertion, decisionmaking, and intellectual daring. Their temptation is to go the other way, to follow the path of least resistance, leading to centralized power. But Herodotus is pointing to the more arduous and prosperous route. The Athenian culture might not be destined to the same decline and fall if it could produce as leaders people willing to dare, to look at choices in an intelligent manner, and to articulate these choices for the consideration of others.

Indicators of a Higher Order:
Gods, Heroes, and the Political Community

To Xenophanes, the distinctions among the gods across civilizations have an obvious source: "Ethiopians have gods with snub noses and black hair, Thracians have gods with grey eyes and red hair."[24] Herodotus seems to have had something parallel in mind in referring to foreign gods by their "equivalent" Greek names, as in his comment that those Ethiopians who live in Meroë "worship alone among gods Zeus and Dionysus" (2.29).[25] For Xenophanes and Herodotus both, contemplating the visible manifestations of religion is one thing, the divine quite

24. Xenophanes, trans. Freeman, *Ancilla*, 22=DK B16 (I.133, 5).

25. Such a scheme cannot be exactly symmetrical, of course, but Herodotus seems to relish the discontinuities. I do not agree wholly with Hall, then, when she concludes that this practice must not have disconcerted Herodotus' Greek audience as it does us: "When he follows his normal practice of using only the Greek name for a foreign god—Aphrodite for Astarte, Zeus for Ahuramazda, Pan for Mendes, or Dionysus for Osiris—he offers no explanation, because he assumed that the identification would seem natural to his audience, which therefore cannot have found them as startling as they sometimes appear to a modern eye" (*Inventing the Barbarian*, 183); she also cites the Ethiopian passage above. On the matter of the gods' names, Herodotus, leaving Xenophanes behind, draws attention to what is his common historiographical assumption: that for better or worse, foreign stories must be recounted in Greek terms. These examples must have been somewhat unnerving to his audience.

another. When confronting the truly divine, Herodotus is dumbstruck; of such things he does not want to speak (2.3). But he freely indulges himself in scathing and significantly negative commentary about a range of overdrawn, misguided, or charlatanistic activities that claim to represent or intuit the realm of religion: "Finally the Magi, using victims and also casting enchantments upon the wind (through their wizards), and, besides this, sacrificing to Thetis and the Nereids, contrived to stop the storm on the fourth day—unless it stopped of its own will" (7.191).[26]

Significantly, Herodotus does not extend the thought that our gods look like us to the animal world, as in the following speculation by Xenophanes: "But if oxen (and horses) and lions had hands or could draw with hands and create works of art like those made by men, horses would draw pictures of gods like horses, and oxen of gods like oxen, and they would make the bodies (of their gods) in accordance with the form that each species itself possesses."[27] If lions had hands, would they draw pictures of lion gods? The Persians have hands, and they draw no Persian gods ("this, in my opinion, is because they do not believe in gods of human form, as the Greeks do" [1.131]); the Egyptians draw gods that look (in part) like lions. If for Herodotus we all know equally about the gods, these conceptions nevertheless are singularly defining of us as peoples.

As with gods, so with heroes: lions are not illuminating of the human situation. The human situation is marked by diversity of conceptions, and the diverse human types that serve as heroes to different communities are of intense interest to Herodotus. When he juxtaposes cultural heroes like Tellus, Boges, and Rhampsinitus, respective heroes of Athens, Persia, and Egypt, we recognize consequential descriptions of the culture that produced them.[28] As usual, the Scythians represent an extreme case. Herodotus describes them gilding the heads of their dead

26. "Religion" as distinct from the "divine" is a target in *The History*—while the divine is of the utmost, if unstated, significance to Herodotus. I take it that this usage is akin to that of Nagy: "the master of ἱστορία is implicitly narrating divine actions as he explicitly narrates human actions" (*Pindar's Homer*, 262), and "It is as if Herodotus merely must have a good sense of judgment in his narration so that the patterns of divine justice could implicitly work their way through his narration" (304).

27. Xenophanes, trans. Freeman, *Ancilla*, 22=DK B15 (1.132, 19).

28. I use "hero" not in the precise sense of Vandiver's *Heroes in Herodotus* ("denizen of the Heroic Age," 19), but in the more ordinary usage of the individual of great courage or nobility; the question of interest to me is what kind of person was most highly regarded in the different cultures.

enemies, which thereafter will be used as their drinking cups: "And when strangers of consequence come to visit, their host brings round these heads and tells, over each one, how they were his kinsfolk but waged war upon him, and how he himself conquered them; and they speak of this as the act of a hero" (4.65). But the deeds of all of these men are extravagant, allowing us to judge, first, in what sense the hero towers over his fellow men, and second, how the heroes appear over against one another.

Boges the Persian is one memorable hero of *The History*. From the Greek point of view, Persian subjects are defined by an eradication of their personal needs, for they relinquish everything in their devotion to the King. Herodotus reinforces this perception of the Persians when he describes Boges, who must rank among the most blessed of his race since he "earned the praise of the Persians and does so still to this day" (7.107). Boges was a viceroy in Eion appointed by Xerxes before the invasion. Afterward, when "the Greeks put out all these Persians," and when Boges "might have marched out under treaty and come home safe to Asia," he refused to do so lest the King judge his survival an act of cowardice; instead, he endured to the end (7.107).

From this setup we might be inclined to expect of Boges some Spartan-like finish, apropos of Thermopylae. What follows, however, is in its own Persian category, for it stretches beyond what we might call heroic sacrifice. For Boges not only offers himself in a gratuitous and dramatic self-sacrifice, he also precedes this with the ceremonial cutting of the throats of "his children, his wife, his concubines, and his servants," and throws all of their bodies into a great fire. Then, after scattering all of the riches of the city, he throws himself into the fire as well. For this act, Xerxes judges him to be the one viceroy who "had proved a good man and true" (7.107). It is the prodigious and superfluous display which is most of note here, for what is praiseworthy to the Persians is to see such behavior unforced. This is the supreme validation of their own (forced) identities.

Another hero who embodies the qualities most esteemed by the Persians is Zopyrus, for in Darius' judgment, "no man has ever surpassed Zopyrus in the rank of the Doers of Good Deeds" (3.160). Zopyrus is essentially of the same order as Boges, and his story shares the same key elements: he initiated a dramatic and uncalled-for sacrifice of lives which involved an incidental reference to the unavoidable slaughter of many other Persians. Zopyrus' good deeds consist in mutilating himself

beyond cure—"he cut off his nose and ears and shaved his hair to dis-
figure himself, and laid lashes on himself" (3.154)—all in an attempt
to convince the Babylonians that he was betraying Darius. And just as
Zopyrus exhibits from the start an unnatural devotion to the Persian
cause, so his strategy calls for an exorbitant sacrifice of lives: seven thousand Persians must die before he will be confident that he has earned the
trust of the Babylonians. The grotesque aims of Zopyrus accomplished,
Herodotus mischievously adds: "It is said that often Darius would say
that he would rather have Zopyrus unblemished of his foul mutilation
than twenty more Babylons added to the existing one" (3.160). The King
himself winces before the Persian hero.

In a different world altogether are the Egyptians. A combination of
passivity and cynicism makes the Egyptians contemptuous of all rule,
native as well as foreign. Their heroes, or perhaps "distinctive figures"
is more accurate, are as far as can be imagined from being apologists
for Egypt. Consider Amasis, a king whom the Egyptians initially hold
in low esteem; they become conciliated only "by his cleverness and his
want of stiff-neckedness" (2.172). These are precisely the qualities which
would intrigue the Egyptians of Herodotus, for elsewhere they are seen
admiring those individuals who can combine cunning, unaffectedness,
and subversiveness. Along this line, the definitive λόγος for Amasis is the
golden footbath that Amasis uses to illustrate his rise from man of the
people to King of Egypt. The story goes that out of a footbath that had
previously been used by the king and his guests, Amasis carved an image
of a god and set it out for the Egyptians to worship. This accomplished,
Amasis gathers his subjects to "make them clear about the matter": "he
said that the image had been made out of a footbath in which formerly
the Egyptians used to vomit and piss and wash their feet, and now they
reverenced it mightily. So now, he said to them, he himself was just like
that footbath" (2.172).

In a humorous comment on Croesus' famous testing of the oracles,
Herodotus has Amasis, too, test them. We recall that Croesus sets up an
elaborate experiment to determine which among the oracles could be
proved to be trustworthy. Croesus comes up with a way to force an unambiguous answer to his turtle soup question ("on the hundredth day
[the messengers] should consult the oracle and ask what it was at that
moment that Croesus, king of Lydia, son of Alyattes, was doing" [1.47]).
Croesus cannot anticipate how the god will proceed to mock his dili-
gence; his great fall is preceded by his utter disregard for human limita-

tions. Here Amasis offers a strikingly different image. Amasis is said to have "gone around stealing" when he was a private person, and consequently to have been "haled to the oracles" by his victims. "Now, as soon as he became king," writes Herodotus, "he took no care at all of those shrines that had acquitted him of thievery, nor would he go there and sacrifice; for he saw them as nothing worth but possessed of lying oracles. But those of them that had strictly convicted him of being a thief, those he took good care of" (2.174). Croesus the Lydian judges the oracles on the basis of an overvaluation of his own abilities, whereas the Egyptian Amasis judges them on the certain evidence of his own base deeds.

The Egyptian penchant for ridiculing authority and for appreciating the wiliness of the lowly subject appears vividly in the Rhampsinitus story. Again, it is an Egyptian king who is being abused. The Rhampsinitus story celebrates the exploits of an unnamed Egyptian thief who begins by raiding the royal treasure house and ends by marrying the King's daughter. The thief is one of two sons of the builder of the king's treasure-house. The builder had the foresight to construct this chamber such that easy access was permitted to anyone who knew the measurements of the stone. The sons of the builder were thus able to abscond with large portions of the king's wealth before the king became suspicious by its steady diminution. At that point, the king set out traps in the chamber, thereupon catching one of the brothers. Realizing his predicament, the one brother called out to the other: "He bade him come in quickly and cut off his head so that he might not be seen and recognized and so destroy his brother as well" (2.121).

Our hero complies without hesitation and returns home with the head of his brother. The king is left mystified the next morning by his discovery of the headless corpse in his treasure chamber. But more trials follow for the thief. He must reclaim the corpse of his brother or be turned in by his mother. Prevailing there, the thief faces a final ordeal, which brings us to the only part of the story that Herodotus explicitly doubts. The king set his daughter in a room, relates Herodotus, "and ordered her to consort with all the men that came to her, alike. But before they enjoyed her, she must compel each to tell her what was the cleverest and wickedest thing he had ever done in his life. Whoever told her the story of the thief, she was to lay hold of" (2.121). The thief, wanting to "surpass the king in resourcefulness," prepared for his meeting by cutting off the arm "of a freshly dead man" as protection against the daughter's hold. From start to finish, we see, the tale overflows with

Egyptian mischief, Herodotus' style. But it is not simply playful, because it marks out their tendency towards certain low and derisive qualities.

Herodotus tells us that the way that the thief combines wickedness with cleverness so appeals to the king that he designates him as "the man who understood more than anyone else in the world" (2.121). This designation makes us recall by contrast the Solon-Croesus conversation of Book I, inasmuch as Solon is certainly the Greek candidate for the man who understood more than anyone. There, we recall, Solon does name the most blessed man of all—Tellus the Athenian. Tellus is significantly less colorful a hero than the Egyptian thief, for his renown comes from his perfect exercise of virtue in the name of the city. His is the most ordinary kind of existence: he was born to a good city, he had good luck with his family, he died nobly, and was honored by his kinsmen. The Egyptian's delight, in contrast, was to ridicule and rob from the authorities; his methods were dazzling, wicked, and immediately successful. Both the Rhampsinitus and Amasis tales show Herodotus centering on the Egyptian disposition to denigrate. In these cases, they denigrate authority, good decorum, and nobility, but broadly speaking, they denigrate humanity altogether.

The unnamed thief's contrast with Solon's second most blessed men is even more intriguing. The Argive brothers Cleobis and Biton, too, are unspectacular champions; their excellence is bodily and spiritual. The Egyptian story also involves two brothers and their mother. But far from sharing deeds of honor, the Egyptian brothers are partners in crime; eventually, the one chops off the head of the other to avoid being caught robbing from the king. The mother's part in the story consists in threatening to betray her son the thief to the authorities. That this family trio stands in such amusing opposition to the Argive three is one small clue that this is no accidental compilation of myths. The Rhampsinitus tale is as pointedly Egyptian as the Solon conversation is Greek. The former glorifies the ability of an anonymous man to be so resourceful and sly as to acquire the king's money and daughter. The latter esteems an ordinary civic life, and remembers the names of its exemplars. When Herodotus juxtaposes cultural preferences as in our extended example of heroes, he provides a view of real alternatives in the ways humans constitute themselves.

Herodotus, as we have come to expect, sets up a prominent opposition between Athenians and Persians. The truth-telling of the Persians in temporal matters has a spiritual counterpart, for they show a rigidity in receiving divine communication as well. This rigidity contrasts sharply with the manner in which the Greeks (and the Athenians in particular) relate to the gods; it is worth closer inspection to highlight the respective characters. The difference can initially be expressed as that which may arise between a people for whom buying and selling in a marketplace is second nature and a people who distrust marketplaces, in the style of Cyrus: "I never yet feared men who have a place set apart in the midst of their cities where they gather to cheat one another and exchange oaths, which they break" (1.153). It seems that daily experiences for the Greeks in an arena that demands give-and-take predisposes them to seek the "best deals" even on the highest plane, whereas the Persians are more likely to accept their portion as set and final. Hence it is a basic point that the Greeks receive their most important communications through the Delphic oracle, where the message is open to competing interpretations; for their part the Persian tyrants most often receive divine communication directly and irrevocably through dreams, where the message is taken to be indisputable.

It is paradigmatic in *The History* that the Great Kings receive direct warnings or signals from the gods. Cyrus, shortly before his death, sees a vision of "the eldest of the sons of Hystaspes with wings on his shoulders, and with one of these wings he overshadowed Asia and, with the other, Europe" (1.209). Likewise, Cambyses sees a vision in his sleep: "There seemed to come to him from Persia a messenger who told him that Smerdis sat on the royal throne and reached for heaven with his head" (3.30). Darius has his accession to the throne endorsed by "a flash of lightning (though the sky was cloudless) and a rattle of thunder" (3.86). Finally, Xerxes' invasion of Greece in the end hinges on a series of dreams in which "a great and handsome man" warns Xerxes that he will not prove "forgiving" should the King choose not to make war (7.12).

Herodotus makes it plain, however, that the gods communicate directly in this way to tyrants, Persian and otherwise. We have before us examples even of Athenian tyrants who are addressed by the gods firsthand: "Hipparchus, the son of Pisistratus, had been killed by Harmodius and Aristogiton. . . . Hipparchus had indeed seen a vision in his dream that very closely foretold what would befall him" (5.55). The treacherous Hippias provides a more sustained illustration of a Greek going native in the Persian world. Here we have a Greek personality, sketched by a Greek historian, illustrating the Persian character. Herodotus carefully draws in Hippias a close resemblance to a Great King, while still conforming to the vivid recollections the Athenians had of their history under the tyrants. By the time of the battle of Marathon, Hippias represents a foreign element to the Athenians; the Athenians had transformed themselves as a people when they rejected their tyrants. Herodotus wholly approved of the transformation: "It is not only in respect of one thing but of everything that equality and free speech are clearly a good; take the case of Athens, which under the rule of princes proved no better in war than any of her neighbors but, once rid of those princes, was far the best of all" (5.78). If Hippias stands for all the Athenians had thrown off, he also fits in the Eastern tradition by being singled out for divine communication. We do not see the individual commanders of the Greeks singled out to receive portentous dreams. And, in fact, the dream of Hippias directly anticipates in important ways the famous dream of Xerxes.

The finality with which Hippias judges his dream is to be noted, for it typifies the way the Persians receive divine communication: no human intervention is presumed to have a chance to affect it. Hippias dreamed that he had lain with his own mother. Rather than draw any inferences about his outrage of custom, he concludes from this dream that "he would return to Athens, and, having reestablished his rule there, would die in his own country, an old man" (6.107). This optimistic reading of a sinister dream is in itself strikingly Persian. But Hippias' interpretation is shaken when a great fit of coughing and sneezing overtakes him, causing one of his teeth to fly out and disappear into the sand. Now Hippias "groaned heavily and said to the onlookers, 'This land is not ours, nor shall we subject it; for the share of it that was mine—the tooth has it'" (6.107). The second reading is as incontrovertible as the first.

As with Hippias, so with the Great Kings: no benefit is to be afforded to the individual chosen as divine medium. It is rather a sign of the obliteration of (an exceptional) free will in a system of tyranny that the divine and cultural necessities converge upon one being. Hence Xerxes assimilates in one thought process the notions of tradition, god, and individual will: "Men of Persia, it is no new law that I initiate among you; it has come to me from the tradition. . . . It is the god that leads us on, and so, when we of ourselves set out our many enterprises, we prosper" (7.8). In the Persian world there is nothing like the reciprocal relation between humans and gods that Greek anthropomorphism suggests. Instead, the Persians consider that so little space is allowed them to exercise free will that the gods will force on their Great King the missteps that lead to destruction. Such a view promotes both hubris and fatalism among its advocates, because it obviates any need for them to reflect on human limitation. Again, Xerxes gives expression to this irresponsible thinking. When Artabanus predicts that the immense Persian force will lack both harbors and food once in Europe, Xerxes replies: "But do not fear everything; do not always take account of everything. As each opportunity arises, if you were to take account of everything that is involved, you would never do anything" (7.50).

Herodotus most explicitly describes the Persian combination of hubristic longings and fatalism in the dream scene of Xerxes. As Xerxes wavers in his decision to attack Greece, he alternately puts forward rash claims ("For the sun will look down upon no country that has a border with ours, but I shall make them all *one* country" [7.8]) and afterthoughts ("Men of Persia, I ask your pardon for the change in plans" [7.13]). The issue is to be settled by a dream. Having made the decision to remain at peace, Xerxes is haunted by the great and handsome man who instructs him to be firm in his first resolve to attack Greece.[29] At this point Xerxes' will is dissolved, for, as he complains to Artabanus: "But now, though I wish to do this, I cannot; for since I have changed and turned from my other purpose, there is a vision keeps haunting me in sleep and will not suffer me to do what I would; even now he has threatened me and vanished" (7.15). So too with Artabanus when he dons the King's garments: the divine message is received that will push the Persians toward destruction. There is no room in this scenario for the Persians to send back for a more propitious message; the communication between the gods and the Persians is one-way. Like Hippias, Xerxes will act against his better judgment. He accepts the inevitability of the attack on Greece.

A final point must be underscored in regard to the Persian interpretation of dreams. The Persians typically receive the divine message as if *it* were unambiguous, and as if *they* were infallible in reading it. The

29. The vision that Xerxes sees in his dream bears a striking relation to his own figure, of which Herodotus comments: "And of those many tens of thousands of men, for handsomeness and size there was none worthier than Xerxes to hold that power" (7.187). Many readers believe with How and Wells (*Commentary,* II.131) that the dream "is modelled on that sent to Agamemnon" (*Iliad* ii.66). That figure is said to have the height and build of Nestor, which hardly seems to illuminate the Herodotean passage. The dreams differ in significant respects (see, among others, Bichler, "Die 'Reichsträume' bei Herodot," 141–142; Crahay, *La littérature oraculaire,* 222). Others have suggested that it is simply the image of Cyrus or Darius, reminding Xerxes of his duties as Great King. Perhaps, but there may be more psychological depth to the image. Xerxes might summon up this domineering personality himself precisely in order to be subject to a necessary force, thus avoiding all the perils and uncertainties of deliberation.

supposition is that this truth-telling is a literal business: the proper response to a divine warning is a human counterstroke. This response does
not serve to relate the human and divine worlds, but to blur the distinction between the two. Thus the Great Kings fail to perceive what is
at stake when the divine presence is felt. Their responses will be either
inadequate because they overestimate their control over events, or misguided because they overestimate their knowledge. Cyrus tries to falsify
his dream by gaining custody of the son of Hystaspes, but his own death
intervenes. Cambyses attempts to control his fate by killing Smerdis, but
he is deceived about the Smerdis in question (as Croesus was deceived
about the empire that was to be destroyed). And if the King should turn
to the Magi for assistance in interpreting the divine message, he is sure
to get an inappropriate reading there, too. A Great King cannot hear
a truth, divine or otherwise, that would cut into the greatness of his
empire, and thus the Magi are reduced to offering simpleminded interpretations. "The vision was this: Xerxes thought that he was crowned
with an olive branch, and from the olives there were shoots that overshadowed all the earth, but that afterwards the crown, which was set
upon his head, vanished" (7.19). The Magi conclude that this vision "referred to all the earth and that all mankind should be slaves to Xerxes."
Xerxes is perfectly satisfied with this response; elsewhere, Herodotus
comments that Xerxes was very pleased with the Magian insight (7.37).

It is inconceivable that the Greeks of Herodotus would assume that
the divine communication is unambiguous or that the human response
could be unequivocal, and this because of their long experience with
the Delphic oracle. Early in their history, the Lacedaemonians learn not
to assume too easily that the god sanctions their objectives. When the
Pythia says "Tegea will I give you, to beat with your feet in dancing/
and with a rope to measure, to fill, her beautiful plainland" (1.66), the
Lacedaemonians scarcely anticipate that it will be as prisoners that they
will measure the land. Such encounters with the oracle teach a wari-
ness in human affairs, an understanding that unlimited power is not for
humans to attain. Correspondingly, the Lacedaemonians must appreciate the limitations of human knowledge as they struggle to ascertain
from the Pythia where the son of Agamemnon is buried:

Somewhere there is Tegea, in Arcadia's level plainland,
where two winds are a-blowing, under dire stress of compulsion;

blow rings answer to blow, and evil is piled upon evil.
There Agamemnon's son is held by the life-giving earth (1.67).

The Greeks are frequently shown having to exert themselves to accomplish the Pythia's bidding. Thus the Theraeans' colonization of Libya involves repeated encounters with the Pythia before the colonists succeed: "The god, you see, would not let them off the project of the colony until they should come to Libya itself" (4.157).

In a more positive sense, too, the Greeks are particular about the divine messages they hear. The Athenians even defy the necessity of certain divinely inspired messages, beginning from the days of Hippocrates, when he refused to hear a prophecy concerning his son, Pisistratus (1.59), right up through the second Persian invasion, when the Athenians sent back to the oracle for a more auspicious response: "My Lord, give us a better oracle about our fatherland; be moved to pity the suppliant boughs with which we come before you, or we will never go away from your shrine but remain right here till we die" (7.141). Similarly, in an earlier series of struggles with the Aeginetans, the Athenians selectively heed an oracle: "but when they heard about the thirty years, they would not put up with the necessity of waiting" (5.89).

In a like vein, the Athenians aggressively appropriate stories that suggest a favorable divine presence among them. Before the battle of Marathon the Athenian herald Phidippides is said to have encountered Pan on his way to rouse the Spartans to battle. Pan's message to the Athenians is one that would serve to invigorate them for the coming fight: "Why do you pay no heed to Pan, who is a good friend to the people of Athens, has been many times serviceable to you, and will be so again?" (6.105). This story seems to have made its way into *The History* because, says Herodotus, "the Athenians were convinced [it] was true" (6.105). The effect, not the truth, of the story is pivotal.

Herodotus seems to be impressed with a people's active structuring of its religious beliefs, and this is where Athens comes in for special praise. Among the Athenian people, Themistocles stands out as an admirable leader in shaping positive responses to the god. In his first appearance in *The History*, Themistocles is shown countering the negative turn in the debate about the meaning of a recent and alarming oracle; Themistocles insists that the threat is to the enemy, not to Athens, and that the oracle is urging resistance. Herodotus reports that the Athenians decide to adopt Themistocles' reading rather than that of the oracle-interpreters: "for the latter would not have them prepare for a sea fight or indeed, to tell the truth, put up a hand's-worth of resistance at all; they should just leave Attica and settle in some other country" (7.143). We are led to conclude that the divine is best felt as a spur to action, as a truly inspiring force. It is under such inspiration that the Athenians become for Herodotus the saviors of Greece: "They chose that Greece should survive free, and it was they who awakened all the part of Greece that had not Medized, and it was they who, under Heaven, routed the King. Not even the dreadful oracles that came from Delphi, terrifying though they were, persuaded them to desert Greece" (7.139). The Athenians chose, awakened, and routed—and all in line with a most upright posture "under Heaven."

That the Athenians draw strength from their system of belief is nowhere more apparent than in their worship of the hero Heracles, who is associated with them significantly in *The History*.[30] The description of the Athenian's hurried defense of the city after the battle of Marathon serves as a poignant example. In the race to Athens, the Athenians "reached it first, before the barbarians came, and encamped, moving from one sanctuary of Heracles—the one at Marathon—to another, the one at Cynosarges" (6.116). The coincidence is significant, for Heracles' double status (2.44) suggests an overlapping in divine and human attributes, and one that the Athenians might bring to bear upon themselves.

In one Egyptian story of Heracles (the same Egyptians from whom the Greeks got "the name of Heracles" [2.43]), Herodotus reports, "Heracles had most earnestly desired to see Zeus, but the god would not be seen by him" (2.42). To fend off the persistent Heracles, Zeus slays a ram, covers himself with the fleece, and so displays himself. Perhaps before Heracles, both gods and humans alike were content to regard the divine in animal form. But in Heracles human intelligence seeks to penetrate the disguise beside which dwells a truth about the ultimate. Heracles represents qualities that define humanity: free and knowledge-seeking, yet fated. The Athenians draw inspiration from this, and it will be the Heracles-like qualities in the Athenians that will determine the course of the Persian War: "They were the first Greeks we know of to charge their enemy at a run and the first to face the sight of the Median

30. Vandiver's insight that Heracles and Perseus "serve as symbolic equivalents for Greece and Persia respectively" is dead right, but the implications go largely unexplored in her account.

dress and the men who wore it. For till then the Greeks were terrified even to hear the names of the Medes" (6.112).

Highly significant from our point of view is the fact that Heracles is not a native of Athens: "Herakles did not belong to the earliest stratum of Attic religion and mythology and therefore his cult was not localized on the Acropolis, Athens' oldest cult center."[31] In *The History,* Heracles is named as the head of three royal families, the Scythian, Spartan, and Lydian, but not the Athenian. The Athenians had to adopt him, or, as Lewis Richard Farnell puts it, "settle him as full citizen in their land."[32] And so they did, making him theirs in thought and in deed. The impact of this becomes clear when we turn back to consider the analogous Persian behavior. At first glance, the Persians seem ready in some parallel way to adopt the practices and convictions of foreign religions. But it turns out that as with customs, so with religions: the Persians adopt foreign ways in only the most superficial sense.[33]

Cyrus is the first to demonstrate the willingness of the Persians to entertain foreign religious notions. After the Persians defeat the Lydians and capture Croesus, Cyrus has the fettered King set atop a huge pyre: "He had in his mind either to offer these first fruits to some god or other, or perhaps he wished to fulfill some vow he had made, or perhaps even, since he had heard that Croesus was a god-fearing man, he set him on the pyre to know whether some one of Those-that-are-Divine would rescue him from being burned alive" (1.86). Cyrus is here staging a scene to discover a religious "truth." It is not far from the scene that Darius orchestrates in regard to custom (3.38), for Cyrus, too, assumes a position of an outside observer, as if the god would play according to his rules.[34] In the end, though, Cyrus interrupts his drama when he senses that he has overstepped his human prerogative ("he recognized that he too was a man" [1.86]). It is a sense that becomes less discernible in his successors.

31. Galinsky, *Herakles Theme,* 40.
32. Farnell, *Greek Hero Cults,* 153.
33. This is where Perseus comes in significantly as the forefather of the Persians. Vandiver writes: "Unlike Heracles, Perseus was of uncertain origin, and his descendants told varying stories about him according to their own circumstances. He does not carry a particular culture with him as Heracles does" (*Heroes in Herodotus,* 201–202). The hero Perseus who carries no particular culture thus stands at the head of a people who indiscriminately adopt the cultural practices of others. One thinks of Rorty's quip about us becoming "so open-minded that our brains have fallen out" (Rorty, "On Ethnocentrism," 526).
34. I discuss the "custom is king" passage in Chapter 5.

On his march to Greece, Xerxes methodically adopts foreign religious practices as a kind of insurance measure. There is never any attempt by the Persians to make the belief *theirs*, as we see with the Athenians and Heracles; rather, they appear merely to be hedging their bets. In Achaea, Xerxes is told a local story "which has to do with the rites of Laphystian Zeus": "Xerxes, when he heard all that had happened, when he came to the grove, kept away from it himself and bade his whole army do so, and treated with reverence both the house and the precinct of the descendants of Athamas" (7.197). At another time, Herodotus reports that the Magi sacrificed to Thetis "because they heard from the Ionians the story" (7.191). Clearly this practice of the Persians of assimilating all sorts of foreign rites does not inspirit them. In one example, after Xerxes observes and inquires about the citadel of Troy, "he sacrificed one thousand cattle to Athena of Ilium, and the Magi offered libations to the heroes." So far was this from strengthening the Persian resolve that on that very night, Herodotus writes, "the host was seized with panic fear" (7.43).

Significantly, it does not matter to the Great Kings whose rite it is they perform, or even who performs it. Thus Xerxes "bade [the Athenians to] go up to the Acropolis and in their own fashion perform the sacrifices." Herodotus comments, "He did this either because he had seen some vision in his sleep or because he began to have scruples about having burned the temple" (8.54). Xerxes assumes the gods will be appeased irrespective of the particular human sacrificers. Herodotus conveys here yet another instance of the Persians abdicating individual responsibility. There will remain for these Persians a gap between reproducing the religious ceremonies of others, and fostering belief in something great towards which they themselves can aspire.

Turning to Egyptian religious beliefs, we note that they are too distinctive even for the Persians to imitate easily, and that Herodotus himself appears to have less than his usual impartial tone in describing them. He seems uncomfortable speaking of their reverence of the subhuman, for this keeps them from holding a constructive ideal of the human. Seth Benardete comments, "They gave their gods, in so far as they had one, an animal shape. They made men look down rather than up, to reverence the subhuman rather than the human, only to despise and never to respect themselves."[35] Certainly it is worth noting the frequency in

35. Benardete, *Herodotean Inquiries*, 46.

Book II of Herodotus' refusal to enter into the details of Egyptian religious ideas, for nowhere else does our author reveal a squeamish side. It seems that in the rare occasion in which his own religious sentiment is offended, he opts for silence rather than overt condemnation: "there is a story told about the matter by the Egyptians; I know it, but it is not quite suitable to be declared" (2.47).

The deprecatory view that the Egyptians have of their relation to the gods seems to translate directly into the low expectations they have of their fellow man, and this is at the heart of the Herodotean criticism. Their cynicism about the motives of others make them unlikely adherents to a noble cause, for they are destined to perpetuate the world of their low imaginings. Thus when Cambyses sends a herald to negotiate a settlement with the Egyptians who were shut up in Memphis, they react with a typical mistrust of motives: "But when the Egyptians saw the ship coming to Memphis they poured out of their fortress, destroyed the ship, cut the men to pieces like very butchers, and dragged them within their walls" (3.13).

If Herodotus seems to see danger in a religion that despises humanity, he seems also to caution against one that takes no heed of human limitation. This pertains to the Persians, who in their undifferentiated worship of "the whole circle of the heaven" seem to lack a sense of the human part in this whole: "They sacrifice, too, to the sun, moon, and earth and to fire, water, and winds" (1.131). The Great King's tendency to fail to consider individual wrongs committed against him has much to do, of course, with his position as tyrant, but there is no doubt a religious influence here as well. Hence Cyrus becomes furious against the river Gyndes for swallowing his white horse, and threatens: "I will make you so feeble that, for the rest of time, even women will easily cross you without wetting their knees" (1.189). A positive religious influence would be one that inspired its adherents to measure the world according to a different hierarchy, one in which the human took its place among the natural, animal, and divine.

The other extreme of the Persians' undifferentiated worship is the obsession with particular observances. The Egyptians, again, err most seriously in this respect: "In their reverence for the gods, they are excessive, more than any others in the world" (2.37). Their daily lives are so bound up with religious prescriptions and rituals that they shield themselves from acting in the human world. This appears to be a distortion of the proper working of the Herodotean hierarchy; instead of humans aspiring to touch the divine, they effectively close off the two realms. The Lacedaemonians, too, are often conveyed in this posture of being so caught up in worship of the gods that they are negligent in matters of life and death. "The Spartans intended, after they had performed the ceremony and left guards in Sparta, to go to the war speedily and in full force" (7.206). Time and again, the good intentions of the Lacedaemonians are sacrificed to the requirements of religion. The Lacedaemonian custom of fighting to the death counteracts, but never obliterates, their fussiness in matters of religious ceremony. Herodotus reserves his full praise for more active postures toward the divine.

Only those who dare to challenge accepted authority can hope to reach out, intellectually and artistically, to know and comprehend the meaning of life and the universe. One small but mysteriously compelling incident gives just this sense. Aristodicus, son of Heraclides, challenges the oracle on behalf of Pactyes, a Lydian rebel against the Persians. He does this in an act of stunning irreverence to the conventions of religion: he violates the oracle's sacred precincts to tear out the swallows' nests from under the eaves of the shrine (1.159). He does so for the purpose of demonstrating the hypocrisy of the god in refusing sanctuary to Pactyes while granting sanctuary to the swallows. Human suppliants are rejected whereas animal suppliants are received, a reversal of the proper hierarchy. Aristodicus thus takes a dramatically challenging approach to the divine in the tradition of Heracles, a tradition of seeking to know, to look behind and beyond the accepted surfaces of society.

To free oneself from the tyranny of the past is a Herodotean imperative, requiring this intellectual and spiritual daring. Success in the human endeavor depends upon this boldness, here described by William James: "It is only risking our persons from one hour to another that we live at all. And often enough our faith beforehand in an uncertified result is the only thing that makes the result come true."[36]

Herodotus appears to find excellence in individuals who think the unthinkable and who resist enslavement to any absolute dictate. Thinking the unthinkable is at the core of Herodotus' praise of Hegesistratus the Elean, for example. Hegesistratus, imprisoned and likely to suffer grisly torture before execution, "managed the bravest act of anyone I

---

36. James, "Is Life Worth Living," in *The Will to Believe*, 59.

know. He calculated that the rest of his foot could slip out of the stocks if he cut it off at the instep" (9.37). He succeeds in resisting enslavement.

Custom is formed by, but also bears against, individual human beings. The most admirable characters seem to be those who manage to assert their freedom and self-sufficiency in the face of overpowering necessities.

CHAPTER 5

The Use of Herodotus in Contemporary Political and Cultural Criticism

From his time to ours, Herodotus has been treated as the father of history the way most fathers are treated: acknowledged but often ignored, or not taken too seriously, except on special occasions. But today, Herodotus is becoming suspiciously fashionable. Evidently something in Herodotus has begun to address issues of contemporary concern in a manner that is found useful to some of the main protagonists in the current debates and controversies on the topics of cultural imperialism, the new historicism, and the Other.

Herodotus is employed variously, as weapon or target, in debates ranging across disciplines: anthropology to literary theory, historiography to hermeneutics.[1] Predominating among them is the Herodotean contribution to the problem of how "we" (the historian, the anthropologist) with our cultural presuppositions can know about "them" (the past, the Other). In this era of diversity and multiculturalism, the answer frequently given is that we cannot know them. But even those scholars who have most extensively denounced one culture's efforts to comprehend another have acknowledged that the task cannot be avoided. According to Said: "Perhaps the most important task of all would be to . . . ask how one can study other cultures and peoples from a libertarian, or a nonrepressive and nonmanipulative perspective."[2]

Looking at the questions today's scholarship poses to Herodotus and the answers it draws from *The History*, we can see that however intriguing it may now be, the meaning of that book remains elusive so long as the imaginative impulse behind this scholarship remains circumscribed. A survey of current postures toward Herodotus reveals a full and mutually incompatible variety. Some readers of Herodotus continue to winnow out facts and employ them for present purposes. Others assert the same degree of certainty about what happened in history, but conclude

---

1. See, for example, in addition to the works that are the subject of this chapter: Shell, *Economy of Literature*, 12–21; Cohen, *Health and the Rise of Civilization*; Smith, *Ethnic Origins of Nations*; McGann, *Beauty of Inflections*; Blumenberg, *Legitimacy of the Modern Age*.

2. Said, *Orientalism*, 24. Unless specifically noted, all references to Said will pertain to *Orientalism*.

that societies of the past as described by Herodotus are time-bound and have nothing universal to offer. Others suggest that the task Herodotus set for himself is impossible: no one era or culture can ever understand or appreciate another in a nonjudgmental way.

These approaches are myriad and inconsonant; not one accounts for the whole of Herodotus' thought. He is appropriated to make some point, to unmake some point, or to prove that we cannot know any particular point. Three contemporary perspectives are provocative in their own right: Martin Bernal and his literal reading of Herodotus, François Hartog and his "decoding" of *The History,* and Edward Said on the Other. They are also provocative in association, for though each comes to Herodotean issues with different purposes, each leaves without coming to terms with the claims to truth implicit in Herodotean historiography.

Martin Bernal and the Cape of Good Hope—Hope

We cannot do better in understanding contemporary modes of thought than to begin with Bernal, whose first volume of his projected four-volume series *Black Athena* "has excited more controversy than almost any other book dealing with Greco-Roman antiquity to have been published in the second half of the twentieth century."[3] Bernal seeks to demonstrate that the Ancient Model, a view of the historical origin of Greece as essentially Levantine, was overthrown and replaced by an Aryan Model in the nineteenth and twentieth centuries by racist and anti-Semitic European historians; these historians, Bernal argues, were anxious to purify their heritage by claiming that classical Greek culture primarily emerged from the Northeast, not the Southwest. Bernal proposes that we revert to a revised version of the Ancient Model, a model he says "had no major 'internal' deficiencies, or weaknesses in explanatory power [but] was overthrown for external reasons." He relies on Herodotus to an extraordinary degree in presenting his argument; even his highly controversial title *Black Athena* is said to have been inspired by Herodotus' portrayal of the Egyptians.[4] Consequently Bernal invites our scrutiny over the kinds of questions he submits to Herodotus.

The most striking characteristic of Bernal's reading of Herodotus is

3. Hall, "When Is a Myth Not a Myth?" 181.
4. Bernal, *Black Athena,* vol. 1: *Fabrication of Ancient Greece,* 2, 53.

that he is both selective and literal.[5] He is not blind to what he labels the fantastic elements in many of the stories of Herodotus; rather, he thinks it is possible to isolate their factual bases.[6] Regarding his particular thesis, Bernal cherishes what we might call the Cape of Good Hope—hope. That is, it sometimes turns out that when Herodotus reports a traditional story that is so far-fetched that he disbelieves it, he provides enough apparently solid information that later readers feel able to deduce the truth of the matter. Herodotus tells the story that King Necos sent the Phoenicians around what we now know as the Cape of Good Hope: "And they declared (what some may believe, though I myself do not) that as they sailed round Libya [Africa] they had the sun on their right" (4.42). In their commentary on Herodotus, W. W. How and J. Wells accept what the historian did not:

> The circumstance disbelieved by Herodotus is strong confirmation; the sun . . . in the southern hemisphere would actually be "on the right," so long as they sailed west, and from the Equator to the Cape of Good Hope the course would be south-west and then west, while on the return journey it would be slightly north-west.[7]

This is the prototype Bernal seems to hold out to us. He refers, for instance, to Herodotus' report that the Egyptians under the pharaoh Sesostris colonized as far into Southwest Asia as Colchis. The standard view that Bernal would like to refute is that Herodotus has mixed together "traditions about Senwosres I and III and Ramesses II and [laced] these with oriental hyperbole."[8] As far as Bernal is concerned, the original Herodotean report has been dismissed too swiftly by mod-

---

5. This criticism has been leveled against Bernal by a number of critics, most notably Lefkowitz, "Not Out of Africa," 33–34; Green, "*Black Athena* and Classical Historiography," 59; Snowden, "Bernal's 'Blacks,' Herodotus, and Other Classical Evidence," 89; and Levine, review of *Black Athena*, 447.

I intend to press these claims further than they have been pressed in regard to Bernal's use of Herodotus. Herodotean scholars tend to consider Bernal a charlatan and therefore not worthy of their serious attention. Yet Bernal's work is widely known, and his claims are often uncritically accepted by audiences who have no grounds for supposing Herodotus to be other than he claims. I take my cue from Herodotus; bad stories should be deflated— even more for the sake of promoting a vital political community than for purposes of correcting our scholarship.

6. Bernal, *Black Athena*, vol. 2: *Archaeological and Documentary Evidence*, 202.

7. How and Wells, *Commentary*, I. 318.

8. Bernal, vol. 2, 236.

ern audiences, which had interests in denying to a single (African) pharaoh such aggressive and ultimately influential behavior.

The burden of proof falls on Bernal here, as the consensus not of two centuries but of more than a millennium of readers has been that Sesostris is something of a compilation. Significantly, although Bernal does believe that he has made a case for the facticity of the Sesostris tradition, he does not insist on it. He contends that he is still closer to the objective truth than were the Aryan model historians of the nineteenth and twentieth centuries. So if the Sesostris tradition is likely to be as true as the Cape of Good Hope story, it need not be:

> Thus, it is extremely probable that . . . there was a local belief in Colchis that their country had been founded by an Egyptian pharaoh, probably Sesostris. It is possible that the tradition was mistaken and arose from a desire to have a respectable cultural ancestry, or, more likely, to explain not only cultic parallels but the African appearance of some of the population.[9]

The very existence of the account that Herodotus relates, says Bernal, tends to undermine the Aryan Model. Elsewhere he elaborates: "We are not concerned here with the rightness or wrongness of [Herodotus'] conclusions, however, but merely with the facts that he himself believed in them and that he was being relatively conventional in doing so."[10] Bernal contends that even in the unlikely case that the Sesostris stories are untrue, their very survival shows that the ancient world preserved different voices and different accounts of historical origins; this contrasts favorably to the whitewashed and unitary reading of the Aryan model. He concludes: "Thus I believe that the chances of finding something approaching objectivity are much greater among the ancient Greeks with their conflicting views than among the more single-minded nineteenth and twentieth century classicists."[11]

Bernal's reading of Herodotus is dated; he mines *The History* for buried facts, distorting and belittling Herodotean historiography in the process. The facts as Herodotus believed in them are considered to be self-evident; his conventional posture in doing so is assumed. All interpretive difficulties vanish. But the immediate textual difficulties do not truly disappear when Bernal extracts and magnifies fragments of He-

9. Ibid., 256.
10. Bernal, vol. 1, 100.
11. Bernal, "*Black Athena* and the APA," 24.

rodotus' Egyptian story. His remarks about Egyptian influence on the
Greeks stem largely from the Herodotean passage at 2.50, which begins,
"The names of nearly all the gods came to Greece from Egypt." This
statement and others similar to it lead Bernal to include Herodotus in his
generalized statement that "the Classical and Hellenistic Greeks themselves maintained that their religion came from Egypt." Later Bernal
comments airily, "In vain does Herodotus tell us that everything comes
from Phoenicia and Egypt."[12] These are surprisingly broad and confident formulations. In the first place, the nature of the historian's belief
on the matter of the gods' names has long puzzled Herodotean scholars; Bernal does not address this as a serious intellectual problem. In the
second place, the literary features of Herodotus' characterization of the
Egyptians that affect Bernal's conclusions are thoroughly neglected.

The thought that Greek religion came from Egypt is odd on the face
of it, inasmuch as it is not immediately apparent what the common religious element is between the world of pyramids, mummification, and the
worship of animal divinities on one hand and that of Homeric heroes
and gods on the other. But there is something to be explained here, for,
odd as it is, Herodotus does stress the role of Egypt in the definition
of Greek deities. And Herodotus does so in spite of his recognition of
the status of Homer and Hesiod in the formation of Greek beliefs ("But
whence each of these gods came into existence, or whether they were
for ever, and what kind of shape they had were not known until the day
before yesterday, if I may use the expression; for I believe that Homer
and Hesiod were four hundred years before my time — and no more than
that" [2.53]). Bernal correctly notes that Herodotus' theory of the Egyptian origin of the gods' names has not been accepted by later readers;
the question is whether this is a consequence of conspiracy.[13]

There are features of Herodotus' presentation that Bernal does not
account for, beginning with the historian's opening remark in Book II

---

12. Bernal, vol. 1, 72, 379.

13. Bernal writes: "For recent detailed attempts to explain this all away, see Froide-
fond . . . [and] Lloyd . . ." (Vol. 1, 458, n 121). For his part, Lloyd attributes Herodotus'
misconception in the matter of the gods' names to a constitutional weakness in logic (Herodotus, it seems, had a failing for *post hoc ergo propter hoc. Herodotus Book II: Introduction*, 147).
Lloyd is hardly a casual reader of Herodotus, and his scholarship does not stand or fall
on this point. Bernal's conclusion remains highly implausible: all critics of Herodotus are
thought to have conspired to suppress any information that is to the credit of the Egyptians. This would represent a unique instance of critical unanimity.

that "I think that all men know equally about the gods" (2.3). And the stubborn fact is that Herodotus does not emphasize the continuity between Greek and Egyptian beliefs, but their discontinuities, and this detracts from the significance of the origin of the names. Bernal does not consider that in Herodotus' claim about the original names of the gods, the Egyptians fulfill their usual role for the Greeks: they are distinctive in being old (perhaps some people are born old? One thinks of Nestor). The Egyptians are rigid in keeping to their ways, and their ways are curious, often opposite to those of other peoples. There is in Herodotus' portrait an ironic comment about the ways Greeks view Egypt and about the self-regard of the Egyptians themselves. The Egyptians, Aristotle maintains, "are held to be the most ancient [of peoples]" (*Pol* 1329b33).

In the account of Psammetichus and his famous experiment, we confronted the irreducible differences of character that Herodotus found in his world. The Egyptians under Psammetichus conclude that they are older than anyone else except for the Phrygians (2.2); their antiquity remains decisive for them, as for Herodotus and his readers.[14] This Bernal does not acknowledge. It is the great age and abiding customs of the Egyptians that lead the Greeks to associate them with the divine; if any people approximates the unchanging and eternal, it is surely Herodotus' Egyptians. This caricature of the Egyptians is set off against that of the Scythians (who "say that their nation is the youngest of all the nations" [4.5], and whose nomadic ways constrain them to Nature); the strong suggestion is that the Greeks have discovered the desirable human mean between these extreme divine and natural models.

The same qualities in the Egyptians that cause such a strong association with the divine have a way of intersecting uncomfortably with the animal world as well. "This Apis-Epaphus is born in the form of a calf from a cow that no longer is able to conceive. The Egyptians say that a lightning bolt from heaven has struck the cow and so from it the calf-Apis is born" (3.28). The worship of animals in Egypt is in keeping with Herodotus' stress on the Egyptians' eminently settled lives. Animals associate and behave by instinct; if there are wonders in the interactions of cats (2.66), there are no changes in behavior. The Egyptians of Herodotus aspire to the same, distinguishing themselves utterly from

14. And the Phrygians? They typically vanish from memory; even Herodotus seems to disregard their claims to antiquity: "No, I believe that the Egyptians . . . have been ever since the race of man was" (2.15).

the Greeks in that way. "They follow their fathers' customs and take no others to themselves at all" (2.79).

Bernal does not see the rigidity that is implied in this portrait of the Egyptians. Thus if Herodotus assuredly does claim that the names of the gods came to Greece from Egypt, this is not the salute to Egypt that Bernal supposes. Bernal misses the implied slight to Egypt that is made every time Greek borrowing is mentioned; for example, in the previous chapter, Herodotus has commented: "Nor will I admit that the Egyptians could have taken these from the Greeks—either these or any other thing of customary usage" (2.49). Out of context, Herodotus appears to favoring the Egyptians, but readers of *The History* know that it is a positive attribute for a people to be able to assimilate the customs of others. Greeks do this, and Greeks are civilized; it is their ability to step out of their customary selves that enables them to defeat the mighty Persians. Egyptians do not accept foreign customs (2.79), and Egyptians are barbarians (2.50); in this quality, they resemble the Scythians in Book IV, surely not a mark of distinction in the eyes of Herodotus. The question of a people's openness to the customs of others is pivotal in *The History,* and if there is a hierarchy of peoples, then at the bottom are those who cannot absorb or consider the conventions of others. Donald Lateiner rightly concludes that "the historian's virtue, and surprisingly, that of Greek civilization in general according to Herodotus, is receptivity to foreign wisdom."[15]

Finally, the description that Herodotus gives of Egyptian religion is not one calculated to serve as a model for the Greeks to emulate as one might infer from Bernal; the Egyptians remain curiosities, through and through. The wit in Herodotus' presentation goes unrecognized:

> Those . . . of the Theban province, all of these sacrifice goats but hold off from sheep. For by no means all Egyptians worship the same gods alike, except for Isis and Osiris, the latter of whom they say is Dionysus. These, it is true, they all alike worship. But those who . . . are of the province of Mendes, these sacrifice sheep but will have none of goats (2.42).

We get the distinct impression that for Herodotus, some of the religious beliefs and practices of the Egyptians are unsavory [why Pan is

15. Lateiner, *Historical Method,* 151.

depicted as a goat "it is not pleasant for me to say" (2.65)]; some are
contradictory; but all are overdone: "In their reverence for the gods, they
are excessive, more than any others in the world" (2.37). When the beliefs conflict, they do so on a massive scale. On the one hand, the Egyptians are famous practitioners of mummification, and Herodotus spares
no details (2.86–88). On the other hand, the Egyptians of Herodotus
tell a story of reincarnation: "The soul of man is immortal and . . . when
the body dies, the soul creeps into some other living thing then coming
to birth. . . . The cycle for the soul is, they say, three thousand years"
(2.123). (One wonders what all the fuss was about in preserving the body,
then.) As Jasper Griffin points out, with this doctrine of reincarnation
Herodotus "ascribed to the Egyptians a set of ideas familiar in Greece
but radically un-Egyptian."[16] Herodotus is strictly in control of this depiction. Our attention ineluctably reverts back to the historian.

On the subject of Egyptian customs, our attention is again made
to shift from the content of the Egyptian customs to the methodology
of the historian. Bernal, however, does not make this move; he is impressed by the historian's candor in deriving "Greek customs from the
East in general and Egypt in particular."[17] But neither does Bernal meet
squarely the contrived character of Herodotus' description of Egyptian
customs: "Just as the climate that the Egyptians have is entirely their
own and different from anyone else's, and their river has a nature quite
different from other rivers, so, in fact, the most of what they have made
their habits and their customs are the exact opposite of other folks'"
(2.35). Sometimes these other folks seem to refer to all of humankind (in
Egypt "the women piss standing upright, but the men do it squatting");
sometimes to the Greeks ("The Greeks write and calculate moving their
hands from left to right, but the Egyptians from right to left"); but in
both cases the exact symmetry is self-consciously constructed. Bernal
ignores this literary element.

Herodotus develops a second symmetry between the Egyptians and
the Scythians; again, it serves to define the Greeks better than it does the

16. Griffin, "Who are These Coming to the Sacrifice?" 26. Elsewhere (3.29), we hear
of another conflicting belief: Apis, an immortal in the form of a calf, is killed by Cambyses. The significance of this according to Benardete is that the Egyptians fail to see any
difficulty: "They maintain both the death and the immortal life of the gods. . . . They do
not see a contradiction as a contradiction" (*Herodotean Inquiries,* 57).

17. Bernal, vol. 1, 100.

Egyptians. Egypt and Scythia are at opposite edges of the world (Greece is at the center) and Egyptian and Scythian customs are extreme and exclusionary (Greek customs are moderate and open). Herodotus neither presents the Egyptian customs in themselves, as Bernal would have it, nor does he establish the origin of Greek custom; rather, he orders his Greek world. James Redfield has explored the Egyptian-Scythian symmetry in some detail, and has found to Bernal's further discredit that the contrasts extend beyond customs to "real" historical events: "The Egyptians stay put while their power expands and contracts; at the point of their furthest advance they got as far as Scythia (2.103). The Scythians, at the furthest limit of their wandering, were induced by the Egyptian pharaoh to turn back (1.105). Each people marks the limit of the other's history." [18] Bernal does not reflect on the historian's procedure, and steadfastly refuses to acknowledge that the Egyptians of *The History* are represented from the perspective that mattered to Herodotus — the Greek.

When Bernal shuns the historiographical challenges of *The History*, he undermines his own allegedly ethical work: "I would argue that the scheme set out in *Black Athena* is better on ethical grounds, that it is more congenial to our general preferences to the general liberal preferences of academia — than that of the Aryan Model." [19] His ethical grounds do not hold up in the end because they are based on blatant distortions of Herodotus. This applies with special force to the most contentious issue of all — the blackness of Black Athena. On the basis of 2.104, where Herodotus declares that "the Colchians are clearly Egyptians," Bernal incorrectly asserts that Herodotus referred to Egyptians as black. At the same *Black Athena* conference, Frank Snowden corrects him: the word Herodotus uses is $\mu\epsilon\lambda\acute{a}\gamma\chi\rho o\epsilon\varsigma$ (2.104), which is not simply equivalent to the word "black" in contemporary usage. [20] This much Bernal was willing to admit, even adding, "I am now convinced that the title of my work should have been *African Athena*." The actual title he attributed

18. Redfield, "Tourist," 107. This does, of course, impinge on Herodotus' objectivity, but it is well to remember Momigliano's comment that Herodotus had "the open mind and the leisure of a historian who has never read a book on historical method." Momigliano, "On Causes of War in Ancient Historiography," in *Studies in Historiography*, 114.

19. Bernal, "*Black Athena* and the APA," 25.

20. Bernal, vol. 1, 242, 435; Snowden, "Bernal's 'Blacks,' Herodotus, and Other Classical Evidence," 84.

to his publisher, who argued: "Blacks no longer sell. Women no longer sell. But black women still sell!"[21] If this were not disreputable enough, Bernal has gone on to rank some forms of racism over others.[22]

Bernal's significance for our purposes is that he selects from among the encyclopedic detail of *The History* items that he chooses to declare to be factually correct. He thus claims to have achieved objectivity in assessing the material found in the most notoriously nonobjective historian, Herodotus. The driving force behind this misrepresentation of Herodotus is Bernal's political agenda: "The political purpose of *Black Athena* is . . . to lessen European cultural arrogance."[23] But *The History* does not sustain Bernal's agenda; the arrogance is elsewhere.

François Hartog: Constructing Images of the Self

In *The Mirror of Herodotus,* Hartog observes that when Herodotus investigates other peoples, he ends up always contemplating the Greeks. This approach places Hartog at the furthest possible remove from Bernal, for he assumes that the historian's interested stance affects the form of the evidence. Without exception, Hartog explains, Herodotus "classifies the reality of others according to Greek categories." Hartog proceeds to give this thesis extreme specificity by examining Herodotus' portrayal of the Scythians in Book IV. Far from accepting Herodotus' statements at face value, he presumes that the Scythians are something of a literary construct:

> [My procedure will be to] . . . treat the proper noun "Scythians" as a simple signifier and track the range of this signifier within the space of the narrative, noting all the predicates that collect around it so as eventually to construct an image of the Scythians. The sum of these predicates constitutes the Scythians of Herodotus.[24]

To his credit, Hartog does not extract selected details, but confronts the Scythians of Herodotus in their totality.

Hartog's terminology and approach suggest his connection to the

21. Bernal, "*Black Athena* and the APA," 31, 32.

22. Bernal, vol. 2, xxii.

23. Bernal, vol. 1, 73.

24. Hartog, *Mirror of Herodotus,* 10, 8. All references to Hartog pertain to this work unless specified.

New Historicist movement; his work is part of the series "The New Historicism: Studies in Cultural Poetics." *The Mirror of Herodotus* is a valuable addition, not least because it seems to validate H. Aram Veeser's claim that New Historicism has "established new ways of studying history and a new awareness of how history and culture define each other."[25] At the same time, *The Mirror of Herodotus* shows signs of the irresolute character that is to be seen in New Historicism as a whole. It seems that Hartog's affiliation with this movement inhibits him from making the bold conclusions his work would support. The problem stems from adhering to one of the "fundamental themes and concerns" of New Historicism: "the idea that autonomous self and text are mere holograms, effects that intersecting institutions produce; that selves and texts are defined by their relation to hostile others . . . and disciplinary power."[26]

To assume so at the outset, or that "no discourse . . . gives access to unchanging truths," is to limit the terms of the discourse unnecessarily.[27] In the case of Hartog, there seems to be a predetermined point beyond which he will not venture in his reading of Herodotus. And that point concerns the most interesting speculation of all: the degree to which Herodotus' narrative is historically viable. Thus the specific insights in *The Mirror of Herodotus* are pointed and irrefutable; only its conclusions are attenuated.

An example of Hartog's strong analysis which remains undeveloped in its larger import is his treatment of Darius' confrontation with the Scythians in Book IV. Hartog is impressed with Herodotus' subtlety in the account of the Scythian-Persian encounter because of the way the historian manages to reconcile the "constraints" of his own narrative with the "shared knowledge" of his audience. That is, for the sake of the narrative coherence of *The History*, the Scythian war functions as a "model for understanding," or a preview, of the Persian War. At the same time, Herodotus has to respect the shared knowledge the Greeks had of the nomadic Scythians if his account is to stand. The intriguing argument Hartog develops is that the narrative constraints and the shared knowledge (or "demands of ethnology") are tugging in precisely opposite directions.[28] Hartog shows Herodotus maneuvering a fine balance:

25. Veeser, *New Historicism*, xiii.
26. Ibid.
27. Ibid., xi.
28. Hartog, 198, 56.

the historian fashions a coherent narrative line while deftly retaining contact with the Scythians as the Greeks knew them.

Hartog outlines the original dilemma. If the Scythian-Persian encounter is to anticipate the Greek-Persian war in *The History*, it is necessary that the Scythians prevail against the imperial army of Darius. On the face of it, this necessity of the narrative is preposterous; to the Greeks, such a match would be presumed to be too uneven for a Scythian victory to be envisioned. Consequently, Herodotus adjusts his Scythian characters to make such a victory conceivable: he temporarily gives the Scythians some Athenian traits that enabled the Athenians and other Greeks to defeat the Persians at Salamis. Thus the Scythian assembly of kings before the encounter with Darius in Book IV predicts almost to the letter the course of the assembly of Greeks before Salamis in Book VIII: "the words of the Scythian delegates to the assembly of kings are close enough to those of the Athenians or the 'Greeks moved by the best of sentiments.'"[29] But, Hartog asks, how can the audience permit this transformation of Scythians into Athenians, when everyone knows that Scythian nomads are the very opposite of Athenians, the paradigmatic city-dwellers?

The solution as Hartog sees it is that Herodotus demonstrates a form of Scythian cunning which the Greeks would appreciate—and find believable. Herodotus locates this cunning in the most obvious, and ingenious, of places:

> For the Scythian nation has made the most clever discovery among all the people we know, and of the one thing that is greatest in human affairs—though for the rest I do not admire them much. This greatest thing that they have discovered is how no invader who comes against them can ever escape and how none can catch them if they do not wish to be caught (4.46).

Hartog observes that Herodotus reads into nomadism a positive value—and herein lies Herodotus' great originality—his "strategic explanation for nomadism."[30] Nomadism becomes a strategic choice rather than merely an enslavement to nature. It is an example of Scythian artifice, and it is clear evidence that the Scythians could prevail against Darius.

As Hartog explains, Herodotus both uses and transforms the Greek conception of the Scythians to reinforce his narrative. In accordance

29. Ibid.
30. Ibid., 202.

with the demands of the narrative, the Scythian battle against Darius becomes an intelligible model for the Athenian battle against Xerxes. In accordance with Greek knowledge, the Scythians are portrayed as nomads, if thoughtful ones (in a strangely familiar way). The merging of Scythian and Athenian identities that takes place is, of course, not as marked in context as out of it, and readers of *The History* are led gradually to accept these Athenian-Scythians. Thus the Herodotean narrative is based on shared knowledge while it simultaneously redefines that knowledge.

The notion of a historian strengthening the demands of the narrative line by expressing and pressing the shared knowledge of the audience is a useful way of thinking about the circumstances in which stories about the past are, or are not, transmitted. Hartog's investigation reveals that Herodotean narrative satisfies two (often competing) claims. First, it makes sense of what would otherwise be unordered past events, and does so in a compelling way; second, it makes contact with the audience's immediate experience of these events, and does so in a way that transforms, even as it recognizes, shared opinion.[31] Hartog suggests further that *The History*—an effective narrative based on shared knowledge—in turn becomes the shared knowledge for subsequent narratives. He observes that *The History* becomes the mirror through which later ages view the world, and he marks the transition "from the work as constituted (the grid used in the work) to the work as an institution (the work used as a grid)."[32]

This analysis intersects significantly with contemporary debates on the nature of historical narrative, and the question must finally surface: what is presumed to be the epistemic status of Herodotean narrative? For what purpose, one might ask, does Hartog collect the predicates that constitute the Scythians of Herodotus? Is the resulting narrative of any historical consequence? It is no small matter, as Carolyn Dewald remarks, whether Herodotus is "interested in finding out as best he can what really happened, or [is only] a gifted writer and abstract thinker with a new and difficult prose rhetoric."[33] To be sure, there are no "displays of epistemological angst" on the part of Herodotus, but when

---

31. Cook describes the criteria of ἱστορία thus: "not only, we may presume, the necessary condition that it be ascertainable as not false, but also the sufficient condition of contributing to what lurks under the story" (*Myth and Language*, 180).

32. Hartog, 356.

33. Dewald and Marincola, "Selective Introduction," 25.

Hartog himself bumps into difficult questions of historical viability, he ducks away:

> What is it in the text that creates an effect? How far-reaching is it? How does it do it? Meanwhile we avoid starting down the dangerous slope of talk of "influences," as well as of hasty "movements outside" the text. . . . It is a question that I can do little more than raise in the present work.[34]

This is insupportable, considering the serious issues Hartog has raised. It is not an innocent position to enter into debates about identity and narrative and textual influences, and then to presume not to confront questions of historical viability. Given the political and intellectual climate of today, the reader is not likely to suppose that truth-telling comes into play.

Hartog surely recognizes profundity in Herodotus, but he interprets it as yet another feature of a polished authorial stance. Another narrative, another code: "It is on the code of power that the narrative is based." And again: "The *Histories* elicit the belief that the difference between Greeks and barbarians is one of power."[35] Why this bland rendering in Hartog of what to Herodotus is an urgent concern with Greek identity, Greek greatness, Greek decline? In my view, it looks to be the company that Hartog keeps, for New Historicists likewise discount any transcendent moral force of historical narrative by casting it as part of its era's clashes of class and power. We may reminisce for the old naive Herodotus when we consider the new historicized one: "To elicit belief in the world that is recounted, inside the world in which one recounts, [Herodotus] cannot do otherwise than deploy and maneuver a whole rhetoric of otherness the figures and procedures of which, in the last analysis, depend on the polarity of two terms, 'them' and 'us,' the 'others' . . . and the 'Greeks.' "[36] By consistently disregarding the moral and epistemological claims of *The History*, Hartog strikes us as not being

---

34. Hartog, 360. The expression in quotations is from Haskell, "Objectivity is Not Neutrality," 153.

35. Hartog, 340.

36. Ibid., 366. Any text is undeniably the product of a particular historic situation. New Criticism of the mid-century without question went too far in disembodying a literary work from its social context. New Historicism may swing the pendulum too far in the other direction if it is employed to discredit the lasting value of any given work. See Bergonzi, *Exploding English*, 174–177.

wrong about Herodotus, but not being true to him, either. His Herodotus is uncommonly abstract and uncommonly odd.

It is not surprising that when Hartog comes to his final assessment of Herodotean historiography, he finds it unfinished: "In the last analysis, [Herodotus'] position may be summed up in the following paradox: even though he is the father of history, he is not really a historian."[37] I submit that, on the contrary, Herodotus is a real historian who does not share our penchant for opposing literary concerns to epistemological ones. In Herodotus truth is, as Oswyn Murray writes, "a question of aesthetics and morality, as much as of fact."[38] This argument can be elaborated by reviewing parallel episodes in Book IV and Book VIII of *The History*. One of these episodes concerns the events of Darius' attack on the Scythians, and so it is outside of historical memory. The second concerns Xerxes' attack on the Greeks, and so it is within historical memory of Herodotus' contemporaries. In Hartog's terms, the degree of shared knowledge varies markedly. At the same time, it is evident that what Hartog calls narrative constraint makes the two episodes decidedly alike in form and content; the one prefigures the other. Now, as Hartog leaves us pondering the imaginary Scythians without providing any follow-up in historiographical terms, he leads us to conclude that the first episode is historically dubious. If the first story is constrained to predict the second, it must be epistemologically or historically unsound. This is the unspoken assumption in *The Mirror of Herodotus* that may be called into question.

The History supports the argument that the epistemological force of the two episodes need not be sacrificed solely because they have comparable aesthetic or literary qualities and the same moral import. In fact, the converse seems to be true: that link establishes the historical credibility. For Herodotus the fundamental point appears to be not how much shared knowledge there is, for shared knowledge always comes down to what is thought to have happened, whether it concerns the mythical Man-Eaters in faraway Scythia of long ago, or the flesh-and-blood Athenians of his own time. As a historian, Herodotus always has more or less shared knowledge available to him, of more or less credibility; he still has to subject it to scrutiny, synthesize it, and translate it for his audience. In Hartog's terms, the truly critical issue for Herodotus is how to achieve the proper balance between shared knowledge (what is thought

37. Ibid., 379.
38. Murray, "Herodotus and Oral History," 107.

to have happened) and narrative constraint (what must have happened). As imprecise as this formulation necessarily is, it points the way to innovative thought on the subject of historical narrative.

Toward this end, we consider first the Herodotean episode which is based on a minimum of shared knowledge. The pivotal moment in the Scythian-Persian encounter in Book IV occurs when the Scythian kings realize that Darius and his men are in cruel circumstances and so send a herald with gifts: "a bird and a mouse and a frog and five arrows" (4.131). Darius does not understand the message, and the messenger does not explain it. Darius therefore strains to construe the message as a sign of surrender to himself ("the mouse is a creature of the earth and eats the same fruit of the earth as man . . . the frog lives in water . . . the bird is likest to a horse; and . . . the surrender of the arrows was a surrender of the people's own valor"). But Gobryas provides a more convincing interpretation: "If you do not become birds and fly away into the sky or become mice and burrow into the lakes, there will be no homecoming for you, for we will shoot you down with our arrows" (4.132). Darius is led to accept this reading only after witnessing the Scythians break ranks to chase a hare: "These people despise us utterly," he reflects, "We will need a very good plan to get safely back home out of this place" (4.134).

The details of this description are unquestionably supplied by Herodotus. Nobody has any specifics about Darius' excursions into Scythia, much less about remnants of the message of frogs and birds. Yet on closer inspection it becomes evident that this account is anchored in what the Greeks did know. Indeed, the shared knowledge and the demands of the narrative are so perfectly integrated as to defy our attempts to break them down. The Greeks know that the Persian Great King has an insatiable drive to conquer, quite apart from the nature of the subjects in question. It would be just like Darius to pursue a people who "has no cities or settled forts . . . [who] carry their houses with them and shoot with bows from horseback" (4.46). The Greeks know that the Great King cannot put himself in the minds of his enemies. It would be just like Darius to convince himself that the Scythians had suddenly decided to surrender. The Greeks know that the Great King will listen to good advice only in dire straits. It would be a hare that was the deciding factor. And so on. This is a marvel of a narrative, because the truth it ascribes comes across with both imagination and power.

Finally, the moral thrust of this narrative is of central importance. Here as elsewhere, *The History* teaches anyone who will learn (including

Persians) how not to be Persian. This is a portrait of a doomed Great
King, whose hubris will prove overwhelming. The political lesson is
transparent. In Herodotus' rendition, it is clear that Darius' escape from
the Scythians is only a temporary reprieve; his fate, like that of all Great
Kings, is settled. Is this, then, a mere self-serving view, fashioned for the
enhancement and glorification of the Greeks? Certainly it is self-serving,
but perhaps not merely so; in the words of George Herbert Mead, "We
always present ourselves to ourselves in the most favorable light possible; but . . . it is quite necessary that if we are to keep ourselves going
we should thus present ourselves to ourselves."[39] What raises Herodotus' account above propaganda is its striving for universal application
of its moral. Power corrupts beyond the borders of Persia, after all, and
there is nothing to prevent the Greeks from taking the Persian lesson to
heart, from seeing themselves as having assumed the Persian role for a
new generation. Such is the consistent message to be gleaned from *The
History*—and an element of its claim to truth.

Rooting himself in the thought of his time, Herodotus thus attempts
to give it more than particular import. This procedure is manifest in
Book VIII as well, when Xerxes encounters the Greeks at Salamis. In
episodes such as this where there is considerably more shared knowledge
for Herodotus to accommodate, his fundamental historiographical procedure remains the same: he incorporates shared knowledge in his narrative, even while pointing beyond its partial circumstances by placing
it within an unmistakably moral schema. Again, the lesson Herodotus
brings home is unambiguous. A human community that perpetuates the
ideas that its members are equal in dignity and liberty will have more resources upon which to draw in times of crisis than a community united
by force alone.

The pivotal moment at Salamis occurs when Themistocles realizes
that Greeks from the Peloponnese intend to retreat to the Isthmus wall:

> There was a meeting . . . some saying that they ought to sail
> off to the Peloponnese and run the danger for that country rather
> than stay and fight for a land that was already a prisoner-of-war
> of the enemy. . . . Themistocles, since he was losing out in the de-
> bates with the Peloponnesians, secretly left the council (8.74–75).

Themistocles thereupon dispatches a messenger to the Persian camp.
In this message, Themistocles informs the Persians that the Greeks are

39. Mead, *Mind, Self, and Society*, 307.

divided and are planning to scatter; the Persian moment to strike pur-
portedly has arrived. So declares the general of the Greeks, who "is indeed an adherent of the King and wants his side to win rather than the
Greeks" (8.75). This note has the intended consequence of drawing the
Persian attack in a confined body of water. When this incident is placed
next to the comparable episode in Book IV, it is evident that despite the
distance between the two episodes in historical memory, they are alike
in historiographical conception.

What knowledge sustains this narrative, and what moral elevates it?
The Greeks know about their adroit leaders, who communicate in complex and sometimes devious ways. It would be just like Themistocles to
come up with this ploy of feigning treason; later on, of course, he was to
drop the feint. The Greeks know that Greeks can get into the minds of
their adversaries. It would be just like Themistocles to predict Xerxes'
swift reaction. The Greeks know that Greeks are contentious and selfish
and short-sighted, and, on occasion, high-minded. It would be just like
the Athenians to have to compel their allies to fight for Greece. None
of this contradicts the Greek experience. More important, all this supports Herodotus' reading of the formation of human communities and
the prospering of communities which value equality and free speech.
Herodotus well understands the art of presenting ourselves to ourselves:
"when held in subjection [the Athenians] would not do their best, for
they were working for a taskmaster, but, when free, they sought to win,
because each was trying to achieve for his very self" (5.78). Greek self-
knowledge leads directly to the universal moral: private interests come
together in common enterprises with most effect and even with unfore-
seeable greatness when they are free and not forced to do so.

This conclusion looks suspiciously like an unchanging truth. And, to
New Historicists, "no discourse . . . gives access to unchanging truths."
It is as if the words of Herodotus or his rhetoric of otherness were interesting only conceptually, for literary rather than truth-telling qualities.
But in Herodotus' own day, Athens had begun to transform herself into
something dangerously Persian. At last glimpse, her leaders are falling
into the κόρος–ΰβρις–ἄτη cycle of the tragic heroes.[40] Herodotus' history
had an immediate and compelling relevance to his contemporary scene,
as Charles Fornara has explored at some length: "Irony, pathos, para-

40. Redfield, "Tourist," 113. "κόρος is the appetite which gains increase by what it
feeds on. . . . κόρος is linked with ΰβρις, violence which overrides proper limits, and also
with ἄτη, a confusion of the mind evidenced by moral and practical error" (Ibid., 112).

dox, and tragedy develop from his tacit dialogue with his audience. . . .
It is a contemporary audience, whose expectations he could predict."[41]

In the last analysis, Hartog pays insufficient attention to the fact that
behind "the polarity of two terms, 'them' and 'us' " there are real people.
How these people appear in the pages of *The History* is a fascinating
study, but not to the exclusion of the status of the truth being told. Wher-
ever that issue of truth leads us, we must start with the actuality that
neither the Greeks, nor the Persians, nor the Egyptians—not even the
long-lived Ethiopians—are mere figments of Herodotus' imagination.

Edward Said, Orientalists, and the Other

The question of where certain images of people come from and how
they become entrenched is precisely the one that Edward Said raises in
Orientalism. In his work, Said examines instances of how Westerners look
at the East; throughout, he denounces the consistently pejorative images
that Western scholars, travelers, and officials have imposed on their
Eastern Other. Said does not focus extensively on Herodotus, though
he might have without affecting the force of his argument. He claims
that Orientalism was "ultimately a political vision of reality whose structure promoted the difference between the familiar (Europe, the West,
"us") and the strange (the Orient, the East, "them")."[42] And Herodotus clearly offers a political vision, dividing the world between Greeks
and barbarians as he announces his intention to preserve memory of the
"great and wonderful deeds" (1.1) of both. Indeed, were one to replace
"reading public" with "listening public" in the following remark by Said,

41. Fornara, *Interpretive Essay*, 62. When Herodotus' audiences (or later, readers) are
mentioned, it is necessary to note that with the rise of postmodernism the balance of power
between author and reader has shifted dramatically, with the reader now empowered to
take over the interpretation of a text from the author regardless of the author's intention.
It should be obvious by this point that this essay is neither an attempt to deconstruct Herodotus or to grow him a pre-postmodern scepter of authorial authority; it is an effort to
draw from the *History* an insight into what is involved when, as Emerson says, "Time dissi-
pates to shining ether the solid angularity of facts" and what that process means politically,
in Herodotus' time and ours.

42. Said, *Orientalism*, 43. (All references to Said in this section will pertain to this
work unless otherwise noted.) Said explains that he is not using the term "Orient" in the
way familiar to most Americans (pertaining to the Far East), but rather as it occurs in the
European Western tradition, particularly among the French and British: "The Orient is
not only adjacent to Europe; it is also the place of Europe's greatest and richest and oldest
colonies, the source of its civilizations and languages, its cultural contestant, and one of its
deepest and most recurring images of the Other" (1).

it might have been attributed to Herodotus and *The History:* the "subject is not so much the East itself as the East made known, and therefore less fearsome, to the Western reading public."[43] There is Orientalism in *The History,* then, which calls forth our response to Said's prominent work.

Said shares important points of contact with Bernal and Hartog as well, even as he sets out a distinctive challenge to Herodotean historiography. His specific readings of the distortions of the Orient as well as his assessments of the historical transmission of these distortions raise fundamental questions about whether knowledge of the Other is possible at all. I have already criticized Hartog for failing to confront this issue; after taking us through an exhaustive account of Herodotus' rhetoric of otherness, he did not proceed to draw conclusions about the justification of this rhetoric. In the end, his claim that Herodotus could not have done otherwise than employ this rhetoric strikes us as a feeble historicist response, and one not in keeping with Hartog's otherwise significant contributions to Herodotean scholarship. Said offers an instructive contrast here, for he is eager to draw conclusions — specifically, principled conclusions — from his survey of Orientalist writings.

Said's affinity is with Bernal in regard to these principled conclusions. As we have seen, Bernal claims an ethical superiority for his *Black Athena* over the Aryan Model histories he investigates ("[my scheme] is better on ethical grounds. . . . It is more congenial to . . . the general liberal preferences of academia"). Both Bernal and Said seem to represent variations of what Turner has termed "Radical Whigs": just as the old Whig historian "knows where history will turn out," so the Radical Whig "thoroughly disapproves of the outcome." Turner continues: the assumptions common to traditional and Radical Whigs are that "moral judgment is part of the task of the historian," and that "judgments about the past relate in one way or another to judgments about the worthiness or unworthiness of the present."[44] In *Black Athena,* Bernal presumes to have righted a past wrong of historical scholarship as a result of his close attention to what ancient writers and Herodotus in particular took to be the objective truth of the past. This has been shown to require a literal and false rendering of Herodotus; accordingly, we have demonstrated that Bernal's high ethical standing is illusory. This conclusion has the merit of being consistent with the influences that *Black Athena* actually

43. Ibid., 60.
44. Turner, "A Dissent," 102.

exerts today, that is, in underscoring "difference rather than similarity, [in furthering] separation rather than mingling, [in proposing] otherness rather than sameness."[45]

Said, though, presents a slightly different form of Radical Whiggism than Bernal, one that requires a broader response. As thoroughly as Said researches and castigates Orientalism in its many manifestations, he nevertheless displays more guarded expectations than Bernal in his ability to correct or even affect the intellectual situation he decries. Said's challenge reaches to the very knowability of the Other. He envisions his book as confronting Orientalism and all it stands for, but more pointedly, he sees his work as a warning

> that systems of thought like Orientalism, discourses of power, ideological fictions—mind-forg'd manacles—are all too easily made, applied, and guarded. . . . If the knowledge of Orientalism has any meaning, it is in being a reminder of the seductive degradation of knowledge, of any knowledge, anywhere, at any time. Now perhaps more than before.[46]

The challenge that Said issues to Herodotus is just this, then: that its systems of thought, its characterizations of non-Greeks, "are all too easily made, applied, and guarded." No doubt he has in mind the kind of ideological fictions that can be culled from *The History* that make it possible, for example, for one of Herodotus' translators to classify the ancient Persians as "clearly marked out from other barbarous races by a lightness and sprightliness of character," who were yet not assimilable to the Greek race, because of "their passionate abandon and slavish submission to the caprices of despotic power."[47] Said would denounce such caricatures as made by those in power, applied canonically, and guarded by those with a stake in the prerogatives of the day.

The relation between knowledge and power is of course notoriously difficult to sort out, and Said recognizes the need for more profound deliberation on this subject. Without entering further into these deliberations, however, he proceeds to attribute the various forms of Orientalism almost exclusively to the relations of power between East and West. The idea is familiar enough in contemporary academic discourse: what typi-

---

45. Levine, review of *Black Athena*, 457.

46. Said, 328.

47. Rawlinson, *History of Herodotus*, cited by Konstan, "Persians, Greeks and Empire," 59.

cally underlies supposedly disinterested Western accounts of the Other is authority and power. "The relationship between Occident and Orient is a relationship of power, of domination, of varying degrees of a complex hegemony, and is quite accurately indicated in the title of K. M. Panik-kar's classic *Asia and Western Dominance*."[48] And, Said notes, the scientific mentality of the West only exacerbates the power imbalance by the insertion of the sense of irrefutable truths: "the sense of Western power over the Orient is taken for granted as having the status of scientific truth."[49]

Said is not mistaken in associating instances of "objective" Western knowledge with a kind of inhumanity, and he is able to marshal countless examples of crude stereotypes that fall under this category: "The European is a close reasoner; his statements of fact are devoid of any ambiguity; he is a natural logician. . . . His trained intelligence works like a piece of mechanism. The mind of the Oriental, on the other hand, like his picturesque streets, is eminently wanting in symmetry. His reasoning is of the most slipshod description."[50] Such deplorable characterizations are, as Said claims, all too widespread and persistent in Oriental studies. Still, there is room to question his assessment of the power and knowledge interplay even if we concur in his readings of single instances. Said himself occasionally complicates his equation ("I do believe in the determining imprint of individual writers upon the otherwise anonymous collective body of texts constituting a discursive formation like Orientalism"), but his overarching principle remains: it is the "pattern of relative strength" between East and West that "enables" this discursive formation.[51]

What remains unsatisfactory in Said's presentation is his explanation of how this discursive formation is perpetuated. The pattern of relative strength between East and West both explains too much and too little, with likeness to many of Foucault's pronouncements ("It is not possible for power to be exercised without knowledge, [and] it is impossible for knowledge not to engender power"[52]). It explains too much because it leaves him no room to account sufficiently for his own transcendence of an entrenched system of thought like Orientalism ("both learned and imaginative writing are never free, but are limited in their imagery, as-

48. Said, 5, 24.
49. Ibid., 46.
50. Ibid., 38.
51. Ibid., 23, 60.
52. Foucault, "Prison Talk," in *Power/Knowledge*, 52.

sumptions, and intentions"[53]). It explains too little because it disregards the realm where imperialism and Orientalism are not coterminous. Indeed, it is clear that Orientalism and Western imperialism did not have the precise overlap that Said suggests; he has made the association of knowledge and power too neat. As Lewis has observed, "The first chair of Arabic in France was founded in the College de France by King Francis I in 1538. The first French incursion into an Arab country was in 1798. One must say that either the French Orientalists were extraordinarily prescient, or the French imperialists were extraordinarily dilatory."[54]

The question must be asked of Said: When two civilizations of roughly equal power interact, are the renderings of the Other then necessarily more accurate, less deleterious? (Does perfectly equal power mean perfect knowledge?) In his conclusion, Said claims to have raised this sort of question ("Is the notion of a distinct culture [or race, or religion, or civilization] a useful one, or does it always get involved either in self-congratulation [when one discusses one's own] or hostility and aggression [when one discusses the 'other']?"[55]). But to ask if such notions are useful is to make no headway on the issue, since in any case we are confronted with different cultures, races, religions, and civilizations. Said's work, like Hartog's, is unfinished.

Said has noted that deconstructionists who should be expert at revealing the interplay between knowledge and power have in practice been ineffective or even complicitous in dealing with the contemporary power structure in which they find themselves. Said, it would seem, sees his scholarship primarily in terms of a present political act.[56] Of course power relations do have a determining role in all our lives. When Richard Bernstein evaluates the positive contribution of deconstruction, he refers approvingly to Derrida's insight that "even the gesture of 'authentic dialogue' can be complicit with an act of violence—where there is a subtle demand that the Other speak in our language and accept our categories and genres."[57] This is a point that demands serious reflection: we distort the Other even in our best faith attempts to understand; we cannot help but impose inappropriate categories of thought. And this

53. Said, 202.
54. Lewis, "Other People's History," 402.
55. Said, 325.
56. See Said, "Opponents, Audiences, Constituencies, and Community."
57. Bernstein, "Reconciliation and Rupture," 306.

insight has come to us from philosophers, anthropologists, feminists, and historians alike. But it does not come to us in equally constructive formats. At best, we can look for it to direct our inquiries, rather than debilitate them.

For Said, "the circumstances making Orientalism a continuingly persuasive type of thought will persist," a prospect he considers "a rather depressing matter on the whole."[58] But we need not share Said's despair about the ways in which human beings misconstrue one another, nor must we assume an infinite staying power in these misreadings. The most that Said hopes for is that there will be others like himself who somehow can resist the "rituals, preconceptions, and doctrines of Orientalism"; he finds such a person in Geertz.[59] Geertz, he thinks, demonstrates an interest in Islam which is "discrete and concrete enough to be animated by the specific societies and problems he studies."[60] I would argue that Geertz is intriguing not because of his discrete and concrete interest in Islam, but because, knowing what Said knows about our unbreachable differences with the Other, and knowing what Said knows about our inveterate wills to power, Geertz nevertheless finds some kind of effort to understand the Other worth making: "The trick is not to achieve some inner correspondence of spirit with your informants; preferring, like the rest of us, to call their souls their own, they are not going to be altogether keen about such an effort anyhow. The trick is to figure out what the devil they think they are up to."[61]

What the devil the natives think they are up to is something Herodotus concerned himself with long before Geertz produced his reflections. With that in mind, we return to Herodotus to consider a compelling alternative to Said's understanding of Orientalism as a system of thought and its transmission from one age to the next.

In order to develop this alternative, I turn to what is surely the most famous vignette of Herodotus' history: the custom-is-king passage. This

58. Said, 326.

59. Or, rather, he once did. In "Orientalism Reconsidered," Geertz is said by Said to offer "standard disciplinary rationalizations and self-congratulatory clichés about hermeneutic circles" (216). We will not presume to keep abreast of who is in and who is out in Said's world, though it seems safe to predict that Bernard Lewis is securely "out." The later Geertz is in good company.

Though Said invariably writes in polemical terms, this is not a reason to ignore his challenges. See note 5 of this chapter on Bernal.

60. Said, 326.

61. Geertz, "From the Native Point of View," 227–228.

brief scene with its accompanying lesson permits us to inspect the Orientalism of Herodotus, and to counter in detail Said's declaration that in Orientalism is a system of thought easily made, applied, and guarded. Although it would be a simple matter to dismiss this passage as an early instance of a Western distortion of the Eastern Other (complete with its successful transmission through the ages), to do so is to sacrifice its enduring intellectual interest.

The passage begins with Herodotus musing on the stances of peoples toward their customs in relation to the customs of others. He claims that the Persian king Cambyses demonstrated his insanity by mocking the customs of other people: "For if there were a proposition put before mankind, according to which each should, after examination, choose the best customs in the world, each nation would certainly think its own customs the best. Indeed, it is natural for no one but a madman to make a mockery of such things" (3.38).

Herodotus proceeds to relate one of many pieces of evidence for this proposition, the particular case of an experiment that King Darius carried out during his rule. Darius assembled a number of Greeks and asked how much money it would take for them to eat their dead fathers. The response was that they would not do so under any condition. Darius then brought in some Indians, whose custom it was to eat their dead fathers. With the Greeks present, he asked how much money it would take for them to burn their dead fathers, to which they "shouted aloud, 'Don't mention such horrors!'" Herodotus interjects, "These are matters of settled custom, and I think Pindar is right when he says, 'Custom is king of all'" (3.38).

The placement of characters by Herodotus seems quite deliberate, as he has differentiated the characters with just a few strokes. The Indians shout out at the mere mention of the Greek custom; the Greeks, on the other hand, may not be prepared to adopt the Indian custom as their own, but they can listen to it with equanimity.[62] This seems to indicate their disposition to evaluate rather than merely inherit their *nomoi*. And while the Persian Darius may be considered open-minded for orchestrating this experiment, it is noteworthy that he is calling into question not his own customs, but those of others. Moreover, it seems significant that he seeks to find the monetary value of these customs; the Shopkeeper is fond of quantifying military strength and valor, not to mention

62. See Benardete, *Herodotean Inquiries*, 81.

his own wealth: "he kept petty accounts for everything" (3.89). The sum total of these impressions might lead one to be suspicious of this lineup: the Greeks are intellectual, the Indians traditional, the Persians cynical. Such an interpretation would seem to vindicate Said's assertion about Orientalism.

Nevertheless, it is evident that these caricatures are not "easily made" at all, if that signifies out of nothing. These depictions are firmly linked to those that stand elsewhere in *The History;* as such, they share the solidity of the portraits as a whole. Herodotus' point of departure is worth highlighting for its own Greek underwriting: he imagines a proposition put before all mankind, a proposition that would be responded to similarly by all (sane) people.[63] He conceives of the human relation to custom impartially. This is not to say he conceives it in a normal or necessarily desirable way; in articulating this scenario, Herodotus is marking himself as a Greek, both in self-image and in the eyes of others. Outside of the Greek tradition, the principle of "strict closure" was the rule for societies, as Castoriadis emphasizes. This principle holds that "our view of the world is the only meaningful one, the 'others' are bizarre, inferior, perverse, evil, or unfaithful."[64]

It is interesting for us today to speculate about how any one society comes to break the closure and comes to care about getting right the representations of others; it was interesting for Herodotus as well. But it is not a characteristic that Herodotus could have opted to remove from his Greeks, or to posit of his barbarians. His enterprise as the first historian reveals him thinking like a Greek, in impartial terms, and doing so with genuine efforts at understanding others. "Greeks learned to *understand,*" writes Hannah Arendt, "not to understand one another as individual persons, but to look upon the same world from one another's standpoint."[65] This is not to deny for a moment that for the Greeks to take on this role of impartial observers serves to present them in the most favorable light possible to themselves. But, as Mead reminds us, this end is settled for any people ("if we are to keep ourselves going"), while the means to this end are not.

63. Herodotus, Greek-like, is attracted to these universal propositions: "But if the constitution of the seasons were changed, and where now stand the winter and the north wind there should stand the summer and the south wind. . . . I say, if these things were to be so" (2.26); see also 2.14 and 7.152.
64. Castoriadis, "Greek Polis," 80.
65. Arendt, "Concept of History," 51.

It is appropriate here to affirm that these Greek, Indian, and Persian approaches to the world as depicted by Herodotus have both positive and negative consequences for their practitioners. Custom is king in three very different ways. It is king most inflexibly for the Callatian Indians, who are so bound to their inherited traditions that they do not easily abide the mere voicing of alternative *nomoi*. In other words, the Callatians are true to their beliefs, and genuine and active exemplars of their culture.[66] For the Persians, custom is literally the king; as Herodotus memorably formulates the Persian "law" elsewhere: he "who was king of Persia could do anything he wished," and this included transgressing previous custom (3.31). We might add that his subjects could do anything the King wished, too. This makes the Persians slavish from one point of view, capable of great works and deeds from another. Custom is king for the Greeks as well, but in their case, custom is neither to be located strictly in their tradition, nor does it evolve in step with their regime. It is to be discerned in general rules, in Redfield's apt formulation: "a person gives particular commands but a *nomos* states only general rules which must be evaluated in the application. Greek custom therefore implies that the Greeks not only have their *nomoi* but think about them, and as they think about them they also talk about them."[67] The talking about *nomoi* is for better or for worse; for better, when a good leader inspires the people to rise above themselves (Themistocles at Salamis), for worse, when the leader himself seeks his own self-interest first (Themistocles subsequently).

The characters as depicted in the custom-is-king passage are neither accidental, nor interchangeable, nor, I would say, particularly distortive. These are not the fictitious ("easily made") characters of Said's Orientalism; they are players in an identifiable mystery Herodotus seeks to unravel: cultures in contact. And each of the characters is to an important degree fixed in role. Persuasion joins Necessity as one of the great Athenian gods. The Greeks are the people who hear with interest the descriptions of customs of other people, and wonder what this differ-

66. Nietzsche has given us a useful contrast to the binding, live culture of the Callatians—the Greco-Western tradition played out after two millennia. Modern culture, Nietzsche claims, is "not a living thing . . . not a real culture at all but only a kind of knowledge about culture. . . . Cultural sensibility then lies quietly within, like a snake that has swallowed rabbits whole and now lies in the sun and avoids all unnecessary movement." Nietzsche, "Uses and Disadvantages of History", 78.

67. Redfield, "Commentary," 252.

ence means. The Greek poet Pindar suggests one meaning, Herodotus another.[68] It is a recognizably Greek conversation. At the opposite extreme are peoples like the Indians, who guard the sanctity of their customs; no conversation is called for. Finally, the Persian role in this shows us a recognizable portrait of the hubris of an all-powerful ruler. Darius does not distinguish between the Greek and Indian reaction; he does not wonder what his experiment means, but orchestrates it to demonstrate what he already knows.

Said's further criticism is about the transmission of distorted views of the Orient; once made, he avows, such stories are applied and guarded all too easily. He speaks of "the management of knowledge by society," the fact that "knowledge—no matter how special—is regulated first by the local concerns of a specialist, later by the general concerns of a social system of authority."[69] Here again, I am impressed by precisely the reverse phenomenon, that is, by the inability of either the specialist or the social system of authority to regulate this knowledge over time. More typically, a story will survive the continued onslaughts of time only when the claims it makes are serious ones to readers who may be unaffected by the power relationship between subject and historian. It is worth recalling that Herodotus seeks to understand his world as a result of an Eastern power attacking the weaker West. It is hard to read Herodotus' view of the East as "a sign of imperial power over recalcitrant phenomena, as well as a confirmation of the dominating culture and its 'naturalization.'"[70] Power relations between East and West have shifted more than once, but Western interest in the Eastern Other has been far more demonstrable than the reverse.[71]

In cases where Said is on firm ground in exposing the powerful West's misrepresentations of the East, he has not succeeded in demonstrating the easy application of these misrepresentations over time. His references to Sacy, whose work "canonizes the Orient," are to the point.

68. See Grene, *History,* 228, on how Herodotus changes the meaning of Pindar's original story. Just as Herodotus corrects Homer's version of the Trojan War (2.116), so in this instance he grounds Pindar's story by filling in real historical characters, thereby adjusting the original moral of the story.

69. Said, 44–45.

70. Ibid., 145.

71. See Lach, *Asia in the Making of Europe,* and Chaudhuri, "The Problematic of 'Polyphonic' History," 24–43. On the shifting of power, see Parkinson, *East and West.* Herodotus' telling of the story of Darius, the Greeks, and the Callatians is a way of pointing out the greater intellectual openness of the West.

Said both attributes an enormous influence to Sacy as inaugurator of Orientalism ("Every major Arabist in Europe during the nineteenth century traced his intellectual authority back to him") and admits that "subsequent Orientalists entirely displaced Sacy's work by supplying their own restored Orient."[72] In this way, Said succeeds in demonstrating that there have occurred numberless facile, offensive characterizations of Orientals by Orientalists in recent centuries, but he has not convinced anyone that those characterizations cannot be amended in time—because of their facile, offensive nature. And although it is no doubt little consolation for victims of racist or ethnic or gender stereotypes to be told that their injustices might be recognized by a future age, it is quite different from saying that they will not.

A story like Herodotus' "custom is king" does not endure because it makes Westerners feel good about themselves at the expense of non-Westerners; its effect is much more enigmatic. As with the Croesus-Solon story, so here the reader must engage with the story to draw what seem to be appropriate conclusions, for the moral that is given resolves almost nothing. (This is Aristotle's complaint.) I have offered a reading of certain plausibility with the understanding that Herodotean readers of a prior century or a century hence or especially of today would find my reading inadequate in some respect or another. Great stories always are read inadequately; they will not stay in place, they will not be determined for all time. If this were not the case, if its meaning were perfectly straightforward, then it would not be addressed meaningfully to the question of understanding the Other.[73]

Said criticizes Orientalists for supposing themselves to be objective when they were not. This is accurate as far as it goes, but it hardly implies the motive Said seems to suspect—in Lewis's terms, a "predatory" or "larcenous" interest in "other people's cultural possessions."[74] Other people's cultural possessions are going to remain resistant to anyone's objective grasp, which is why they are interesting in the first place. Thus, although we have the duty to correct lies and misrepresentations in our dealings with the Other, getting the facts straight is not going to resolve our differences or eliminate our disorientation.

72. Said, 129, 130.

73. This does not mean that any interpretation will do. As Hartog demonstrates, neither the demands of the narrative nor the demands of our shared knowledge may be sacrificed if the story is to endure.

74. Lewis, "Other People's History," 399.

In the end, it is the question of objectivity that needs to be sorted out for Bernal, Hartog, and Said. Bernal assumes that Herodotus is objective, at least selectively; from there, Bernal is led to any number of equally unsubstantiated assertions. Hartog assumes that Herodotus is not objective, but he does not go on to speculate on what claim to truth *The History* might have, leaving his readers mystified about the impulse behind his detailed reading. Finally, Said is cognizant of the false claims of Orientalists to objectivity, but he sees this as an Orientalist failing, rather than an intellectual limitation within which human beings must work. None of these thinkers has done justice to the historiographical teaching in *The History*. Herodotus could be better used.

CHAPTER 6

Before Objectivity, and After

Inclusivity and Attached Meaning

The Herodotean first principle of evidence—inclusivity—derives from Herodotus' absorption in cultures and in cultural self-descriptions. Most conspicuously, he seems to delight as much in evidence "tainted" by human influence as he does in verifiable information. In David Grene's phrase, there is no bump in the narrative as Herodotus moves from what seem to be radically different types of evidence. Describing how Croesus was besieged by Cyrus, Herodotus remarks casually that "this was the only place [in the citadel] where the former king of Sardis, Meles, had not carried round the lion cub that his concubine had borne him" (1.84). Elsewhere the historian includes the most precise information about Croesus' dedications to Delphi: "When the sacrifice was over, he melted down a vast deal of gold and made out of it ingots, on the long side six palms' length, on the short side three, and in height one palm" (1.50). For Herodotus the two types of evidence are not radically different; fact and fiction are presumed to coexist in human remembrances.

Facts for Herodotus are not regarded as some enduring component of the original moment, but rather as always a form of remembrance in their own right. That is, facts provide a framework of factors, such as the ethnic makeup of an army or the exact location of a battle, on which the truly important story can be elaborated. But the historical moment itself is not assumed to be retrieved, as if the historian with the facts at his disposal had somehow gotten hold of transcendent entities. Herodotus recognizes the compelling quality of factual material without granting it primacy; he is not inclined to enumerate each piece of verifiable information he happens on. In his rendering of the continuity between past and future, facts play only supporting roles. Emerson expressed this best possible relation: "The facts fall aptly and supple into their places; they know their master, and the meanest of them glorifies him."[1]

Every factual note about a people in *The History* contributes in some way to their assigned place; this holds true for the shortest note about the

---

1. Emerson, "History," in *Essays*, 24.

Scythians to the most protracted listings of the Persian satrapies (3.89–97). In this way, when Herodotus discusses the Scythian invasion during the reign of Cyaxares, the facts are assimilated in his narrative description of the Scythians as a fiercely independent, roving, uncivilized, and uncivilizable people: "For twenty-eight years, then, the Scythians were masters of Asia, and all was wasted by their violence and pride; for apart from their exacting of tribute, which they laid upon each man, apart from the tribute they rode around and plundered whatsoever it was that anyone possessed" (1.106). This is the sum total of information with which we are provided on the Scythian hegemony, and it is predictable information: they rode around and plundered. Those twenty-eight years have no other meaning, and we are in need of no further elaboration. Extraneous factual material, whatever does not further the historian's portrait of a people, is allowed to fade away.

This managing of facts is evident, too, in regard to the Herodotean theme of the archetypal clash of civilized and barbaric nations. From his original account of the Median-Persian skirmish to his ominous hints about the impending Athenian-Spartan encounter, Herodotus repeatedly dramatizes the transformations that occur when the two extremes of human life come into contact. This pattern is an effective guidepost to the world of the Persian War, and it is brought to bear on confrontations throughout *The History*. It follows that Herodotus requires facts that will confirm this pattern. Consequently, when he recounts a battle he calls the most severe ever fought among the barbarians, that between the Persians and the Massagetae (1.214), Herodotus furnishes factual information that still corroborates his pattern of barbaric and civilized nations in conflict. The relevant information about the Massagetae turns out to distinguish their level of barbarity from that of the Persians, so that it is not simply two barbarian peoples at war after all, but a version of the conflict between barbarism and civilization. As François Hartog has noted, the narrative of Herodotus will accommodate two, and not three, terms.[2] So the historian calls on evidence that will demonstrate where the real barbarism takes place:

> When a man of the Massagetae desires a woman, he hangs his quiver on the front of her wagon and lies with her, fearlessly. There is no definite limit to life other than this: when a man grows very old, all his relatives come together and kill him, and

2. Hartog, *Mirror of Herodotus*, 49.

sheep and goats along with him, and stew all the meat together and have a banquet of it. That is regarded as the happiest lot (1.216).

Next to this portrait, the Persians are the picture of urbanity. Thus does Herodotus bridge factual evidence (the battle between the Persians and the Massagetae) and meaning (the softening effects of empire on warriors).

The corollary of Herodotus' measured use of factual material is his uncommon handling of stories and myths.[3] Far from being exclusively concerned with facts, he is inclusively concerned with the immeasurable remembrances of the past that grow up around a historical moment. The stories and myths that Herodotus relates generate meaning that is even more difficult to appraise than the factual information he includes. He typically accentuates this effect by offering no explanation for their uncertain sense. In reading Herodotus it often seems that the facts or best-available information he includes are less illuminating of the past than these sometimes dubious stories that his characters, or he himself, recounts.[4]

3. It is important to keep in mind the distinction between the highly complicated issues surrounding *myth* and the Herodotean *stories* as sources of political community that we here are examining. The distinction might be illustrated by a look at Gates's writing on the Yoruba, which, he makes clear, does not deal with the historical story of the Yoruba diaspora beyond Africa, but with a myth of origins that outlines principles of black signification. In contrast is the story of Zulu identity as elaborated by its present leadership in terms of territorial, martial, and political qualities and duties. See Gates, *Signifying Monkey*, and Harries, "Imagery, Symbolism and Tradition in a South African Bantustan," 105–125. Herodotus is interested in myths but examines and incorporates them as elements, where apt, in stories. The question of when a story becomes a myth, or when a myth takes on the role of a story, deserves continuing study. See Blumenberg, *Work on Myth*, 35–36; Veyne, *Did the Greeks Believe in their Myths?*; and Levin, "Some Meanings of Myth," 19–31.

4. Flory analyzes a single anecdote ("the captain's reward" [8.118–119]) to demonstrate that Herodotus self-consciously opposes two types of evidence, facts and anecdotes, as part of his ironic recognition that a historian's means of conveying what happened are always problematic and inadequate. It is part of Herodotus' sophisticated humor, according to Flory, to take great pains to verify a fact when that fact must be recognized by his audience to be utterly trivial. Then again, he may relate a true story blandly and without comment, while making grand digressions and editorial comments on the admittedly false version. Flory, *Archaic Smile*, 49–79.

Cook expresses a similar point by contrasting the loose way that Herodotus relates the particular to the general, next to the tighter pattern of Thucydides: "Thucydides has one story to tell, a totally exemplary one. Herodotus' stories hover between the one and the many; and the uncertain or certain presence of mediation between divine favor, human intelligence, and ethnic proclivity keeps the single exemplum from holding" ("Act of Inquiry," 41).

In the essay "The Storyteller," Walter Benjamin appreciates the provocative nature of a Herodotean story by contrasting it with information: "The value of information does not survive the moment in which
it was new. It lives only at that moment; it has to surrender to it completely and explain itself to it without losing any time. A story is different. It does not expend itself. It preserves and concentrates its strength
and is capable of releasing it even after a long time."[5] Of the story of
Psammenitus in Book III, Benjamin observes that it is exactly because
Herodotus refrains from comment, after delivering the story in the driest
possible terms, that it "is still capable after thousands of years of arous-
ing astonishment and thoughtfulness."[6] This story tells how Psammenitus was the target of deliberate injury by Cambyses, who "made trial
of the very soul of him" (3.14). The Egyptian was forced to look on as
his daughter was paraded in the rags of a slave, and then again while
his son was set at the head of a death procession. Psammenitus "looked
fixedly at them first, took it all in, and then . . . bowed himself to the
ground." Psammenitus subsequently noticed an elderly man, one of his
former drinking companions, now reduced to the condition of begging
from Cambyses' army. This sight brought forth from Psammenitus the
most visible signs of grief and distress. Pressed by Cambyses to explain
the strange discrepancy in his behavior, Psammenitus replied: "Son of
Cyrus, my own griefs were too great to cry out about, but the sorrow of
this friend is worth tears; he had much, and much happiness, and has lost
all and become a beggar when he is upon the threshold of old age" (3.14).

Herodotus no sooner arouses our astonishment and thoughtfulness
at this episode than he moves us on to another plane—here, with dark
humor. Croesus is said to burst into tears at Psammenitus' reply (the
scene has been deemed "worth tears"), only to be followed by all of the
Persians present, and, Herodotus marvels, "a kind of pity entered Cambyses himself." What follows is Cambyses' fruitless attempt to overturn
the son's death verdict. No intervention by Apollo closes the scene; the
boy was to be "the first cut down" (3.15).

There is no single interpretation that is decisive for this story, though
Croesus' presence surely reminds us that the blasphemous son of Cyrus
never assumes the role of his father. Herodotean stories are open-ended
and unsettling, like discursive thinking itself: "discursive thinking cannot

5. Benjamin, "Storyteller," in *Illuminations*, 90.
6. Ibid.

simply arrive at truth or uncoveredness (ἀλήθεια). Λόγος itself conceals what it reveals or reveals in a concealed manner."[7] But if these stories have ranges of meaning beyond that of factual material, they still comprise just one facet of the historian's spectrum of evidence. They have their place as part of the whole composition, so that they illumine and are illumined by other forms of evidence. Thus Herodotus does not attempt to cut through the multiple stories to arrive at the real evidence, because to him the stories are not only real, but also the most rooted loci of meaning.

In Herodotus' discussion of the Corinthian role in the battle of Salamis, we see another illustration of the way in which stories function as evidence. Here Herodotus repeats a slanderous tale told by the Athenians about how the Corinthians were in the midst of deserting when they learned of the favorable turn of events for the Greeks; only then did they rejoin the fleet, to find the action finished. "Such is the story told about them by the Athenians," he reports, and adds: "The Corinthians themselves do not agree but think that they were the first in the engagement; and the rest of Greece bears them witness" (8.94). The question is why Herodotus has recounted the Athenians' derogatory version at all, inasmuch as the rest of Greece concurred in the defense of the Corinthians.

Because Herodotus does not sanction the near-universal praise of the Corinthians, it is certainly possible that we were meant to retain some skepticism about their role in the battle. Additionally, with this inclusion Herodotus impresses on his audience a picture of the Greeks winning an improbable victory (as in his account of Marathon), not one that had anything fated about it. Even in their highest moment the Greeks are shown squabbling, with individual cities claiming and disclaiming credit. It seems that this victory was no selfless achievement; the quarrels between the Greek cities began before the Persian invasion, persisted throughout, and were to extend menacingly into the future. A distortion of this historical instance might well have consisted in a historian settling on the good behavior of the Corinthians at Salamis without taking note of the Athenian rejoinder. But to this historian the clashing voices in the retellings were of the highest significance then and afterward. Attempts by historians to isolate what really happened, in contrast, would have closed off the meaning of these retellings; in this instance, they would have promoted a misleading impression of Greek selflessness. As

7. Rosen, *Question of Being*, 58.

Carolyn Dewald comments, "Malevolent and mythic λόγοι sometimes receive his attention because he wants to present belief in them as a significant fact—one that can explain subsequent actions undertaken by the individuals who believe in the λόγος."[8]

At the heart of Herodotean historiography is attentiveness to these diverse amplifications that occur in the discourse about events. For Herodotus the purpose of writing history seems to be to articulate the meaning that a particular people attaches to a past event based on the way the event has affected and continues to affect present circumstances; this meaning may serve as the basis for them to think constructively about the future. In the absence of this attached meaning, the original moment is without dignity or historical use. As John Herington suggests, Herodotus is the community's philosopher, on the understanding that the community itself provides the impetus for this philosophy. Carl Becker has something similarly Herodotean in mind when he describes the function of the historian as one that intersects with those of bards, storytellers, and priests: "to preserve and perpetuate the social tradition . . . to the end that 'society' (the tribe, the nation, or all mankind) may judge of what it is doing in the light of what it has done and what it hopes to do."[9] Inclusivity is a central tenet in this evidentiary method, for the attached meaning could be discernible in any number of forms. The historian's needs are not in the first instance for documentary evidence. They are more basic: a good sense of sight (ὄψις: a sharper agent of belief than hearing, says Candaules [1.8]); proper hearing (ἀκοή: "man can hear wrongly insofar as he does not catch what is essential"[10]); appropriate judgment (γνώμη, which includes the sense of how much to rely on sight and hearing); and a delight in ἱστορίης ἀπόδεξις—the setting forth and showing off of one's researches.

The History *and the Historians*

Modern critics tend to be suspicious of historians with an agenda, and the idea of a historian hearkening to a people's sense of its past with a view to articulating its future sounds dangerously close to an agenda. From this point of view, there is much in *The History* to give pause. On several occasions, Herodotus makes remarks that seem unimportant to

---

8. Dewald, "Narrative Surface," 166.
9. Becker, "Everyman His Own Historian," 231.
10. Heidegger, *Early Greek Thinking*, 65.

the topic at hand but that have a clear relation to the contemporary scene. Sometimes this takes the form of an isolated comment: "This woman married Xanthippus . . . and in her pregnancy saw a dream in which she brought forth a lion. A few days later she brought forth Pericles" (6.31).[11] Or Herodotus may suggest the long view, alluding to the shared knowledge of his readers: "So because the Athenians knew this, they put up no resistance, but yielded, but only so long as they had urgent need of the others, as they later proved" (8.3).[12] These scattered remarks have proven intriguing to readers, but even those critics who explore these instances to best effect have tended to disavow their historical legitimacy.

Charles W. Fornara argues convincingly in one analysis that the historian's depictions of Themistocles and Pausanias were composed so as to heighten the irony among readers who were able to fill in the endings to Herodotus' accounts. He writes of Herodotus: "He has created a drama to which the audience, as the 'dramatist' well knows, and indeed demands, will bring a level of comprehension that altogether changes its point."[13] Because Herodotus assumes that his audience well recalls the inglorious end of both of these heroes of the Persian War, he could sketch their dispositions in a way that almost imperceptibly presages their decline but that comes across with force in the narrative at hand. As Fornara claims, this procedure allows Herodotus to work on different levels of comprehension. The effect is striking, of the sort that Shelley produces with his *Ozymandias:*

> And on the pedestal these words appear:
> "My name is Ozymandias, king of kings:
> Look on my works, ye Mighty, and despair!"
> Nothing beside remains. Round the decay

11. The dream is intriguing. Herodotus has described for us earlier the breeding patterns of lions: "But the lioness, which is the strongest and most daring of animals, gives birth only once in her life and to but one cub. When she gives birth, she expels the womb with the cub. The reason is that, when the cub in the womb begins to stir, it has the sharpest nails of any creature and tears at the womb; as it grows bigger, the scratching grows worse, and, when the birth is near, there is hardly any of the womb left whole" (3.108). It is true that this is complete nonsense: "If lions bred in this way, there would be no lions" (Redfield, "Tourist," 104). But the passages together do indicate something of the leonine nature of Pericles: he is to be Athens' pride and strength and perhaps its undoing.

12. See also 6.91, 7.133, 7.233, and 9.73.

13. Fornara, *Interpretive Essay,* 65.

Of that colossal wreck, boundless and bare,
The lone and level sands stretch far away.[14]

The immediate scene cannot be viewed with dispassion; we are ineluctably raised to a more pensive state of mind. Such also is the consequence of Herodotus' dramatizations. Yet many critics resist such literary accomplishments. Even though Fornara strenuously tries to demonstrate his thesis, he goes on in another work to claim that Herodotus misrepresents the past by so dramatizing it: "It is a question of how far this technique can be reconciled with the elementary rules of "objective" historical composition; for if Herodotus was guided in his selection of fact by contemporary considerations, it unfortunately follows that (through him) we have been viewing the Persian Wars through a distorted lens."[15] Kurt A. Raaflaub concurs; historians should avoid imposing their present-day perspective on the past. He sees difficulties in having to consider the speeches of Herodotus as "expressions of his own thought; they serve his specific purposes of illumination and interpretation."[16]

The elementary rules of objectivity are yet worth reconsidering, for as Herodotus demonstrates in his work and as the Western tradition has come to recognize, there is nothing elementary about the demands of objectivity, nor are these demands subject to rules on which anyone can agree. Novick's researches into the contemporary state of the historical discipline elicit the following conclusion: "As a broad community of discourse, as a community of scholars united by common aims, common standards, and common purposes, the discipline of history [has] ceased to exist. Convergence on anything, let alone a subject as highly charged as 'the objectivity question' [is] out of the question."[17]

The objective tradition is, of course, one in which Herodotus had little role to play; with this tradition in decline, his example holds new interest. For just as Aristotle succeeded in establishing analysis as the

14. Shelley, "Ozymandias," *Complete Poetical Works,* vol. 2, pp. 319–320.

15. Fornara, *Nature of History,* 105.

16. Raaflaub, "Herodotus, Political Thought, and the Meaning of History," 235. Consider also Finley: "I do not believe that it is possible to 'save' even Thucydides once it is held that the issue is one of honesty, of morality, in twentieth-century terms" (*Ancient History,* 13).

17. Novick, *That Noble Dream,* 628.

ideal for philosophy, so Thucydides established objectivity as the ideal for history—with Herodotus serving as the backdrop in both cases.

Thucydides was the first historian to throw a disapproving look toward our writer; he contrasted his own work, a history for "everlasting possession" (1.22), with that of his predecessor, a history alleged to have been publicly read and popularly acclaimed. If Thucydides could not lay claim to being the first historian, he could still stake out a position as the first serious historian. The Western tradition was to accept this assertion of greater seriousness on the part of Thucydides; Herodotus' conception and presentation of evidence was to be supplanted almost immediately by the Thucydidean legacy.[18] His appeal centered on his systematic approach to evidence, inasmuch as in his hands this seemed to promise a far more reliable historical account. His point, as we have seen, was to elucidate the event before it was irretrievably lost in mythical accrual, and thereby to approach certain knowledge about the past. This bounded nature of the evidence for *The Peloponnesian War* proved decisive for later historians, and was to eventuate in a (decidedly anti-Thucydidean) maniacal quest for just the facts.

As later historians tended to follow Thucydides' lead in demarcating historical evidence, so too did they imitate his presentation of the evidence. The key factor here is Thucydides' practice of compressing the space between his account of the past and the past itself. This is the narrative technique that Dewald labels transparent: "This does not mean," she explains, "that the narrative has not been artfully shaped. But in Thucydides the shaping occurs in the narrative itself: the choice of nouns and verbs, the selection of significant narrative detail, the arrangement of the narrative sequence and the narrated thoughts and words of the participants in events."[19]

When Thucydides relates the alleged causes of the outbreak of the Peloponnesian War, he traces a chronological series of skirmishes among the Greeks that set off the momentum toward war. The account is written to convey the sense of immediate access to the order of events. The Epidamnians put themselves under the protection of the Corinthians, which caused the Corcyraeans to lay siege to the city, and so on; one event follows another in a plausible and tight sequence that closes the door on doubts or questions about the validity of the account. Thucydi-

18. "Legacy" is especially to be underlined here, though, for Thucydides' own writings often bore little resemblance to later formulations put forward in his name.

19. Dewald, "Narrative Surface," 148.

des does not present the possibility that there may have been conflicting versions of events, or that there were gaps or uncertainties in the account he selects; indeed, he allows very little attention to be focused on the account itself. Later historians interpreted this to mean that there could be a perfect translation from clear evidence to factual presentation; evidence that was recent, nonmythical, and as exact as possible would fall into place almost by itself. The task of historians came to be seen as one of marshaling the available data and then letting the facts speak for themselves. Given the historians' responsible perusal of the factual evidence, and absent their interference with this data on account of some private agenda, it seemed that they could not help but compose a true historical account.[20]

The concept of historical objectivity that grew up around these premises about the nature and presentation of evidence has terminated in one of the most vexatious debates of modern times. It is manifest that the Thucydidean model is no longer the compelling criterion it once was; its fundamental tenets are considered unrealistic by contemporary historians concerned with justifying their methodology. ("Hoping to find something without looking for it," Becker muses, "expecting to obtain final answers to life's riddle by resolutely refusing to ask questions."[21]) However, the situation today is not one of straightforward work by historians to replace an outmoded concept with a widely accepted improvement. On one hand, it has been largely and inexplicably unnecessary

20. Perhaps the most probing attempt to address this matter can be found in the thought of Dilthey, the German philosopher and historian of ideas who imported the term "hermeneutics" from theology to history, and ultimately to all the human sciences. Not just a sacred text but life itself required exegesis. Dilthey's thought led him to the hermeneutical circle: "Description, which is based on observation, demands the construction of concepts; the concept and its definition presupposes a classification of the phenomena; if this classification is to be an orderly totality, if the concepts are to express the essence of the facts which they represent—then they presuppose a knowledge of the whole. There arises a circle here. At base it is an artistic process in which the power, the universality, and the objective character of the intuitions determine the value of the results" (*Gesammelte Schriften*, 11.258).

As Ermath points out, the hermeneutic circle pertaining to all interpretation is unresolvable in theory, but in practice it proves to be a productive rather than a vicious circle (not unlike Bacon's view of the scientific method). To Herodotus, anticipating Dilthey, it seems indeed to be an artistic process with the artist (Arion) sensing from the people the meaning which they would wish to attach to their experience, past and present, and then offering an artistic rendition for their approval. (Ermath, *Wilhelm Dilthey*, 252). On the hermeneutic circle, see also Spiro, "Cultural Relativism and the Future of Anthropology"; Müller-Vollmer, ed., *Hermeneutics Reader;* and Ormiston, ed., *Hermeneutic Tradition.*

21. Becker, "Everyman his own Historian," 233.

for some modern historians to scrutinize their assumptions about objectivity in order for them to write histories that are highly acclaimed. On the other hand, the indiscriminate dismissal of the objective tradition has by no means proved to be a universally heartening experience for the historical discipline. James Kloppenberg describes the best-case scenario: "Even if we concede that the objectivist dream of 'eternal and universal Truth about human behavior is an unattainable goal,' we can still work to make our versions of the past truer because they are more comprehensive, more multidimensional, more frankly tentative in tone, and more sensitive to the diversities of human cultures than our predecessors' accounts have been."[22]

In practice, however, rarely are the tones less tentative or the versions of the past more comprehensive when modern historians seek out new standards for judging the excellence of a work. Historians are still seeking the middle ground between those who may find value "in every scrap of writing, no matter how vulgar . . . so long as it happened to have been produced by an approved victim group" (or, stated less polemically, those who see no point in discussing any fact or reality apart from its representation), and those who hope to restrict their view of history to political, economic, or military matters that can be examined relatively uninfluenced by the observer.[23] There are scholars today who remain intent on adhering to objectivist goals, as in Carr's older formulation: "the belief in a hard core of historical facts existing . . . independently of the interpretation of the historian," or in Richard Bernstein's more recent one: "the basic conviction that there is or must be some permanent, ahistorical matrix or framework to which we can ultimately appeal in determining the nature of rationality, knowledge, truth."[24] At the same time, there are even more who have abandoned all pretense of aspiring toward that goal; they are relativists of various degrees who hold that rationality, knowledge, and truth are alike "relative to a specific conceptual scheme, theoretical framework, paradigm, form of life, society, or culture."[25]

The striking fact (well documented by Bernstein) is that objectivists and relativists contribute alike to the contemporary dilemma in history. The well-known trend for historians is to carve out their specialties from ever smaller segments of the past and to formulate questions to which

22. Kloppenberg, review of *That Noble Dream*, 1028.
23. McMillen, "Controversial Anthology of American Literature," A22.
24. Carr, *What is History?*, 10; Bernstein, *Beyond Objectivism and Relativism*, 8.
25. Ibid.

some kind of answer is possible, verifiable or not. It is certainly safer for scholars under current conditions to master a narrow area rather than to expose themselves to charges of superficiality by embarking on a general theme. And so the questions narrow, the subjects shrink, and the peer groups diminish in size. Meanwhile, the possible subjects of historical study seem to multiply endlessly, as groups that were scarcely visible in older accounts succeed in arguing for a place of prominence in current histories. This heterogeneity could be enriching, and it is, to the extent that questions of excellence in historical writing remain alive. But few scholars today are disposed to entertain questions of such magnitude, or even to raise the simplest of Herodotean questions about the past: what is worth remembering? Lacking the determination to confront this question, lacking the energy to argue for the significance and context of our historical inquiries, we may revert to the lowest common denominator in judging one another's work: does the author have her facts straight?[26] Such a state may be more insidious even than that imagined by Nietzsche when he wrote of "idlers in the garden of knowledge" who have lost control of their critical pens, and "instead of directing them are directed by them."[27]

We return, then, to the refreshing and irresistible "secret of lightness" inhering in the Herodotean model.[28] Its suggestions concerning the seriousness of the proven story deserve our renewed attention. That a history is retold through the ages signifies that the particular story rings true for the experience of a larger humanity; such a history must have rung true for the original audience as well. This seems evident of *The History*, for Herodotus presents an image of cultures that has an explicit connection to the way people thought and told stories about themselves and each other. His declarations that stories must be heeded simply by virtue of being told are not superficial; his depictions respond to what people believe happened in order to stay close to human meaning. He often disagrees with their thinking: "At this point I am forced to declare an opinion that most people will find offensive; yet because I think it

26. Novick writes of the current situation: "the only grounds for anything resembling an evaluative consensus on an historical work [is] whether it had its facts straight" (*That Noble Dream*, 595).

27. Nietzsche, "Uses and Disadvantages of History," 59, 87.

28. "The sudden agile leap of the poet-philosopher who raises himself above the weight of the world, showing that with all his gravity he has the secret of lightness" was chosen by Calvino as an "auspicious image for the new millennium" (Calvino, *Six Memos for the Next Millennium*, 12).

true, I will not hold back" (7.139). But he does not attempt to lift himself out of his time and place to summon up a detached view of peoples
(and thereby lessen his accountability). Even in evidence that has fought
its way into the country of myth, past credence, Herodotus sees a rich,
not a forbidding topic of historical inquiry. To evoke what is of enduring
significance for peoples across his world, Herodotus looks to what has
endured in their stories.

It is therefore not the objective truth of *The History* that constitutes
its force (Herodotus wrote "before" objectivity), but its perceived authenticity. Herodotus offers the Greeks a way to understand their past
that hearkens to them, that inspires and admonishes them. He self-
consciously connects with his audience and with his time; in the words
of Adam Parry, "the history of the early fifth century *is* like the style
of Herodotus."[29] As an interested Greek thinker, then, Herodotus sets
down his Greek signature in the larger process of asserting a peremptory
stance as the historian of the Persian War. This seems not to be because
he supposed that he had produced the one true rendition of the events
in question, but because he offered a compelling perspective grounded
in inherited thought and knowledge that did not fail to take hold among
his contemporaries.

Neither does Herodotus betray any relativist misgivings. Cultures
that differ greatly confront each other, and when they do, Herodotus
goes to the heart of the matter: each culture has a right to its own particular outlook, but one may be better equipped for the future than
another. Darius called Greeks and Indians before him in order to observe the cultural confrontation. One party could not even contemplate
the practices of the other, whereas the other shows readiness to assess
and consider practices utterly alien to their own. Herodotus leaves no
doubt which is better suited for success in a global world. And he lays
out examples of political behavior that any and every society, whatever
their own practice might be, may consider for adoption. It is as if for
Herodotus the world were composed of many laboratories with distinct
experiments set up to answer the basic question of human association
and political definition. Each laboratory reaches a different result; each
is worthy of the most serious attention; but it is possible, at least tenta-
tively, to choose the better ways. Herodotus exercises his ability to dis-

29. Parry, *Logos and Ergon*, 143. He continues: "and the history of the later 5th century
is like the style of Thucydides."

criminate among what Bernstein has called "those particulars that have *exemplary validity*."[30]

Our experience with Herodotus suggests that although historians may never have the last word on their subject matter, a great historian may have the decisive word. With the passage of time, new stories of explanation unfold that may or may not displace the old. But when an old story does persist across generations, it is because it has succeeded in striking a balance between the solidity of its description of particulars and the universality of its import; it has proven its own exemplary validity, even if in some cases its social, economic, cultural, or political impact may be detrimental. It seems that the oldest of our forebears in the historical discipline brings us face to face with the most current of our preoccupations: canonicity.

White Whales and Dead White Males: Herodotus in a Neo-Canonical World

Herodotus did not inherit from his predecessors a sense of what is worth telling, worth knowing, or worth recording; his historiography is self-formulated. Previous historians (Hecataeus) or poets (Homer, Hesiod) did not offer him a sufficiently principled method for determining which stories about the past should be retained; his classic is about canons and canon-making. According to Herodotus, time will draw the color from most of the creations of mankind. He strives therefore to resist this process by gathering stories that seem to vie for recognition, and thus looks to demonstrate what I risk calling *the* human project. He makes clear that human beings differ from animals in not existing in close, prescribed social organizations in accordance with instinct, genes, or inheritance. No such instinct guides our species; fate, or the gods, or whatever force lies behind the visible world, none has implanted a way of governance in our sector of the living world. Thus exists the requirement of political activity. So Herodotus proceeds to reveal that each tribe, culture, society, or nation of the human world organizes itself in its own way. The human project is political theory and the assessment of the ensuing practice. How this has been done, how it is perpetuated, comes by way of a society's canon—the stories it tells itself about its origins and distinctive development, and the continuing puzzles that it presents each

30. Bernstein, *Beyond Objectivism and Relativism*, 218.

succeeding generation for contemplation. These puzzles are so fundamental to the human condition as to exceed our ability to solve them
once and for all in other than slow and piecemeal ways of advance.

The analogy to today's canon debates is straightforward: the place
of stories in Herodotus' history is like the place of the great books in
our canon. For what are our great books but the stories we tell ourselves, and what is our canon but the sum total, or history, of the stories
that have endured? Consider the record of one of the two most famous
white whales in history: *Moby-Dick.* O'Brien unkindly wrote in 1853 that
"Mr. Melville does not improve with time,"[31] while a year earlier a Boston literary journal judged *Moby-Dick* to be a new disappointment: "It is
a curious mixture of fact and fancy. . . . Over this mixture is thrown a veil
of a sort of dreamy philosophy and indistinct speculation just sufficient to
obscure the value of the facts stated, and which in our opinion does not
improve the quality of the tale."[32] The quality of the tale was not to be
generally acknowledged for several decades to come. Quite apart from
its unsettling mixture of factual information and "dreamy philosophy"
(a charge, it should be noted, also commonly directed at Herodotus),
Moby-Dick was not initially favored by educators because it was thought
to be a retrograde look at a dying industry (whaling) at a time when far
more interesting industries (railroads, banks) merited attention.

Moby-Dick did get into the canon, however, and it got in by fighting its way in, by being able to provide insights into enduring human
concerns. *Moby-Dick* spoke more truthfully to human nature and more
powerfully of the human condition than did its early critics, and it outlasted them. In 1984 Malcolm Cowley could write that one of the crucial events of the twentieth century's critical and academic history "was
the discovery about 1920 of a great American novel—of course it was
Moby-Dick—that had gone almost unread for sixty years."[33] The near-
universal judgment of sixty years of educators was not to prevail.

The point is more than that time must pass before a great work receives its due recognition. Here the example of *The History* of Herodotus
is illuminating. In century after century, educators disparaged this history as less than serious, even while it rose again and again in the canon.
The historiography was judged deficient, yet its endurance was never

31. Fitz-James O'Brien, "Our Young Authors—Melville," *Putnam's Monthly,* vol. 1
(Feb. 1853): 155–164, quoted in Parker and Hayford, eds., *Moby-Dick As Doubloon,* 94.
32. *Today: A Boston Literary Journal,* January 10, 1852, quoted in *Doubloon,* 85.
33. Cowley, *Portable Malcolm Cowley,* 431.

affected. The ability of a work to carve out a niche for itself without anyone's blessing can be more than a little disconcerting.

Contemporary debates on the topic of the canon yet raise a crucial question: whether a canon exists, or can be shaped, that presents fundamental issues without being culture-bound, without manifesting the imposed preferences of an empowered elite. These would be stories, problems, conundrums, and precedents that require the thinker to grapple with what must be done in facing the elemental human predicament. Canonical works might be a source of pride, of history-telling, of insight into human relations for a culture. Might they also be mere reflections of a society's power structures?

Some readers of Herodotus would reply affirmatively: when he writes about his fellow Greeks, issues of influence and power come into play, for he decides which voices count as representative; he decides which voices are to be discounted as marginal or dissenting. Like all historians, Herodotus had prejudices or interests that led him to promote or demote certain subjects, characters, and events at the expense of others. In the words of Joan Wallach Scott, it is a given that "there will always be a plurality of stories, that telling them involves contests about power and knowledge, and that the historian's mastery is necessarily partial."[34] And the partiality of the historian stands in the way of a comprehensive interpretation of cultures: the Greekness of Herodotus would make him ill suited to act as witness and judge of Egyptian, Persian, and Scythian cultures. The most highly esteemed qualities of Herodotus' own culture become the unacknowledged basis for characterizing the cultures of others. For such readers, Matthew Arnold's formulation of the idea of the canon—"the acquainting ourselves with the best that has been known and said in the world, and thus with the history of the human spirit"[35]—leaves unexplained how it is that authors traditionally recognized in the canon of which Herodotus forms a part are manifestly more male than female, more white than black, more Christian than Muslim.

Our Melville example will serve us again, for *Moby-Dick* appears to be in new trouble. For reasons which have nothing to do with its now-acknowledged literary merit, *Moby-Dick* has become part of the issue of the canon because of its putative lack of diversity. The complaint is about perspective, for the canon seems to be made up of authors of suspi-

34. Scott, "History in Crisis?" 691.
35. Arnold, *Literature and Dogma*, xi.

ciously comparable backgrounds. Here is where the slogan "dead white male" enters, for it is meant to label this uniformity of perspective. (The understanding is implicit that the deadness of the author is the least objectionable quality.) Melville is one of these dead white males, and he writes, in turn, about white males and white whales. More pointedly, the reasons for Melville's being considered profoundly suspect at the moment were dutifully listed off by a graduate student attending the 1990 Modern Language Association convention: "There is not a woman in his book, the plot hinges on unkindness to animals and the black characters mostly drown by Chapter 29."[36]

This memorable formulation refers to the recent phenomenon of critics basing their readings of works on the author's original perspective or background. Such an approach represents from our point of view an indefensible leap from the recognition that all peoples have their own perspective, and that some have had and continue to have more advantage than others, to the claim that we should decide beforehand what perspectives to accept. The belief that the original point of departure should meet certain specifications is determinist, and shockingly so for an age that prides itself on its openness. Earlier, less open ages regarded the particular horizon within which authors worked as representing the condition and not the essence of the work. So Jane Austen, for example, could move the wider world within her two inches of ivory: "The little bit (two inches wide) of ivory on which I work with, so fine a brush as produces little effect after much labour."[37] And so Melville could attract the interest of an audience wider than white male cetacean enthusiasts: "There's another rendering now; but still one text. All sorts of men in one kind of world, you see."[38]

A close reading of *The History* would suggest that educators of any age do not have the prerogative of adding to, deleting from, or simply preserving the canon; as much as we argue among ourselves about what has been and what should be featured in the canon, its makeup is not determined by institutional authority. The point is not to enshrine works in a canon; they cannot be enshrined. To Herodotus, every canonical story fights its way into contemporary consciousness, and if it loses the

36. Richard Abowitz, quoted by Anne Matthews, "Deciphering Victorian Underwear and Other Seminars," *New York Times Magazine*, February 10, 1991, 58.
37. Jane Austen to J. Edward Austen, December 16, 1816, in John Bartlett, *Familiar Quotations*, 15th ed. (Boston: Little, Brown and Company, 1980), 588.
38. Melville, *Moby-Dick*, 444.

fight, it falls away. As Wright Morris puts it, "every classic is open to re-appraisal. We might go further and say that until reappraised it is not a classic. We know the classic as a book too deep to know itself."[39] No item can be lastingly inserted in the canon by curriculum change. The canonical text proves itself "by being able to withstand changing assaults of interpretation without ever seeming to be exhausted."[40] There is an openness to the canon beyond our specific control.

Newcomers who can meet these stringent standards are to be welcomed to the company of great books, while traditional texts should not be shelved without a fresh look to assess their political as well as cultural richness. The old metaphor of the conversation across the ages remains constructive; we "therefore have the advantage of being able to preserve the modernity of our choices without surrendering the right to add to them, even to exclude members of them, not by means of difficult administrative procedures but simply by continuing a conversation."[41] Frank Kermode adds that we may quarrel in this conversation, "but on the whole everybody knows what is being talked about."[42] It is because everyone knows what is being talked about that we can justify in the last analysis Arnold's famous quest for "culture, the acquainting ourselves with the best that has been known and said in the world, and thus with the history of the human spirit." If Arnold sets out an ideal, it is a highly defensible one: that we culture-bound humans can unbind ourselves and speak across cultures on issues we all recognize as fundamental. The dignity of such writing depends on our conviction that there are writers and readers alike who are capable of distinguishing between self-serving and thoughtful remembrances.

How, then, are we to justify the elements of caricature that seem always to mar our portraits of alien cultures? Herodotus corrects some misperceptions ("There are pygmies in central Africa," Terrot Glover recounts, "not quite so small as Homer said; they are bigger than your fist."[43]) and perpetuates others ("These Ethiopians . . . have customs very different from everyone else, especially in regard to their monar-

39. Morris, foreword to Twain, *Tragedy of Pudd'nhead Wilson*, vii. See Nagy, who describes the scene of Croesus on the pyre as illustrative of the "Classical ideal": "the ideology of an ideal audience, listening to an ideal performance of an ideal composition, the message of which applies to all humanity" (*Pindar's Homer*, 249).

40. Lentricchia, preface to Kermode, *Forms of Attention*.

41. Kermode, *Forms of Attention*, 79.

42. Ibid.

43. Glover, *Herodotus*, 164.

chy. For whichever of their citizens they judge to be tallest . . . him they think fit to be their king" [3.20]). Redfield has noted of *The History* that the depiction of the civilized Greeks' overcoming the barbarous Persians would have seemed an odd reading to the Persians of that age: "for them, I would suppose, the campaigns of 480–479 represented a moment at which a developing barbarian district resisted incorporation in the administrative structure of civilised power."[44] But to expect the historian to be above such character-drawing is to entertain old objectivist expectations about the nature of historical knowledge; all historians have to work with what is thought and said in their own time. And our criticism of the received opinion of earlier ages tends to be more acute than that directed toward contemporary times. The Persians or Egyptians or Scythians would have emerged quite differently if depicted from a native point of view, but that is of very little consequence for the truth-telling status of Herodotus' history. There is and always was ample space for other historians to contribute their perspectives and to challenge that of Herodotus. His perspective has survived.

Herodotus proceeds as if there were no other way to look at the past except through the perspective of his present. He opens *The History* by locating himself: "I, Herodotus of Halicarnassus, am here setting forth my history . . ." (1.1). He is forthright ever after about the Greek bearings of the stories he recounts. This self-referencing does not seem to cause him any discomfort, as if he were supposed to be uncovering a past independent of any perspective. He is a Greek exploring character and custom for other Greeks, and his origins are not something he tries to overcome. He affirms his perspective in the most offhand comments: "When the Nile comes out upon the country, only the cities show above the watery surface, very much like islands in the Aegean Sea" (2.97). His treatment of the gods of mankind is startling in this regard: "In the Egyptian language, Apollo is Horus, Demeter is Isis, and Artemis is Bubastis" (2.156). When he professes his intent to memorialize "those great and wonderful deeds manifested by both Greeks and barbarians," it is understood that the (relatively) undifferentiated barbarians—all non-Greeks —are his subjects, not his audience. Without overlooking either the deficiencies of the Greeks or the capacities of the barbarians, Herodotus sets out the prospect of his world through the eyes of his people: "For in the days of Darius . . . Xerxes . . . and Artaxerxes . . . more ills befell Greece

---

44. Redfield, "Commentary," 251.

than in all twenty generations before Darius" (6.98). At the same time that he embraces his particular Greek circumstances, he locates these circumstances in a much larger imaginative setting. He interests us not because he reflects a fifth-century Halicarnassian mind-set but because he puts forward a provocative interpretation of the place of the Greeks in his world, and of the world of his Greeks.

Stories at the Origin

Herodotus is unabashed in his attempts to describe the past with an eye toward affecting the character of his fellow Greeks. His message is Heraclitean: "One should quench arrogance ($\H{v}\beta\rho\iota\varsigma$) [sooner than a raging fire]."[45] When he closes *The History* with the warning from Cyrus, Great King of Persia ("From soft countries come soft men. It is not possible that from the same land stems a growth of wondrous fruit and men who are good soldiers" [9.122]), it is his Greek audience that is called to attention by the surprise ending: "So the Persians took this to heart and went away; their judgment had been overcome by that of Cyrus, and they chose to rule, living in a wretched land, rather than to sow the level plains and be slaves to others" (9.122). The audience knows better. But does the audience know better? Their version was yet unfinished. Storytellers only tell stories; they do not enforce them. You might draw a protective ring around the fire with all due care (2.66); some of the cats will hurl themselves into the fire all the same.

Aristotle and Herodotus intersect on this insight: neither the $\phi\rho\acute{o}\nu\iota$-$\mu o \varsigma$ nor the historian can assume the prerogative of merely applying general principles; they might use their experience and wisdom to deliberate correctly about the best actions to take in contingent circumstances, but they recognize the limited effect of their truth-telling.[46] Aristotle's final line in the *Nicomachean Ethics* is as startling as Herodotus' in *The History:* "let us make a beginning of our discussion" ($\lambda\acute{e}\gamma\omega\mu\epsilon\nu$ $o\H{v}\nu$ $\mathring{a}\rho\xi\acute{a}\mu\epsilon\nu o\iota$). His late acknowledgment of the need to buttress his philosophical arguments with the force of law is reminiscent of his apparent afterthought in the *Politics* to take note of the visible manifestations of character in the cities of Greece and nations of the inhabited world (1327b21–24). The most elevated analyses prove inadequate to the task of subsuming

45. Heraclitus, trans. in Freeman, *Ancilla*, 27=DK B 43 (I.160, 12).
46. Clark, *Aristotle's Man*, 134.

those complicated beings we call human. Davis observes that the ordinary effect of Aristotle's neat division of the sciences is that he leaves out something important: "The things treated by the sciences are less precise than the sciences that treat them."⁴⁷ This is quietly acknowledged by Aristotle, even with high humor.

But whereas Aristotle's humor is an acquired taste and a difficult taste to acquire, Herodotus' is both more open and infectious. To the last, their divergences are illuminating. Aristotle pronounced Herodotus ὁ μυθολόγος; the term was pejorative, and forever after, μῦθος and λόγος would be kept straight. The Philosopher might allow that "even" the lover of myth could be accorded a certain respect (myths are "composed of wonders," and "it is owing to their wonder that men both now begin and at first began to philosophize" [Met 982b12-19]); still, the implication is clear that for Aristotle the paths of μῦθος and λόγος had long ago been disconnected, and for the best of reasons. Hence when he writes that the lover of myth is "in a sense" (πῶς) a lover of wisdom, the force of his qualification should not be undervalued. "There is much in that πῶς,"⁴⁸ W. K. C. Guthrie remarks, and we concur: Aristotle and the tradition following him disparaged the historian who afforded respect, at least potentially, to the community as philosopher. The severance of μῦθος and λόγος would assure the philosopher's preeminence. This was more than a departure from long Greek usage; it was the intentional forgetting of the single idea of μυθολογος, the philosophic storyteller.

Reading Herodotus' *History*, it is still possible to gain a sense of how μῦθος and λόγος were once thought of as being together in the Greek world. Zaslavsky observes that of the numerous renderings of μῦθος and λόγος in the Liddell-Scott lexicon, the two fundamental ones for both "seem to be 'speech' and 'account,' initially without any distinction of true and false."⁴⁹ Eventually, myth was to be associated with "false account" and λόγος with "true," but this was a gradual development, not true in original uses of the terms. Jean-Pierre Vernant explains:

> The Greek word μῦθος means formulated speech, whether it be a story, a dialogue, or the enunciation of a plan. So μῦθος belongs to the domain of λέγειν [to say, speak, tell, recount] . . . and does not originally stand in contrast to λόγοι, a term which has

47. Davis, *Aristotle's Poetics*, 168, n 102.
48. Guthrie, "Aristotle as a Historian of Philosophy," 40.
49. Zaslavsky, *Platonic Myth and Platonic Writing*, 11.

a closely related semantic significance and which is concerned with the different forms of what is said.[50]

To be sure, for Herodotus the words had become so far differentiated that on one hand he upbraids the poets for resorting to myth for lack of a more responsible explanation (2.23), whereas on the other he acknowledges a ruling necessity in his λόγος (as in, "I go back to the former track of my λόγος" (1.140), or "I do not record the names of these because it is not necessary for the purpose of my *History* [τῶν ἐγώ, οὐ γὰρ ἀναγκαίη ἐξέργομαι ἐς ἱστορίης λόγον, οὐ παραμέμνημαι (7.96)]. But the division is not easily or strictly maintained. Murray notes that Herodotus himself does not explicitly contrast λόγος, ἱστορία and μῦθος: "though the words clearly have different connotations for him, he was not aware of our problems."[51] This is not to say that our problems begin with Aristotle, only that it was the inclination of Aristotle, as it was not of Herodotus, to associate λόγοι with "demonstrative rationality."[52] Λόγοι for Herodotus could embrace virtually any living tradition, from the most rationalistic (Persian chroniclers) to the most poetic (Greeks). In our time of imaginatively constricted scholarship, we have particular cause to attend to Herodotus' more expansive conception of what counts as formative for our political selves.

For Herodotus, the true origins of the political community are spoken by the community. The historian or poet or philosopher with ears to hear, eyes to see, and a mind alert and lively enough to assimilate those perceptions might succeed in making these origins accessible. But the route of the λόγοι is not an easy one. Dewald speaks of Herodotus as a heroic warrior struggling with and overcoming a beastlike antagonist, a "polymorphously fearsome oddity": "it consists of the λόγος, or collection of λόγοι, that comprise the narrative of the *Histories*."[53] The image is a good one, and appropriately evinces Herodotus battling with a worthy combatant: stories, myths, and exaggerated speeches vying for notice and survival. Some of these speeches are more irrepressible than others, but the historian's challenge is a genuine one: time draws the color from all human creations. In seeking to subdue the given λόγοι by establishing his λόγος, Herodotus resists the blurring effects of time.

50. Vernant, *Myth and Society*, 186.
51. Murray, "Herodotus and Oral History," 99.
52. Vernant, *Myth and Society*, 188.
53. Dewald, "Narrative Surface," 147.

As Seth Benardete has noted, it is Herodotus' great achievement "to understand the given without destroying the given."[54] From our point of view, the important point to recognize is that Herodotus accomplishes this through his receptivity to an infinite range of λόγοι; the inescapable thought is that λόγος as implying demonstrative rationality is insufficient for preserving the given. It loses touch with the fighting element in the λόγοι and therefore loses touch.

Vernant claims that by the time of Aristotle, the realms of μῦθος and λόγος had become so distant that communication between the two was no longer possible; his example is from the *Metaphysics* (1000a11–20), where Aristotle is shown reading a myth "as if it were a philosophical text." He concludes, "For a historian of religion the interest lies in the misplaced, not to say misguided character of Aristotle's remarks where myth is concerned."[55] Misplaced, misguided, and deliberate, we would add; the defense of the philosophic life was coterminous with the assertion that the highest life was one that could best account for itself on essentially rational terms. Nicholas Lobkowicz reminds us that Aristotle had his own agenda, that he had an ideological component to his discussions that served "to justify the way of life of the philosopher who pursues interests which, at first glance, have nothing to do with the problems of society."[56] The all-important divide remains: Aristotle was post-Socratic.

To disclose one's story fully and constructively is no light matter. The Persian chroniclers adapted the stories of others to compile their version of the past; the result was that they imposed and did not propagate a view. Obedience to the story of the Great King was not necessarily belief in the story. Truth-tellers can shape the experience that others merely live, but this requires meaningful contact with the shared knowledge of the community, a sense of one's own unique narrative, and the energy to defend it. In the best case, a story will be worth telling to all humankind, regardless of the ultimate fate of its proponents. What the Greeks did or did not do with the story Herodotus told is now beside the point. The lessons are still there for us concerning the never-ending process of storytelling that is at the root of any political community. Storytelling no doubt found a more respectful welcome in the pre-Socratic world; Xenophanes here seems to encourage an expansive μυθολόγος: "One should hold such converse by the fire-side in the winter season, lying on

54. Benardete, *Herodotean Inquiries*, 4.
55. Vernant, *Myth and Society*, 193.
56. Lobkowicz, "On the History of Theory and Praxis," 15.

a soft couch, well-fed, drinking sweet wine, nibbling peas: 'Who are you among men, and where from? How old are you, my good friend? What age were you when the Mede came?' "[57]

But for communities pre- or post-Socratic, the story exists at its core, whether it is a good story or bad, whether attention is paid to it or not. It can be constructed and it can be deconstructed, should a political community wish to do so. "The self we serve is one that we create," Stephen Clark concludes, and "the only reasonable self to create is a loving one."[58] Herodotus keeps in sight our reasonable and unreasonable propensities alike, and in the process he fully engages his audience. That his truth-telling elicits a consistently appreciative audience makes it untimely, not unimportant. In our time, to be able to conceive of a poetic historian who is philosophically engaging is to think the unthinkable.

57. Xenophanes, trans. Freeman, *Ancilla*, 23=DK B 22 (I.134, 13).
58. Clark, *Aristotle's Man*, 113. In his unusual and intriguing study Clark brings Aristotle very close to Herodotus in such phrases.

Afterword:
Arion's Leap

One of the most attractive and intriguing images surviving from antiquity is the boy on a dolphin, reproduced today on book colophons, institutional seals, and fountain statuary. The boy is Arion the poet and singer, born in Lesbos, who prospered at the court of the Corinthian despot Periander. Arion had lived among the Corinthians, sung their story, assessed the character of their community, and trusted them.

At sea, where the Corinthians are out of their element, they abandon their custom, their character, and that which makes them a community. They throw off that which distinguishes human from nonhuman society. Facing death at the hands of the Corinthian pirates, Arion is forced to choose. He can leap into the sea unclothed (in a sense thereby shedding his human qualities) and perhaps survive. Instead, Arion elects to exercise his creative powers, his artistry, in the face of grave danger. He sings and then leaps into the sea, even though the weight of his bardic gear will certainly make him sink like a stone. This does not happen. Arion's performance persuades a dolphin to carry him to shore, where he confronts his would-be killers. Arion has saved himself by reaffirming his culture and creative character in a moment of crisis and even when out of his element. Arion's partner in this successful outcome is the dolphin, symbol of questing intelligence in the animal world, constantly seeking to extend itself beyond the limitations of its situation, as it repeatedly breaks the surface of the sea.

The task then is to fulfill the human vocation, to create history through art and to form community by means of that perception. To be human is to engage history, for history is all we have. What we make of it will shape a common destiny. If shaped well, the community may thrive; if not, it may crumble when out of its element or confronted with crisis. Arion's story stirs us toward courage, creativity, and a readiness to leap into an unknown future.

Bibliography

Ackrill, J. L. "Aristotle on *Eudaimonia*." In Amélie Oksenberg Rorty, ed., *Essays on Aristotle's Ethics*, pp. 15–33. Berkeley: University of California Press, 1980.

Adkins, A. W. H. "*Theoria* versus *Praxis* in the *Nicomachean Ethics* and the *Republic*." *Classical Philology* 73 (1978): 297–313.

———. "The Connection between Aristotle's *Ethics* and *Politics*." *Political Theory* 12 (1984): 29–49.

Ahmad, Aijaz. *In Theory: Classes, Nations, Literatures*. New York: Verso, 1992.

Aly, Wolf. *Volksmärchen, Sage und Novelle bei Herodot und seinen Zeitgenossen: Eine Untersuchung über die volkstümlichen Elemente der altgriechischen Prosaerzälung*. Göttingen: Vandenhoeck and Ruprecht, 1921. Reprint, 1969.

Äppfel, Helmut. *Die Verfassungsdebatte bei Herodot (3.80–82)*. Erlangen, Ph.D. dissertation, 1957. Reprint, New York: Arno Press, 1979.

Arendt, Hannah. "The Concept of History: Ancient and Modern." In *Between Past and Future*, 41–90. New York: Penguin Books, 1980.

Aristophanes. *The Acharnians*. Translated by Douglass Parker. Ann Arbor: University of Michigan Press, 1961.

Aristotle. *De Arte Poetica Liber*. Edited by Rudolfus Kassel. Oxford: Clarendon Press, 1965.

———. *Ars Rhetorica*. Edited by W. D. Ross. Oxford: Clarendon Press, 1959.

———. *The Complete Works of Aristotle*. 2 vols. Edited by Jonathan Barnes. Princeton: Princeton University Press, 1984.

———. *Eudemian Ethics*. Translated by H. Rackham. Cambridge: Harvard University Press, 1935.

———. *Generation of Animals*. Translated by A. L. Peck. Cambridge: Harvard University Press, 1963.

———. *Historia Animalium*. Translated by A. L. Peck. 3 vols. Cambridge: Harvard University Press, 1965.

———. *Metaphysica*. Edited by Werner Jaeger. Oxford: Clarendon Press, 1957.

———. *Nicomachean Ethics*. Translated by H. Rackham. Cambridge: Harvard University Press, 1982.

———. *On the Heavens*. Edited by D. J. Allan. Oxford: Clarendon Press, 1936.

———. *Parts of Animals*. Translated by A. L. Peck. Cambridge: Harvard University Press, 1937.

———. *Politica*. Edited by W. D. Ross. Oxford: Clarendon Press, 1957.

———. *The Politics*. Translated by Carnes Lord. Chicago: University of Chicago Press, 1984.

Armayor, O. Kimball. "Did Herodotus Ever Go to Egypt?" *Journal of the American Research Center in Egypt* 15 (1978): 59–73.

———. "Did Herodotus Ever Go to the Black Sea?" *Harvard Studies in Classical Philology* 82 (1978): 45–62.

———. *Herodotus' Autopsy of the Fayoum: Lake Moeris and the Labyrinth of Egypt.* Amsterdam: J. C. Gieben, 1985.

———. "Herodotus' Catalogues of the Persian Empire in the light of the Monuments and the Greek Literary Tradition." *Transactions of the American Philological Association* 108 (1978): 1–9.

———. "Sesostris and Herodotus' Autopsy of Thrace, Colchis, Inland Asia Minor, and the Levant." *Harvard Studies in Classical Philology* 84 (1980): 51–74.

Arnhart, Larry. *Aristotle on Political Reasoning: A Commentary on the Rhetoric.* DeKalb, Ill.: Northern Illinois University Press, 1981.

Arnold, Matthew. *Literature and Dogma: An Essay Towards a Better Apprehension of the Bible.* Boston: James R. Osgood and Company, 1873.

Atkinson, R. F. *Knowledge and Explanation in History: An Introduction to the Philosophy of History.* Ithaca, N.Y.: Cornell University Press, 1978.

Ax, Wolfram, ed. *Memoria Rerum Veterum: Neue Beiträge Zur Antiken Historiographie Und Alten Geschichte.* Stuttgart: Franz Steiner Verlag, 1990.

Ayo, Nicholas. "Prolog and Epilog: Mythical History in Herodotus." *Ramus* 13, 1 (1984): 31–47.

Bailyn, Bernard. "The Challenge of Modern Historiography." *American Historical Review* 87 (Feb. 1982): 1–24.

Ball, Terence, ed. *Political Theory and Praxis: New Perspectives.* Minneapolis: University of Minnesota Press, 1977.

Barnes, Jonathan, Malcolm Schofield, and Richard Sorabji, eds. *Articles on Aristotle: II. Ethics and Politics.* London: Gerald Duckworth, 1977.

Barth, Hannelore. "Einwirkungen der vorsokratischen Philosophie auf die Herausbildung der historiographischen Methoden Herodots." *Neue Beiträge zur Geschichte der Alten Welt.* Vol. 1: *Alter Orient und Griechenland.* (1964): 173–183.

———. "Zur Bewertung und Auswahl des Stoffes durch Herodot." *Klio* 50 (1968): 93–110.

Barthes, Roland. "The Death of an Author." In *Image/Music/Text,* 142–148. Translated by Stephen Heath. New York: Hill and Wang, 1977.

———. "Historical Discourse." In Michael Lane, ed., *Introduction to Structuralism,* pp. 145–155. Translated by Peter Wexler. New York: Basic Books, 1970.

———. "Introduction to the Structural Analysis of Narrative." Translated by Lionel Duisit. *New Literary History* VI, 2 (Winter, 1975): 237–272.

Beck, Ingrid. *Die Ringkomposition bei Herodot und ihre Bedeutung für die Beweistechnik.* New York: G. Olms, 1971.

Becker, Carl. "Everyman His Own Historian." *American Historical Review* 37 (Jan. 1932): 221–236.

———. "What are Historical Facts?" In Hans Meyerhoff, ed., *The Philosophy of History in our Time,* pp. 124–131. Garden City, N.Y.: Doubleday Anchor Books, 1959.

Benardete, Seth. *Herodotean Inquiries.* The Hague: Martinus Nijoff, 1969.

Benjamin, Walter. "The Storyteller." In *Illuminations*. Translated by Harry Zohn. New York: Harcourt, Brace and World, 1979.

Bergonzi, Bernard. *Exploding English: Criticism, Theory, Culture*. Oxford: Clarendon Press, 1991.

Bernal, Martin. *Black Athena: The Afroasiatic Roots of Classical Civilization*. Vol. 1: *The Fabrication of Ancient Greece 1785–1985*. New Brunswick, N.J.: Rutgers University Press, 1987.

———. *Black Athena: The Afroasiatic Roots of Classical Civilization*. Vol. 2: *The Archaeological and Documentary Evidence*. New Brunswick, N.J.: Rutgers University Press, 1991.

———. "*Black Athena* and the APA." *Arethusa: Challenge of 'Black Athena'* Special Issue (Fall 1989): 17–37.

Bernstein, Richard J. *Beyond Objectivism and Relativism: Science, Hermeneutics, and Praxis*. Philadelphia: University of Pennsylvania Press, 1988.

———. "Reconciliation and Rupture: The Challenge and Threat of Otherness." In Frank Reynolds and David Tracy, eds., *Discourse and Practice*, pp. 295–314. Albany: State University of New York Press, 1992.

Bichler, Reinhold. "Die 'Reichsträume' Herodots. Eine Studie zu Herodots schöpferischer Leistung und ihrer quellenkritischen Konsequenz." *Chiron* 15 (1985): 125–147.

Blanco, Walter. *The Histories*. New York: Norton, 1992.

Bleicken, Jochen. "Zur Entstehung der Verfassungstypologie im 5. Jahrhundert v. Chr. (Monarchie, Aristokratie, Demokratie)" *Historia* 28 (1979): 148–172.

Blumenberg, Hans. *The Legitimacy of the Modern Age*. Translated by Robert M. Wallace. Cambridge: MIT Press, 1983.

———. *Work on Myth*. Translated by Robert M. Wallace. Cambridge: MIT Press, 1985.

Boedeker, Deborah. "Protesilaos and the End of Herodotus' *Histories*." *Classical Antiquity* 7 (April 1988): 30–48.

———. "The Two Faces of Demaratus." *Arethusa* 20 (Spring and Fall 1987): 185–201.

Bornitz, Hans-Friedrich. *Herodot-Studien: Beiträge zum Verständnis der Einheit des Geschichtswerkes*. Berlin: De Gruyter, 1968.

Bowersock, G. W. "Herodotus, Alexander, and Rome." *The American Scholar* 58 (Summer 1989): 407–414.

Brannan, Patrick. "Herodotus and History: The Constitutional Debate Preceding Darius' Accession." *Traditio* 19 (1963): 427–438.

Braudel, Fernand. *Afterthoughts on Material Civilization and Capitalism*. Translated by Patricia Ranum. Baltimore: Johns Hopkins University Press, 1977.

———. *The Mediterranean and the Mediterranean World in the Age of Philip II*. Vol. 2. New York: Harper and Row, 1973.

Bringmann, Klaus. "Die Verfassungsdebatte bei Herodot, 3.80–82, und Dareios' Aufstieg zur Königsherrschaft." *Hermes* 104, 3 (1976): 266–279.

Brown, Truesdell S. "Herodotus and his Profession." *American Historical Review* 59 (1954): 829–843.

Buell, Frederick. *National Culture and the New Global System.* Baltimore: Johns Hopkins University Press, 1994.

Burger, Ronna. *Plato's Phaedrus: A Defense of a Philosophic Art of Writing.* University, Alabama: University of Alabama Press, 1980.

Burn, Andrew R. *Persia and the Greeks: The Defence of the West, c. 546–478.* New York: St. Martin's Press, 1962.

Bury, J. B. *The Ancient Greek Historians.* London: St. Martin's Press, 1962.

Bury, J. B., S. A. Cook, and F. E. Adcock, eds. *The Cambridge Ancient History IV: The Persian Empire and the West.* Cambridge: Cambridge University Press, 1926.

Calvino, Italo. *Six Memos for the Next Millennium.* Cambridge: Harvard University Press, 1988.

Cameron, Averil, ed. *History as Text.* London: Gerald Duckworth, 1989.

Carr, David. "Narrative and the Real World: An Argument for Continuity." *History and Theory* 25, 2 (1986): 117–131.

———. *Time, Narrative, and History.* Bloomington: Indiana University Press, 1986.

Carr, Edward Hallett. *What is History?* New York: Vintage Books, 1961.

Castoriadis, Cornelius. "The Greek Polis and the Creation of Democracy." *Graduate Faculty Philosophy Journal* 9, 2 (Fall 1983): 80.

Cerri, G., and Bruno Gentili. *History and Biography in Ancient Thought.* Amsterdam: J. C. Gieben, 1988.

Chaudhuri, K. N. "The Problematic of 'Polyphonic' History (Europe and Asia 1500–1800)." *Common Knowledge* 2, 3 (Winter 1993): 24–43.

Chiasson, C. "Tragic Diction in Herodotus: Some Possibilities." *Phoenix* 36 (1982): 156–161.

Clark, Stephen R. L. *Aristotle's Man: Speculations upon Aristotelian Anthropology.* Oxford: Clarendon Press, 1975.

Clifford, James. *Person and Myth: Maurice Leenhardt in the Melanesian World.* Berkeley: University of California Press, 1982.

Cobet, Justus. *Herodots Exkurse und die Frage der Einheit seines Werkes.* Wiesbaden: Franz Steiner Verlag, 1971.

———. Review of *Die Quellenangaben bei Herodot* by Detlev Fehling. *Gnomon* 47 (1974): 737–746.

———. "Wann wurde Herodots Darstellung der perserkriege publiziert?" *Hermes* 105 (1977): 2–27.

Cohen, Mark Nathan. *Health and the Rise of Civilization.* New Haven: Yale University Press, 1989.

Condren, Conal. *The Status and Appraisal of Classic Texts: An Essay on Political Theory, Its Inheritance, and the History of Ideas.* Princeton: Princeton University Press, 1985.

Connor, Walter Robert. "Commentary on the Conference." *Arethusa* 20, 1 and 2 (Spring and Fall 1987): 255–262.

———. "The *Histor* in History." In Ralph M. Rosen and Joseph Farrell, eds., *Nomodeiktes: Greek Studies in Honor of Martin Ostwald,* pp. 3–15. Ann Arbor: University of Michigan Press, 1993.

————. *The New Politicians of Fifth-Century Athens.* Princeton: Princeton University Press, 1971.

Cook, Albert. "Herodotus: The Act of Inquiry as a Liberation from Myth." *Helios* 3 (May 1976): 23–66.

————. *History/Writing.* New York: Cambridge University Press, 1988.

————. *Myth and Language.* Bloomington: Indiana University Press, 1980.

Cornford, Francis M. *Thucydides Mythistoricus.* London: Edward Arnold, 1907.

Crahay, Roland. *La littérature oraculaire chez Hérodote.* Paris: Les Belles Lettres, 1956.

Dandamayev, M. A. "Herodotus' Information on Persia and the Latest Discoveries of Cuneiform Texts." *Storia della Storiografia* 7 (1985): 92–100.

Darbo-Peschanski, Catherine. *Le discours du particulier: Essai sur l'enquête hérodotéenne.* Paris: Editions du Seuil, 1987.

Davis, Michael. *Aristotle's "Poetics": The Poetry of Philosophy.* Lanham, Md.: Rowman & Littlefield, 1992.

Derrida, Jacques. *Of Grammatology.* Translated by Gayatri Chakravorty Spivak. Baltimore: Johns Hopkins University Press, 1978.

Develin, Robert. "Herodotos and the Alkmeonids." In John W. Eadie and Josiah Ober, eds., *Craft of the Ancient Historian: Essays in Honor of Chester G. Starr,* pp. 125–139. Lanham, Md.: University Press of America, 1985.

Dewald, Carolyn. "Narrative Surface and Authorial Voice in Herodotus' *Histories.*" *Arethusa* 20, 1 and 2 (Spring and Fall 1987): 147–170.

————. "Practical Knowledge and the Historian's Role in Herodotus and Thucydides." In *The Greek Historians: Literature and History: Papers Presented to A. E. Raubitschek,* pp. 47–63. Saratoga, Cal.: ANMA Libri, 1985.

————. "Women and Culture in Herodotus' *Histories.*" In Helene P. Foley, ed., *Reflections of Women in Antiquity,* pp. 91–125. New York: Gordon and Breach Science Publishers, 1981.

Dewald, Carolyn, and Marincola, John. "A Selective Introduction to Herodotean Studies." *Arethusa* 20, 1 and 2 (Spring and Fall 1987): 9–40.

Diels, Hermann. "Herodot und Hekataios." *Hermes* 22 (1887): 411–444.

Diels, Hermann, and Walther Kranz, eds. *Die Fragmente der Vorsokratiker.* 3 vols. Berlin: Weidmannsche Buchhandlung, 1934.

Dihle, A. "Herodot und die Sophistik." *Philologus* 106 (1962): 207–220.

Diller, Hans. "Die Hellenen-Barbaren Antithese im Zeitalter der Perserkriege." In *Grecs et Barbares,* 39–82. Fondation Hardt, Entretiens 8. Vandoeuvres-Genève, 1961.

Dilthey, Wilhelm. *Gesammelte Schriften.* 18 vols. Stuttgart: B. G. Teubner, and Göttingen: Vandenhoeck & Ruprecht, 1914–1977.

Dionysius of Halicarnassus. *The Critical Essays In Two Volumes.* Translated by Stephen Usher. Cambridge: Harvard University Press, 1985.

Dodds, E. R. *The Greeks and the Irrational.* Berkeley: University of California Press, 1951.

Drews, Robert. "The First Tyrants in Greece." *Historia* 21, 2 (1972): 129–144.

————. *The Greek Accounts of Eastern History.* Washington, D.C.: Center for Hellenic Studies, 1973.

Eadie, John W. *Craft of the Ancient Historian: Essays in Honor of Chester G. Starr.* Lanham, Md.: University Press of America, 1985.

Ehrenberg, Victor. "Origins of Democracy." *Historia* 1 (1950): 515–548.

Else, Gerald F. *Aristotle's Poetics: The Argument.* Cambridge: Harvard University Press, 1967.

Emerson, Ralph Waldo. *Essays by Ralph Waldo Emerson.* New York: Harper Colophon Books, 1951.

Erbse, Herbert. "Das erste Satz im Werke Herodots." In H. Erbse, ed., *Festschrift Bruno Snell*, pp. 209–222. Munich: Beck, 1956.

Ermath, Michael. *Wilhelm Dilthey: The Critique of Historical Reason.* Chicago: University of Chicago Press, 1981.

Euben, J. Peter. "The Battle of Salamis and the Origins of Political Theory." *Political Theory* 14, 3 (Aug. 1986): 359–390.

———. "Creatures of a Day: Thought and Action in Thucydides." In *Political Theory and Praxis: New Perspectives*, 28–56.

Evans, J. A. S. "Despotes Nomos." *Athenaeum* 43 (1965): 142–153.

———. "The Dream of Xerxes and the 'Nomoi' of the Persians." *Classical Journal* 57, 2 (Nov. 1961): 109–111.

———. "Father of History or Father of Lies: the Reputation of Herodotus." *Classical Journal* 64, 1 (Oct. 1968): 11–17.

———. *Herodotus.* Boston: Twayne Publishers, 1982.

———. *Herodotus, Explorer of the Past.* Princeton: Princeton University Press, 1991.

———. "Notes on the Debate of the Persian Grandees in Herodotus 3.80–82." *Quaderni Urbinati di Cultura Classica* 36 (1981): 79–84.

Farnell, Lewis Richard. *Greek Hero Cults and Ideas of Immortality.* Oxford: Clarendon Press, 1921.

Faulkner, Donald W., ed. *The Portable Malcolm Cowley.* New York: Viking Penguin, 1990.

Fehling, Detlev. *Die Quellenangaben bei Herodot.* Berlin: De Gruyter, 1971.

———. *Herodotus and his "Sources": Citation, Invention and Narrative Art.* Translated by J. C. Howie. Leeds: Francis Cairns, 1989.

Finley, Moses I. *Ancient History: Evidence and Models.* New York: Viking Press, 1986.

———. *The Use and Abuse of History.* New York: The Viking Press, 1975.

Fischer, David Hackett. *Paul Revere's Ride.* Oxford: Oxford University Press, 1994.

Flashar, H., ed. *Synusia: Festgabe für Wolfgang Schadewaldt.* Pfulingen: Neske, 1965.

Flory, Stewart. *The Archaic Smile of Herodotus.* Detroit: Wayne State University Press, 1987.

———. "Arion's Leap: Brave Gestures in Herodotus." *American Journal of Philology* 99, 4 (Winter 1978): 411–421.

———. "Laughter, Tears and Wisdom in Herodotus." *American Journal of Philology* 99, 2 (Summer 1978): 145–153.

———. "Who Read Herodotus' *Histories?*" *American Journal of Philology* 101, 1 (Spring 1980): 12–28.

Foley, Helene P. *Reflections of Women in Antiquity.* New York: Gordon and Breach Science Publishers, 1981.

Fornara, Charles W. *Herodotus: An Interpretative Essay*. Oxford: Clarendon Press, 1971.

———. "Herodotus' Knowledge of the Archidamian War." *Hermes* 109, 1 (1981): 149–156.

———. *The Nature of History in Ancient Greece and Rome*. Berkeley: University of California Press, 1983.

———. "The 'Tradition' About the Murder of Hipparchus." *Historia* 17, 4 (1968): 400–424.

Foucault, Michel. *Power/Knowledge: Selected Interviews and Other Writings 1972–1977*. Edited by Colin Gordon. New York: Pantheon Books, 1980.

Fränkel, Hermann. "Eine Stileigenheit der frühgriechischen Literatur." In Franz Tietze, ed., *Wege und Formen frühgriechischen Denkens: Literarische und philosophiegeschichtliche Studien*, pp. 40–96. Munich: Beck, 1955.

Frede, Dorothea. "Necessity, Chance, and 'What Happens for the Most Part' in Aristotle's *Poetics*." In Amélie Oksenberg Rorty, ed., *Essays on Aristotle's "Poetics"*, pp. 197–219. Princeton: Princeton University Press, 1992.

Freeman, Kathleen. *Ancilla to the Pre-Socratic Philosophers*. Cambridge: Harvard University Press, 1983.

Friedlander, Saul, ed. *Probing the Limits of Representation*. Cambridge: Harvard University Press, 1992.

Frisch, Peter. *Die Träume bei Herodot*. Meisenheim am Glan: A. Hain, 1968.

Fritz, Karl von. "Aristotle's Contribution to the Practice and Theory of Historiography." *University of California Publications in Philosophy* 28, 3 (Sept. 1958): 113–137.

———. "Der gemeinsame Ursprung der Geschichtsschreibung und der exakten Wissenschaften bei den Griechen." *Philosophia Naturalis* 2 (1952): 200–223.

———. *Die griechische Geschichtsschreibung*. Vol. 1. Berlin: De Gruyter, 1967.

———. "Herodotus and the Growth of Greek Historiography." *Transactions of the American Philological Association* 67 (1936): 315–340.

Gabba, Emilio. "True History and False History in Classical Antiquity." *Journal of Roman Studies* 71 (1981): 50–62.

Galinsky, G. Karl. *The Herakles Theme*. Totowa, N.J.: Rowman and Littlefield, 1972.

Gammie, John G. "Herodotus on Kings and Tyrants: Objective Historiography or Conventional Portraiture?" *Journal of Near Eastern Studies* 45, 3 (July 1986): 171–195.

Gates, Henry Louis, Jr. *The Signifying Monkey: A Theory of Afro-American Literary Criticism*. New York: Oxford University Press, 1988.

Geertz, Clifford. "Anti Anti-Relativism." *American Anthropologist* 86 (June 1984): 263–278.

———. "From the Native Point of View: On the Nature of Anthropological Understanding." In Paul Rabinow and William M. Sullivan, eds., *Interpretive Social Science*, pp. 225–241. Berkeley: University of California Press, 1979.

Gentili, Bruno, and G. Cerri. *History and Biography in Ancient Thought*. Amsterdam: J. C. Gieben, 1988.

————. *Poetry and its Public in Ancient Greece.* Translated by A. Thomas Cole. Baltimore: Johns Hopkins University Press, 1988.

Gill, Christopher. "Plato on Falsehood—not Fiction." In Christopher Gill and T. P. Wiseman, eds., *Lies and Fiction in the Ancient World*, pp. 38–87. Exeter: University of Exeter Press, 1993.

Glover, Terrot R. *Herodotus.* Berkeley: University of California Press, 1924.

Gomme, Arnold W. *The Greek Attitude to Poetry and History.* Berkeley: University of California Press, 1954.

————. *A Historical Commentary on Thucydides.* 5 vols. Oxford: Clarendon Press, 1945–1981.

————. *More Essays in Greek History and Literature.* New York: Garland, 1987.

Goody, Jack, and Ian Watt. "The Consequences of Literacy." In Jack Goody, ed., *Literacy in Traditional Societies*, pp. 27–68. Cambridge: Cambridge University Press, 1968.

Gordon, Colin, ed. *Power/Knowledge: Selected Interviews and Other Writings 1972–1977.* New York: Pantheon Books, 1980.

Gould, John. *Herodotus.* New York: St. Martin's Press, 1989.

Green, Tamara M. "*Black Athena* and Classical Historiography: Other Approaches, Other Views." *Arethusa: Challenge of "Black Athena"* Special Issue (Fall 1989): 55–65.

Grene, David. "The Historian as Dramatist." *Journal of Philosophy* 58, No. 18 (Aug. 1961): 477–488.

————. "Introduction." Herodotus, *The History*, 1987.

Griffin, Jasper. "Die Ursprünge der Historien Herodots." In Wolfram Ax, ed., *Memoria Rerum Veterum: Neue Beiträge Zur Antiken Historiographie Und Alten Geschichte*, pp. 51–82. Stuttgart: Franz Steiner Verlag, 1990.

————. "Who Are These Coming to the Sacrifice?" Review of *Black Athena: The Afroasiatic Roots of Classical Civilization*, Vol. 1, by Martin Bernal. *Times Literary Supplement*, June 15, 1989, pp. 25–27.

Groningen, B. von. *In the Grip of the Past: Essay on an Aspect of Greek Thought.* Leiden: E. J. Brill, 1953.

Gulley, Norman. "The Concept of ἱστορία in Aristotle's *Poetics.*" *Trivium* 15 (1980): 1–9.

Guthrie, W. K. C. "Aristotle as a Historian of Philosophy: Some Preliminaries." *Journal of Hellenic Studies* 77 (1957): 35–41.

Hall, Edith. *Inventing the Barbarian: Greek Self-Definition through Tragedy.* Oxford: Oxford University Press, 1989.

————. "When Is a Myth Not a Myth?" *Arethusa* 25 (1992): 181–201.

Halliwell, Stephen. *Aristotle's "Poetics".* London: Gerald Duckworth, 1986.

Hample, Franz. *Geschichte als Kritische Wissenschaft.* Darmstadt: Wissenschaftliche Buchgesellschaft, 1975–1979.

Handlin, Oscar. "History: A Discipline in Crisis?" *The American Scholar* 40, 3 (Summer 1971): 447–465.

Hardie, W. F. R. *Aristotle's Ethical Theory.* Oxford: Clarendon Press, 1968.

Harlan, David. "Intellectual History and the Return of Literature." *American Historical Review* 94 (June 1989): 581–609.

Harries, Patrick. "Imagery, Symbolism and Tradition in a South African Bantustan: Mangosuthu Buthelezi, In Katha, and Zulu History," *History and Theory* 32 (1993): 105–125.

Harris, William V. *Ancient Literacy.* Cambridge: Cambridge University Press, 1989.

Hart, John. *Herodotus and Greek History.* New York: St. Martin's Press, 1982.

Hartog, François. "Herodotus and the Historiographical Operation." Translated by Wayne R. Hayes. *Diacritics* 22, 2 (Summer 1992): 83–93.

———. *The Mirror of Herodotus: The Representation of the Other in the Writing of History.* Translated by Janet Lloyd. Berkeley: University of California Press, 1988.

Harvey, F. D. "The Political Sympathies of Herodotus." *Historia* 15 (1966): 254–255.

Haskell, Thomas L. "Objectivity is Not Neutrality: Rhetoric vs. Practice in Peter Novick's *That Noble Dream.*" *History and Theory* 29, 2 (1990): 129–157.

Hatab, Lawrence J. *Myth and Philosophy: A Contest of Truths.* LaSalle, Ill.: Open Court, 1990.

Havelock, Eric A. *The Literate Revolution in Greece and its Cultural Consequences.* Princeton: Princeton University Press, 1982.

———. *Preface to Plato.* Oxford: Oxford University Press, 1963.

Hedrick, Charles W., Jr. "The Meaning of Material Culture: Herodotus, Thucydides, and Their Sources." In Ralph M. Rosen and Joseph Farrell, eds., *Nomodeiktes,* pp. 17–37. Ann Arbor: University of Michigan Press, 1993.

Hegyi, D. "Historical Authenticity of Herodotus in the Persian 'Logoi.'" *Acta Antiqua Academiae Scientiarum Hungaricae* 21 (1973): 73–87.

Heidegger, Martin. *Early Greek Thinking: The Dawn of Western Philosophy.* Translated by David Farrell Krell and Frank A. Capuzzi. San Francisco: Harper and Row, 1984.

———. *Poetry, Language, Thought.* Translated by Albert Hofstadter. New York: Harper and Row, 1971.

Herington, John. "The Poem of Herodotus." *Arion* 1, 3 (Fall 1991): 5–15.

———. *Poetry into Drama: Early Tragedy and the Greek Poetic Tradition.* Berkeley: University of California Press, 1985.

Herodotus. *Historiae.* 2 vols. Edited by Carolus Hude. Oxford: Clarendon Press, 1927.

———. *The Histories.* Edited by Walter Blanco and Jennifer Tolbert Roberts; translated by Walter Blanco. New York: Norton, 1992.

———. *The History.* Translated by David Grene. Chicago: University of Chicago Press, 1987.

Hignett, Charles. *Xerxes' Invasion of Greece.* Oxford: Oxford University Press, 1963.

Himmelfarb, Gertrude. *The New History and the Old.* Cambridge: Harvard University Press, 1987.

———. "Some Reflections on the New History." *American Historical Review* 94 (June 1989): 661–670.

Hobbes, Thomas. *Leviathan.* Edited by Richard Tuck. Cambridge: Cambridge University Press, 1991.

Hooker, J. T. "Arion and the Dolphin." *Greece and Rome* 36, 2 (1989): 141–146.

Hornblower, Simon. *Thucydides.* London: Gerald Duckworth, 1987.

How, W. W., and J. Wells. *A Commentary on Herodotus.* 2 vols. Oxford: Clarendon Press, 1928 (1979).

Huber, Ludwig. "Herodots Homerverständnis." In H. Flashar and K. Gaiser, eds., *Synusia: Festgabe für Wolfgang Schadewaldt,* pp. 29–52. Pfulingen: Neske, 1965.

Hughes, H. Stuart. *History as Art and Science.* New York: Harper and Row, 1964.

———. "Is Contemporary History Real History?" *The American Scholar* 32, 4 (Autumn 1963): 516–525.

Humphreys, Sally. "Law, Custom and Culture in Herodotus." *Arethusa* 20 (Spring and Fall 1987): 211–220.

Hunter, Virginia. *Past and Process in Herodotus and Thucydides.* Princeton: Princeton University Press, 1982.

Immerwahr, Henry R. "Aspects of Historical Causation in Herodotus." *Transactions of the American Philological Association* 87 (1956): 241–280.

———. "Ergon: History as a Monument in Herodotus and Thucydides." *American Journal of Philology* 81, 3 (1960): 261–290.

———. *Form and Thought in Herodotus.* Cleveland: APA Philological Monographs 23, 1966.

———. "Historical Action in Herodotus." *Transactions of the American Philological Association* 85 (1954): 16–45.

Jacoby, Felix. "Herodotos." In August F. Pauly, George Wissowa, and Wilhelm Kroll, eds., *Pauly's Real-Encyclopädie Supplement-band,* vol. 2, pp. 205–520. Stuttgart: J. B. Metzler, 1913.

James, William. "Is Life Worth Living?" In *The Will to Believe and Other Essays in Popular Philosophy.* New York: Dover Publications, 1956.

Kagan, Donald. *The Great Dialogue: History of Greek Political Thought from Homer to Polybius.* New York: Free Press, 1965.

Kamen, Michael. "Clio and the Changing Fashions." *The American Scholar* 44, 3 (Spring 1975): 484–496.

Kermode, Frank. *The Genesis of Secrecy: On the Interpretation of Narrative.* Cambridge: Harvard University Press, 1979.

Kirk, G. S., J. E. Raven, and M. Schofield. *The Presocratic Philosphers: A Critical History With a Selection of Texts.* Cambridge: Cambridge University Press, 1957 (1983).

Kloppenberg, James. Review of *That Noble Dream* by Peter Novick. *American Historical Review* 94 (1989): 1011–1030.

Knapp, Steven, and Walter Benn Michaels. "Against Theory." *Critical Inquiry* 8 (Summer 1982): 723–742.

———. "Against Theory 2: Hermeneutics and Deconstruction." *Critical Inquiry* 14 (Autumn 1987): 49–68.

Konstan, David. "Persians, Greeks and Empire." *Arethusa* 20 (1987): 59–73.

———. "The Stories in Herodotus' *Histories:* Book I." *Helios* 10, 1 (1983): 1–22.

Koselleck, Reinhart. *Futures Past: On the Semantics of Historical Time.* Translated by Keith Tribe. Cambridge: MIT Press, 1985.

Krischer, Tilman. "Herodots Prooimion." *Hermes* 93 (1965): 159–167.

Kuklick, Bruce. "The Mind of the Historian." *History and Theory* 8, 3 (1969): 313–331.

Lach, Donald F. *Asia in the Making of Europe.* 2 vols. Chicago: University of Chicago Press, 1965–1977.

Lachenaud, Guy. *Mythologies, religion et philosophie de l'histoire dans Hérodote.* Lille: Université de Lille, 1978.

Lane, Michael, ed. *Introduction to Structuralism.* New York: Basic Books, 1970.

Lang, Mabel L. *Herodotean Narrative and Discourse.* Cambridge: Harvard University Press, 1984.

Larsen, J. A. O. "The Judgment of Antiquity on Democracy." *Classical Philology* 49 (1954): 1–14.

Lasserre, François. "Hérodote et Protagoras: le débat sur les constitutions." *Museum Helveticum* 33, 2 (1976): 65–84.

———. "L'historiographie grecque à l'époque archaïque." *Quaderni di Storia* 4 (1976): 113–142.

Lateiner, Donald. "The Failure of the Ionian Revolt." *Historia* 31, 2 (1982): 129–160.

———. "Herodotean Historiographical Patterning: The Constitutional Debate." *Quaderni Di Storia* 20 (1984): 257–284.

———. *The Historical Method of Herodotus.* Toronto: University of Toronto Press, 1989.

———. "Limit, Propriety, and Transgression in the *Histories* of Herodotus." In *The Greek Historians,* pp. 87–100. Palo Alto: ANMA Libri, 1985.

———. "No Laughing Matter: A Literary Tactic in Herodotus." *Transactions of the American Philological Association* 107 (1977): 173–182.

———. "Nonverbal Communication in the *Histories* of Herodotus." *Arethusa* 20, 1 and 2 (Spring and Fall 1987): 83–107.

———. "A Note on the Perils of Prosperity in Herodotus." *Rheinisches Museum für Philologie* 125, 2 (1982): 97–101.

Latte, Kurt. "Die Anfänge der griechischen Geschichtsschreibung." In *Histoire et historiens dans l'antiquité,* pp. 3–20. Fondation Hardt, Entretiens 4. Vandoeuvres-Genève, 1956.

Lattimore, Richmond. "The Composition of the *Histories* of Herodotus." *Classical Philology* 53 (1958): 9–21.

———. "The Wise Advisor in Herodotus." *Classical Philology* 34 (1939): 24–35.

Laurot, Bernard. "Idéaux grecs et barbarie chez Hérodote." *Ktema* 6 (1981): 39–48.

Lefkowitz, Mary. "Not Out of Africa." *The New Republic,* Feb. 10, 1992: 29–36.

Legrand, Philip E. *Hérodote: Introduction.* Paris: Les Belles Lettres, 1954.

———. "De la 'malignité' d'Hérodote." In *Mélanges Gustave Glotz.* 2 vols. Paris: Presses Universitaires de France, 1932.

Lentricchia, Frank. Preface to Frank Kermode, *Forms of Attention.* Chicago: University of Chicago Press, 1985.

Lesky, A. "Tragödien bei Herodot?" In K. H. Kinzel, ed., *Greece and the Eastern Mediterranean in Ancient History and Prehistory*, pp. 224–230. New York: W. De Gruyter, 1977.

Levick, Barbara, ed. *The Ancient Historian and His Materials*. Westmead, England: Gregg International, 1975.

Levin, Harry. "Some Meanings of Myth." In H. Levin, ed., *Refractions: Essays in Comparative Literature*, pp. 19–31. London: Oxford University Press, 1966.

Levine, Molly Myerowitz. Review of *Black Athena: The Afroasiatic Roots of Classical Civilization*, Volume 1: *The Fabrication of Ancient Greece, 1785–1985* by Martin Bernal. *American Historical Review* April 1992: 440–460.

Lewis, Bernard. "Other People's History," *The American Scholar* 59 (Summer 1990): 397–405.

Lewis, David M. "Persians in Herodotus." In *The Greek Historians*, pp. 101–117. Palo Alto: ANMA Libri, 1985.

Leyden, W. von. "Spatium Historicum: The Historical Past as Viewed by Hecataeus, Herodotus, and Thucydides." *Durham University Journal* 11 (1949–1950): 89–104.

Linforth, Ivan M. "Greek Gods and Foreign Gods in Herodotus." *University of California Publications in Classical Philology* 9 (1926): 1–25.

———. "Herodotus' Avowal of Silence in His Account of Egypt." *University of California Publications in Classical Philology* 7 (1924): 269–292.

Lloyd, Alan B. *Herodotus Book II: Introduction*. Leiden: E. J. Brill, 1975.

———. *Herodotus Book II: Commentary 1–98*. Leiden: E. J. Brill, 1976.

———. *Herodotus Book II: Commentary 99–182*. Leiden: E. J. Brill, 1988.

———. "Herodotus on Egyptians and Libyans." In *Hérodote et Les Peuples Non Grecs*, pp. 215–244. Fondation Hardt, Entretiens 35. Vandoeuvres-Genève, 1988.

Lloyd, G. E. R. *Magic, Reason and Experience*. Cambridge: Cambridge University Press, 1979.

Lobkowicz, Nicholas. "On the History of Theory and Praxis." In *Political Theory and Praxis: New Perspectives*, 13–27.

———. *Theory and Practice: History of a Concept from Aristotle to Marx*. South Bend, Ind.: University of Notre Dame Press, 1967.

Locke, John. *Two Treatises of Government*. Edited by Peter Laslett. Cambridge: Cambridge University Press, 1988.

Longinus. *On Sublimity*. Translated by D. A. Russell. Oxford: Clarendon Press, 1965.

Lord, Carnes, and David K. O'Connor, eds. *Essays on the Foundations of Aristotelian Political Science*. Berkeley: University of California Press, 1991.

Louis, Pierre. "Le mot *historia* chez Aristote." *Revue de Philologie* 29 (1955): 39–44.

Macan, Reginald Walter. *Herodotus, the Fourth, Fifth and Sixth Books*. 2 vols. London: Macmillan, 1895.

———. *Herodotus, the Seventh, Eighth, and Ninth Books*. 2 vols. London: Macmillan, 1908.

Malinowski, Bronislaw. *A Diary in the Strict Sense of the Term*. Translated by Norbert Guterman. London: Routledge & Kegan Paul, 1967.

Manuel, Frank E. *Shapes of Philosophical History*. Palo Alto: Stanford University Press, 1965.

Marg, Walter, ed. *Herodot, Eine Auswahl aus der neueren Forschung*. Munich: Beck, 1962.

Marincola, John. "Herodotean Narrative and the Narrator's Presence." *Arethusa* 20, 1 and 2 (Spring and Fall 1987): 121–137.

Marincola, John, and Carolyn Dewald. "A Selective Introduction to Herodotean Studies." *Arethusa* 20, 1 and 2 (Spring and Fall 1987): 9–40.

McGann, Jerome J. *The Beauty of Inflections: Literary Investigations in Historical Method and Theory*. Oxford: Clarendon Press, 1988.

McMillen, Liz. "Controversial Anthology of American Literature: Ground-Breaking Contribution or a 'Travesty'?" *Chronicle of Higher Education*, January 16, 1991, A22.

McNeill, William H. "Mythistory, or Truth, Myth, History, and Historians." *American Historical Review* 91, 1 (Feb. 1986): 1–10.

Mead, George Herbert. *Mind, Self, and Society*. Edited by Charles W. Morris. Chicago: University of Chicago Press, 1962.

Megill, Allan. "Recounting the Past: Description, Explanation, and Narrative in Historiography." *American Historical Review* 94 (June 1989): 627–653.

Meier, Christian. *The Greek Discovery of Politics*. Translated by David McLintock. Cambridge: Harvard University Press, 1990.

————. "Historical Answers to Historical Questions: The Origins of History in Ancient Greece." *Arethusa* 20, 1 and 2 (Spring and Fall 1987): 41–57.

Melville, Herman. *Moby-Dick*. Edited by Tony Tanner. New York: Oxford University Press, 1989.

Meyerhoff, Hans. *The Philosophy of History in Our Time*. Garden City, N.Y.: Doubleday Anchor Books, 1959.

————. *Time in Literature*. Berkeley: University of California Press, 1955.

Moles, J. L. "Truth and Untruth in Herodotus and Thucydides." In Christopher Gill and T. Wiseman, eds., *Lies and Fiction in the Ancient World*, pp. 88–121. Exeter: University of Exeter Press, 1993.

Momigliano, Arnaldo. *Alien Wisdom: The Limits of Hellenization*. Cambridge: Cambridge University Press, 1990.

————. *The Development of Greek Biography*. Cambridge: Harvard University Press, 1971.

————. "Greek Historiography." *History and Theory* 17, 1 (1978): 1–28.

————. "The Historians of the Classical World and their Audiences: Some Suggestions." *Annali della Scuola Normale Superiore di Pisa* 8, 1 (1978): 59–75.

————. "The Place of Herodotus in the History of Historiography." *History* 43 (1958): 1–13.

————. "The Rhetoric of History and the History of Rhetoric: On Hayden White's Tropes." In E. Schaffer, ed., *Comparative Criticism: A Yearbook*, pp. 259–268. Cambridge: Cambridge University Press, 1981.

————. *Studies in Historiography*. London: Weidenfeld and Nicolson, 1966.

Morris, Wright. Foreword to Mark Twain, *The Tragedy of Pudd'nhead Wilson*. New York: New American Library, 1964.

Morrison, J. S. "The Place of Protagoras in Athenian Public Life." *Classical Quarterly* 35, 1 (1941): 1–16.

Müller, Dietram. "Herodot—Vater des Empirismus? Mensch und Erkenntnis im Denken Herodots." In Gebhard Kurz, Dietram Müller, and Walter Nicolai, eds., *Gnomosyne: Menschliches Denken und Handeln in der frühgriechischen Literatur*, pp. 299–318. Munich: Verlag C. H. Beck, 1981.

Müller-Vollmer, Kurt, ed. *The Hermeneutics Reader: Texts of the German Tradition from the Enlightenment to the Present*. New York: Continuum, 1985.

Munson, Rosaria Vignolo. "Artemisia in Herodotus." *Classical Antiquity* 7 (April 1988): 91–106.

————. "The Celebratory Purpose of Herodotus: The Story of Arion in *Histories* 1.23–24." *Ramus* 15, 2 (1986): 93–104.

Murray, Oswyn. "Herodotus and Oral History." In Helen Sancisi-Weerdenburg and Amélie Kuhrt, eds., *Achaemenid History II: The Greek Sources*, pp. 93–115. Leiden: Nederlands Instituut voor het Nahije Oosten, 1987.

Myres, John L. *Herodotus, Father of History*. Oxford: Oxford University Press, 1953.

Nagy, Gregory. *The Best of the Achaeans: Concepts of the Hero in Archaic Greek Poetry*. Baltimore: Johns Hopkins University Press, 1979.

————. "Herodotus the *Logios*." *Arethusa* 20, 1 and 2 (Spring and Fall 1987): 175–184.

————. *Pindar's Homer: The Lyric Possession of an Epic Past*. Baltimore: Johns Hopkins University Press, 1990.

Nestle, Wilhelm. *Vom Mythos zum Logos*. New York: Arno Press, 1942 (1978).

Nichols, Mary P. *Citizens and Statesmen: A Study of Aristotle's "Politics"*. Savage, Md.: Rowman & Littlefield, 1992.

Nietzsche, Friedrich. *On the Genealogy of Morals and Ecce Homo*. Translated by Walter Kaufmann and R. J. Hollingdale. New York: Vintage Books, 1989.

————. "On the Uses and Disadvantages of History for Life." In *Untimely Meditations*, pp. 57–123. Translated by R. J. Hollingdale. Cambridge: Cambridge University Press, 1983.

Norman, Andrew P. "Telling It Like It Was: Historical Narratives On Their Own Terms." *History and Theory* 30, 2 (1991): 119–135.

Novick, Peter. *That Noble Dream: The Objectivity Question and the American Historical Profession*. Chicago: University of Chicago Press, 1988.

Ormiston, Gayle L., and Alan D. Schrift, eds. *The Hermeneutic Tradition: From Ast to Ricoeur*. Albany: State University of New York Press, 1990.

Ostwald, Martin. *Nomos and the Beginnings of the Athenian Democracy*. Oxford: Oxford University Press, 1969.

Parker, Hershel, and Harrison Hayford. *Moby-Dick As Doubloon*. New York: Norton, 1970.

Parkinson, C. N. *East and West*. Boston: Houghton Mifflin, 1963.

Parry, Adam. *Logos and Ergon in Thucydides*. New York: Arno Press, 1981.

Pauly, August F., George Wissowa, and Wilhelm Kroll, eds. *Pauly's Real-Encyclopädie Supplement-band*. Vol. 2. Stuttgart: J. B. Metzler, 1913.

Pausanias. *Description of Greece*. Translated by W. H. S. Jones. New York: G. P. Putnam's Sons, 1918.

Pearson, Lionel. "Credulity and Skepticism in Herodotus." *Transactions of the American Philological Association* 72 (1941): 335–355.

———. "*Prophasis* and *Aitia*." *Transactions of the American Philological Association* 83 (1952): 205–223.

———. "Real and Conventional Personalities in Greek History." *Journal of the History of Ideas* 15, 2 (1954): 136–145.

Pfeiffer, Rudolf. *History of Classical Scholarship*. Oxford: Clarendon Press, 1968.

Pippidi, D. M. "Aristote et Thucydide." In *Mélanges à J. Marouzeau*, pp. 483–490. Paris: Belles Lettres, 1948.

Plato. *Timaeus*. Translated by Benjamin Jowett. In *The Collected Dialogues of Plato*. Edited by Edith Hamilton and Huntington Cairns. Princeton: Princeton University Press, 1978.

Plutarch. *Moralia*. Translated by Lionel Pearson and F. H. Sandbach. Volume 11. Cambridge: Harvard University Press, 1965.

Pocock, J. "The Origins of Study of the Past: A Comparative Approach." *Comparative Studies in Society and History* 3 (1961): 209–246.

Pohlenz, Max. *Herodot, der erste Geschichtschreiber des Abendlandes*. Stuttgart: B. G. Teubner, 1961.

Powell, J. E. *A Lexicon to Herodotus*. Cambridge: Cambridge University Press, 1958.

Pratt, M. L. *Toward a Speech Act Theory of Literary Discourse*. Bloomington: Indiana University Press, 1977.

Press, Gerald A. *The Development of the Idea of History in Antiquity*. Montreal: McGill-Queen's University Press, 1982.

Pritchett, W. Kendrick. *The Liar School of Herodotus*. Amsterdam: J. C. Gieben, 1993.

———. "Some Recent Critiques of the Veracity of Herodotus." In *Studies in Ancient Greek Topography: Part IV*, pp. 234–285. Berkeley: University of California Press, 1982.

Quinn, Kenneth. *Text and Contexts: The Roman Writers and their Audience*. London: Routledge and Kegan Paul, 1979.

Raaflaub, Kurt A. "Herodotus, Political Thought, and the Meaning of History." *Arethusa* 20, 1 and 2 (Spring and Fall 1987): 221–248.

Rabinow, Paul. *Interpretive Social Science*. Berkeley: University of California Press, 1979.

Raubitschek, Antony E. *The School of Hellas: Essays on Greek History, Archaeology, and Literature*. Edited by Dirk Obbink and Paul A. Vander Waerdt. Oxford: Oxford University Press, 1991.

———. "What the Greeks Thought of Their Early History." *Ancient World* 20 (1989): 39–45.

Rawlinson, George. *The History of Herodotus*. 4 vols. New York: 1860–1893.

Redfield, James. "Commentary on Humphreys and Raaflaub." *Arethusa* 20, 1 and 2 (Spring and Fall 1987): 249–253.

———. "Herodotus the Tourist." *Classical Philology* 80 (April 1985): 97–118.

———. *Nature and Culture in the Iliad*. Chicago: University of Chicago Press, 1975.

Regenbogen, Otto. "Die Geschichte von Solon und Krösus: Eine Studie zur

Geistesgeschichte des 5. und 6. Jh." In Walter Marg, ed., *Herodot*, pp. 375–403. Munich: Beck, 1962.

Reinhardt, Karl. *Vermächtnis der Antike: Gesammelte Essays zur Philosophie und Geschichtschreibung.* Edited by Carl Becker. Göttingen: Vandenhoeck and Ruprecht, 1960.

Reynolds, Frank, and David Tracy. *Discourse and Practice.* Albany: State University of New York Press, 1992.

Ricoeur, Paul. *Time and Narrative.* Vol. 1. Translated by K. McLaughlin and D. Pellauer. Chicago: University of Chicago Press, 1984.

Roberts, Deborah H. "Outside the Drama: The Limits of Tragedy in Aristotle's *Poetics.*" In Amélie Oksenberg Rorty, ed., *Essays on Aristotle's Poetics,* pp. 133–153. Berkeley: University of California Press, 1980.

Rokeah, D. "Speeches in Thucydides: Factual Reporting or Creative Writing?" *Athenaeum* 60 (1982): 386–401.

Romilly, Jacqueline de. *The Rise and Fall of States According to Greek Authors.* Ann Arbor: University of Michigan Press, 1977.

———. "La vengeance comme explication historique dans l'oeuvre d'Hérodote." *Revue des études grecques* 84 (July–Dec. 1971): 314–337.

Rorty, Amélie Oksenberg, ed. "Introduction." In *Essays on Aristotle's Ethics.* Berkeley: University of California Press, 1980.

———. *Essays on Aristotle's Poetics.* Princeton: Princeton University Press, 1992.

Rorty, Richard. *Contingency, Irony, and Solidarity.* Cambridge: Cambridge University Press, 1989.

———. "On Ethnocentrism: A Reply to Clifford Geertz." *Michigan Quarterly Review* 25, 3 (Summer 1986): 525–534.

Rosellini, Michèle, and Suzanne Saïd. "Usages des femmes et autres nomoi chez les 'sauvages' d'Hérodote." *Annali della Scuola normale superiore di Pisa* 8, 3 (1978): 949–1005.

Rosen, Ralph. *Nomodeiktes: Greek Studies in Honor of Martin Ostwald.* Ann Arbor: University of Michigan Press, 1993.

Rosen, Stanley. *Hermeneutics As Politics.* New York: Oxford University Press, 1987.

———. "Herodotus Reconsidered." In Herodotus, *The Histories,* pp. 332–356. Translated by W. Blanco. New York: Norton, 1992.

———. *Plato's Sophist: The Drama of Original and Image.* New Haven: Yale University Press, 1983.

———. *The Quarrel Between Philosophy and Poetry.* New York: Routledge, 1993.

Rosenmeyer, Thomas G. "History or Poetry? The Example of Herodotus." *Clio* 11:3 (Spring 1982): 239–259.

Rousseau, Jean-Jacques. *The First and Second Discourses and Essay on the Origin of Languages.* Edited and translated by Victor Gourevitch. New York: Harper and Row, 1986.

Said, Edward W. "Opponents, Audiences, Constituencies, and Community." *Critical Inquiry* 9 (September 1982): 1–26.

———. *Orientalism.* New York: Vintage Books, 1979.

———. "Orientalism Reconsidered." In F. Barker, ed., *Literature, Politics, and Theory,* 210–229. London: Methuen, 1986.

Saïd, Suzanne. "Guerre, intelligence et courage dans les Histoires d'Hérodote." *Ancient Society* 11 (1980): 83–117.

Saïd, Suzanne, and Michèle Rosellini. "Usages des femmes et autres nomoi chez les 'sauvages' d'Hérodote." *Annali della Scuola normale superiore di Pisa* 8, 3 (1978): 949–1005.

Ste. Croix, G. E. M. de. "Aristotle on History and Poetry (*Poetics* 9, 1451a36–11)." In Barbara Levick, ed., *The Ancient Historian and His Materials.* Westmead, England: Gregg International, 1975.

Salkever, Stephen G. "Aristotle's Social Science." In Carnes Lord and David K. O'Connor, eds., *Essays on the Foundations of Aristotelian Political Science*, pp. 11–48. Berkeley: University of California Press, 1991.

—. *Finding the Mean: Theory and Practice in Aristotle's Political Philosophy.* Princeton: Princeton University Press, 1990.

Saxonhouse, Arlene W. *Fear of Diversity: The Birth of Political Science in Ancient Greek Thought.* Chicago: University of Chicago Press, 1992.

Schadewaldt, W. "Die Anfänge der Geschichtsschreibung bei den Griechen." *Die Antike* 10 (1934): 144–168.

Schepens, Guido. "Ephore sur la valeur de l'autopsie." *Ancient Society* 1 (1970): 163–182.

—. *L'"autopsie' dans la méthode des historiens grecs du cinquième siècle avant J.-C.* Brussels: Paleis der Academiën, 1980.

—. "Some Aspects of Source Theory in Greek Historiography." *Ancient Society* 6 (1975): 257–274.

Schmittenhenner, Walter, and Renata Zoepffel, eds. *Studien zur Alten Geschichten.* 2 vols. Hildesheim: G. Olms, 1982.

Schwabl, H. "Das Bild der fremden Welt bei den frühen Griechen." In *Grecs et barbares*, pp. 3–23. Fondation Hardt, Entretiens 8. Vandoeuvres-Geneve, 1961.

Scott, Joan Wallach. "History in Crisis? The Others' Side of the Story." *American Historical Review* 94 (June 1989): 680–692.

Searle, John R. "Rationality and Realism." *Daedalus* 122, 4 (Fall 1993): 58.

—. *Speech Acts: An Essay in the Philosophy of Language.* Cambridge: Cambridge University Press, 1978.

Segal, Charles. "*Kleos* and Its Ironies in the *Odyssey*." In Harold Bloom, ed., *Homer's The Odyssey*, pp. 127–149. New York: Chelsea House, 1988.

Shell, Marc. *The Economy of Literature.* Baltimore: Johns Hopkins University Press, 1978.

Shelley, Percy Bysshe. *The Complete Poetical Works of Percy Bysshe Shelley.* 4 vols. Edited by Neville Rogers. Oxford: Clarendon Press, 1975.

Shimron, Binyamin. *Politics and Belief in Herodotus.* Stuttgart: Franz Steiner Verlag, 1989.

Sinclair, Thomas A. *A History of Greek Political Thought.* London: Routledge and Kegan Paul, 1952.

Smith, Anthony D. *The Ethnic Origins of Nations.* Oxford: Basil Blackwell, 1986.

Snell, Bruno. *Philologische Untersuchungen: Die Ausdrücke für den Begriff des Wissens in der vorplatonischen Philosophie.* Berlin: Weidmannsche Buchhandlung, 1924.

Snowden, Frank M., Jr. "Bernal's 'Blacks,' Herodotus, and Other Classical Evidence." *Arethusa: Challenge of "Black Athena"* Special Issue (Fall 1989): 83–95.

Solmsen, Lieselotte. "Speeches in Herodotus' Account of the Battle of Platea." *Classical Philology* 39 (Jan.–Oct. 1944): 241–253.

———. "Speeches in Herodotus' Account of the Ionic Revolt." *American Journal of Philology* 64, 2 (1943): 194–207.

Spiro, Melford E. "Cultural Relativism and the Future of Anthropology." In George E. Marcus, ed., *Rereading Cultural Anthropology*. Durham, N.C.: Duke University Press, 1992.

Stadter, P. A., ed. *The Speeches in Thucydides*. Chapel Hill: University of North Carolina Press, 1973.

Stahl, Hans-Peter. "Learning through Suffering? Croesus' Conversations in the History of Herodotus." *Yale Classical Studies* 24 (1975): 1–36.

Steiner, George. *Martin Heidegger*. New York: Viking Press, 1979.

———. *Real Presences*. Chicago: University of Chicago Press, 1991.

Stocking, George W., Jr. *Observers Observed: Essays on Ethnographic Fieldwork*. Madison: University of Wisconsin Press, 1983.

Strasburger, Hermann. "Herodot und das perikleische Athen." *Historia* 4, 1 (1955): 1–25.

———. *Homer und die Geschichtsschreibung*. Heidelberg: Carl Winter Universitätsverlag, 1972.

———. *Studien zur Alten Geschichten*. 2 vols. Edited by Walter Schmittenhenner and Renata Zoepffel. Hildesheim: G. Olms, 1982.

Stroheker, Karl F. "Zu den Anfängen der monarchischen Theorie in der Sophistik," *Historia* 2, 4 (1953–1954): 381–412.

Sulek, Antoni. "The Experiment of Psammetichus." *Journal of the History of Ideas* 50, 4 (1989): 645–651.

Swanson, Judith A. *The Public and the Private in Aristotle's Political Philosophy*. Ithaca, N.Y.: Cornell University Press, 1992.

Tessitore, Aristide. "Making the City Safe for Philosophy: *Nicomachean Ethics*, Book 10." *American Political Science Review* 84, 4 (Dec. 1990): 1251–1262.

Thomas, Rosalind. *Literacy and Orality in Ancient Greece*. Cambridge: Cambridge University Press, 1992.

Thucydides. *The Peloponnesian War: The Complete Hobbes Translation*. Notes and introduction by David Grene. Chicago: University of Chicago Press, 1989.

Tietze, Franz. *Wege und Formen frühgriechischen Denkens: Literarische und philosophiegescchichtliche Studien*. Munich: Beck, 1955.

Toynbee, Arnold J. *Greek Historical Thought From Homer to the Age of Heraclitus*. London: J. M. Dent and Sons, 1924.

Turner, Frank M. "Martin Bernal's *Black Athena*: A Dissent," *Arethusa: Challenge of "Black Athena"* Special Issue (Fall 1989): 97–109.

Vander Waerdt, P. A. "The Political Intention of Aristotle's Moral Philosophy." *Ancient Philosophy* 5 (1985): 77–89.

Vandiver, Elizabeth. *Heroes in Herodotus: The Interaction of Myth and History*. New York: Peter Lang, 1991.

Veeser, H. Aram, ed. *The New Historicism*. New York: Routledge, 1989.

————. *The New Historicism Reader.* New York: Routledge, 1994.

Verdin, Herman. *De Historisch-Kritische Methode van Herodotus.* Brussels: Verhandelingen Kon. VI. Acad., Klasse der Letteren, XXXIII, 69. English summary.

————. "Notes sur l'Attitude des Historiens Grec à l'Égard de la Tradition Locale." *Ancient Society* 1 (1970): 183–200.

————. "Hérodote historien? Quelques interprétations récentes." *L'Antiquité Classique* 44 (1975): 668–685.

Vernant, Jean-Pierre. *Myth and Society in Ancient Greece.* Translated by Janet Lloyd. Atlantic Highlands, N.J.: Humanities Press, 1980.

Vernant, Jean-Pierre, and Pierre Vidal-Naquet. *Myth and Tragedy in Ancient Greece.* Translated by Janet Lloyd. New York: Zone Books, 1988.

Versenyi, Laszlo. "The Quarrel Between Philosophy and Poetry." *Philosophical Forum* 2, 2 (Winter 1970–1971): 200–212.

Veyne, Paul. *Did the Greeks Believe in Their Myths? An Essay on the Constitutive Imagination.* Translated by Paula Wissing. Chicago: University of Chicago Press, 1988.

Vlastos, Gregory. "Isonomia." *American Journal of Philology* 74, 4 (1953): 337–366.

Walbank, F. W. "History and Tragedy." *Historia* 9 (1960): 216–234.

Wardman, A. E. "Herodotus on the Cause of the Greco-Persian Wars." *American Journal of Philology* 82, 2 (1961): 133–150.

————. "Myth in Greek Historiography." *Historia* 9 (1960): 403–413.

Waters, Kenneth H. *Herodotos the Historian: His Problems, Methods and Originality.* Norman: University of Oklahoma Press, 1985.

————. "Herodotos and Politics." *Greece and Rome* 19 (1972): 136–150.

————. *Herodotos on Tyrants and Despots: A Study in Objectivity.* Wiesbaden: Franz Steiner Verlag, 1971.

————. "The Purpose of Dramatisation in Herodotos." *Historia* 15 (1966): 157–171.

Weber, Hans Alois. *Herodots Verständnis von Historie: Untersuchungen zur Methodologie und Argumentationweise Herodot.* Bern: H. Lang, 1976.

Weil, Raymond. *Aristote et l'Histoire: Essai sur la "Politique".* Paris: Librairie C. Klincksieck, 1960.

————. "Aristotle's View of History." In Jonathan Barnes, Malcolm Schofield, and Richard Sorabji, eds., *Articles on Aristotle: 2. Ethics and Politics,* pp. 202–217. London: Gerald Duckworth, 1977.

Weiler, Ingomar. "Greek and Non-Greek World in the Archaic Period." *Greek, Roman, and Byzantine Studies* 9 (1968): 21–29.

Wells, J. *Studies in Herodotus.* Oxford: Oxford University Press, 1923.

————. "The Persian Friends of Herodotus." *Journal of Hellenic Studies* 27 (1907): 37–47.

West, Stephanie. "Herodotus' Epigraphical Interests." *Classical Quarterly* 35 (1985): 278–305.

————. "Herodotus' Portrait of Hecataeus." *Journal of Hellenic Studies* cxi (1991): 144–160.

White, Hayden. "The Burden of History." *History and Theory* 5, 2 (1966): 111–134.

————. "Historicism, History, and the Figurative Imagination." *History and Theory* 14 (1975): 48–66.

————. *Metahistory: The Historical Imagination in 19th Century Europe.* Baltimore: Johns Hopkins University Press, 1973.

————. "The Question of Narrative in Contemporary Historical Theory." *History and Theory* 23 (1984): 1–33.

Will, Edouard. Review of *Die Quellenangaben bei Herodot* by Detlev Fehling. *Revue de Philologie* 49 (1975): 102–113.

Wilson, J. "What Does Thucydides Claim for his Speeches?" *Phoenix* 36 (1982): 95–103.

Wood, Henry. *The Histories of Herodotus.* The Hague: Mouton, 1972.

Wüst, Karl. *Politisches Denken bei Herodot.* Munich: Ph.D. dissertation, 1935. Reprint, New York: Arno Press, 1979.

Yack, Bernard. *The Problems of a Political Animal.* Berkeley: University of California Press, 1993.

Zaslavsky, Robert. *Platonic Myth, Platonic Writing.* Washington, D.C.: University Press of America, 1981.

Index